The Beauty of Impermanence
A Woman's Memoir

Frances Curtis Barnhart

The Beauty of Impermanence: A Woman's Memoir
By Frances Curtis Barnhart
© 2016

ISBN-13: 978-1535229692
ISBN-10: 1535229691

Original artwork: Frances Curtis Barnhart
Editor: Gina Mazza
Cover design and interior layout: Lee Ann Fortunato-Heltzel, Creative One
Art photography and author photo: Tran Song
More art photography: Dan McDilda

While the text inside some of the art photography is
not legible, the essence of the wording is in the art itself.

Frances Curtis Barnhart
Roanoke, VA
www.TheBeautyofImpermanence.com

The feather carries beauty

'Though it once was on the bird

Or is that a leaf drifting from a tree?

One flower blossoms, while another gives way

A healing hand ages and becomes wiser

A heart expands

A pretty face leaves bone as eyes see deeper

Our spirals mark our time.

PART I: There Is Some Kiss

PART II: Two Realities

PART III: Fire In The Heart, Heart In The Fire

PART IV: Revealing The Concealed

PART V: Stillness In The Field

"Our deepest fear is not that we are inadequate.

Our deepest fear is that we are powerful beyond measure.

It is our light, not our darkness, that most frightens us.

We ask ourselves, who am I to be brilliant, gorgeous, talented, fabulous?

Actually, who are you not to be?

It is not just in some of us, it is everyone.

And as we let our own light shine,

we unconsciously give other people permission to do the same."

—Nelson Mandela

First, my deepest love and gratitude to the God That is All, Everywhere and in Everyone. My desire is that I have been true to that love and that through my words, personal as they are, I am passing that love on to you, the reader.

In grateful memory of my parents, grandparents, nephew Dan and dear friends who are already on the other side: Judy, Joanna, Joanie, Naomi, Anna, Roy and Wanda. Maybe you've all met each other by now and are dancing in the light together.

With joyful enthusiasm, I dedicate my heart to the loves of my life, without whom I would not be me: My children, Adam Curtis, Jennifer Prax and Elizabeth Moss; their spouses, Louise, Brian and Ben; the rising future, my precious grandchildren, Jacob, Jessica, Rachael, Jordan, Evelyn Rose, Curtis Blaze, Lincoln, Maine, Hannah and Easton; and to Ron Curtis, my ex-husband and friend, their Daddy and Grandpa; and to my cherished sister, Nancy Slonim Aronie, who has walked with me hand in hand across the years with laughter, grief and beauty. I want to also acknowledge the treasured four who have now joined our family: Portia, Rob, Asher and Kendall.

A special and humble thanks to my many teachers, both long-term and fleeting, including dear friends who have, in various ways, impacted my life: Dick Riddington, Dorothy Mason, Elinor Cohen, Fran Blackwell, Jocelyn Audet, Rhonda Mattern, Abby Shahn and the loyal Sandra Katz, who found me in a sandbox when we were three and who remains a friend to this day; to my Aunt Shirley and Uncle Yuddie, and to all the many who are so dear to me but too numerous to mention here.

Kudos to my patient initial editor April Bacon, who got me started on this book and kept me organized and inspired; and largely to my dedicated editor and genius Gina Mazza, who helped me whip this lifelong project into shape. After the writing there was even more to do, and I thank my creative team Lee Ann Fortunato-Heltzel, Doug Morrison and Beth Gartz.

NOW lastly, with profound and abundant gratitude, I thank my rare and wonderful husband, Maurice, my rock and playmate who gave me the encouragement, time, space and humor with which to finish this project. You knew, Maur, this was something I needed to do and I thank you for your love.

With time comes new perspective, insight and meaning. What feels certain to me now can change, so I hold loosely to the beauty of impermanence. That is the power of evolution, the evolution of each of us individually and as a collective. My personal story is one microcosm within the macrocosm that is the story of us all.

One reason I am writing this memoir is for my children and their children, who might be bored with my stories by now, but who probably don't know all that I'd like them to know—the good and the bad, if there is such a thing. Kids tend to keep us semi-frozen in their childhood perceptions and sometimes find it hard to hear the evolving voices of their parents. Therefore, I would like to leave my personal history to all of my kids—not that it is a stellar lifetime, but it is my lifetime. Since they do not sit at my knee to listen to these stories, I am writing them down.

In doing so, I suspect that in some peculiar way, my story might inspire your own. Everyone longs to be known and we all want to know: Who were our people? What was their legacy? What will be ours?

Writing this memoir has given me much insight into my life—and life, in general. I just cannot get over how much we can learn about ourselves by looking at our lives from a distance, thinking we've got it finally, and still not being sure of anything. I made lists and lists of my major turning points and no matter how hard I tried there was no chronology that made sense. As I came to the end of writing these pages, I began to realize that no matter how we judge ourselves or others, we rarely ever see the whole picture. How we are doing or what we've achieved can never be determined by the facts of our lives. Whether we should have stayed or whether we should have gone, whether we were weak or whether we were strong can never be truly evaluated because of the minute nuances of every unique life.

As individuals, we are made up of so many layers, colors and tones, pasts, presents and futures all at the same time so that how we perceive ourselves is often reduced to selecting one color from a kaleidoscope. It all depends on which lens we are looking through at the time.

We all come in with our own uniqueness, our predispositions, our particular lessons that need to be learned and the mode of suffering we will endure. Poet Jane Hirshfield says: "The psyche's work is in no small part to discover what you will do in your life with the suffering that has been given you." Most of us are raised by imperfect parents with the best of intentions and how we react to that will determine who we become. There are often hidden reasons for all of our choices, and our beliefs largely determine our reality, so the question becomes: What determines those beliefs?

My belief at this point is that although I have done nothing particularly monumental in this life, it is a relief to be able to finally say, "That's okay." It is liberating to discover that what I did and how I did it was good enough. Only distance could have brought me to this sense of liberation and now I can exhale sweetly knowing the truth of *The Beauty of Impermanence.*

Kate Morton's protagonist in *House at Riverton* sums this up so well: "Wars make history seem deceptively simple. They provide clear turning points, easy distinctions: before and after, winner and loser, right or wrong. True history, the past, is not like that. It isn't flat or linear. It has no outline. It is slippery, like liquid; infinite and unknowable, like space. And it is changeable: Just when you think you see a pattern, perspective shifts, an alternative version is proffered, a long forgotten memory resurfaces. In real life turning points are sneaky. They pass by unlabeled and unheeded and are only uncovered later, by historians who seek to bring order to a lifetime of tangled moments. Time is the master of perspective."

A time came during menopause when I was changing drastically and a new me was emerging. Growing up, I had always thought that *Frances* was my middle name because that's what they told me. But in my twenties, I discovered the truth. So as I was emerging into someone new,

somewhere between fifty and fifty-five, I dropped *Marjorie* and claimed *Frances*, my true first name. I already had an affinity for Saint Francis of Assisi, the animal lover, and Saint Francis de Sales, the writer; and I was born in St. Francis Hospital on December twenty-eighth, the day and month of de Sales' death, so it felt utterly natural to switch. Once I did that, I felt taller. That said, there should be no confusion regarding those two names. They each had their season as me.

There Is Some Kiss

"There is some kiss we want
with our whole lives,
the touch of Spirit on the body."
—Rumi

Letter to Myself
From this photo I came across last night
taken over sixty years ago, I still remember you,
a little girl on a bad day.

There you are on the front porch stoop
in your dimity dress with the eyelet trim,
your unruly hair squeezed
down into a butterfly barrette,
face swollen from another hour of tears.
It's September and the first day of school.

The Touch of Spirit on the Body

ways wanted   to b
ng my around desire
ong
strong

minist

ong

strong

re is some kiss
 wan't our who

The Touch of Spirit on The Body

Dark Time

A Quick Switch: Who is This Girl?

Another Hour of Tears, A Praying Mantis, Hearing the Mysterious, Gram Knows Best

The streetlights in this Village at Tinker Creek shine eerily into the room, giving me a glimpse of the mountains, grounding me to the here and now. My robe is red and cozy like the jacket Daddy bought me the winter I was twelve.

Staring out at those village lights dotting the darkness, I find myself melting into the past, present and future all at once. But just for a minute. It's one fifty-nine in the morning on December 16, 2014. I'm seventy-seven and looking both forward and back to not too long ago when I walked out, finally, after forty-four years of marriage with no money and nowhere to go. I'm remembering all the history that brought me to that moment, and how afterward, I somehow managed to land exactly where I am now, where I needed to be. I can't sleep this night so I sit here staring at the mountains through the dark of the window in my fleecy robe, facing certain memories that have been sneaking uninvited into the present.

It turns out, I was never a real child, carefree, footloose, skipping down the sidewalk somewhere, but I was something else that I was yet to discover.

It was 1947 and I knew my parents had no money for that red jacket. I remember being so happy to be alone with Daddy, out on a dark, snowy night shopping at G. Fox for Christmas presents in the very best store on Main Street. We walked through those silvery deco doors and everything was luminous. Life-sized Santa, his elves and reindeer soared high above. Red and gold and green and silver boughs and bells hung across ceilings and over balconies. Everything shone like crystal. Even though we were Jewish, we celebrated Christmas. Hanukah was good, but Christmas was magic and the whole world was doing it.

We got off the elevator on the fifth floor, the girl's department. Just for fun and longing, I tried on this beautiful red jacket with big pearly buttons. I looked good in red and Daddy loved the way I looked, too, so much so he got that grin on his face that just kept spreading up to the corners of his eyes.

"We'll take it," he told the clerk, just like that. "We'll take it."

"Mommy is going to kill me, Margie," he said with a shrug that told me I was privy to something I shouldn't be.

I loved that night with Daddy, with everyone bustling around, heads bent against the flurry of snow, juggling pretty packages of all shapes and sizes, carols blaring through loud speakers and a real Santa ringing his bell by the Salvation Army kettle. It was a beautiful night before Christmas but it was the last good thing I would remember about Daddy.

Cozy in my robe gazing at these mountains, I'm thinking these are the things I have to tell you from my childhood to set the stage before we move on:

Summer was fast approaching and my little sister, Nancy, and I walked across the yard between our house and Mr. Murphy's house after school. I was crazy about my little sister and loved taking care of her. When she was born and I was four, Mommy said, "What do you think we should name your baby sister?

"Jack," I replied.

"That's a boy's name. Let's name her Jill. She

will be Nancy Jill."

Unlike me, Nancy loved to do cartwheels and climb trees, but like me, she loved visiting Lucky, who lived in the doghouse in Mr. Murphy's yard. Lucky had white hair that flopped in his eyes. He was so old that when I petted him, his back felt as hard as a shell. But Lucky would muster up excitement when he saw us and run in circles wagging his tail as fast as he could. That always made us laugh and whenever I'd talk to him in a high-pitched voice, he'd always answered with a little humming sound.

Mr. Murphy lived in the only paint-weathered house on our street. He'd sit in the doorway of his shed every afternoon and when we stole into his yard, he'd cheerily hoist himself up from his rickety chair. With a twinkle and a grin, he'd take us on a tour of his hollyhocks, grapevines, gooseberries and irises. His grass seemed greener and softer than anyone else's and felt good under our bare feet. His yard smelled of wild roses and sweet honeysuckle.

"D'ya have a song in yer pocket?" he typically asked, which meant that he wanted us to sing. Mr. Murphy was old, too, but both he and Lucky made my sister and me happy.

"White coral bells upon a slender stalk, lilies of the valley on my garden walk," we'd sing in harmony, then he'd pluck two flowers and place them in our hair.

My best friends Sandy, Naomi, Judy, Paula and Susan decided to form a private club. We named it The Happy Huddle, or H.H. for short. We typically convened at my house because no one was ever home. One Saturday, we all took the bus downtown to Fox's Department Store (yes that same store), rode the escalator to the sewing department and each bought two blue H's to sew onto white sweatshirts. Our plan was to learn to cook and sew, and make trips to the library because they had a giant photography section where you could go through pictures of all kinds of things.

During the school year, our school showed a movie every Wednesday night for just a nickel. It wasn't really "night" but in the winter, it was dark and quite a big adventure for us to be out in the snowy cold air by ourselves. We all met at my house for our own movie night, too, because I lived right across the street from the school. We were silly young girls and probably pretty cliquish. We didn't much think about the other kids because we liked each other so much, maybe even loved each other.

The movies were shown on the top floor of the school auditorium. There were a lot of stairs leading up to this floor and for some reason it was hard for me to climb them. My legs typically felt like they were made of lead and none of the adults in my life knew why. My parents just thought I was lazy. But the H.H. girls always waited for me to catch up. After the film, all the kids would rush outside and if there was any snow on the ground, snowball fights would ensue. They'd always start with one snowball thrown by Petey, the class clown, at his best friend, Jimmie, and in mere seconds, all of the kids would be running and shouting and forming teams while I watched.

When I was in sixth grade, Mommy brought home a tiny book titled Growing Up.

"It's time for you to know these things," she said and left me alone with the book. I looked at the pictures and started to scan the text but decided it would be best for the H.H. to read it together. That week, we crowded into the bathroom—it was the only room in our house with a lock—and sat on the floor.

"You're getting them!" Susan giggled. When she said this, I wasn't as embarrassed as the time when the stupid pediatrician congratulated me for getting "ice cream cones."

"Let me see yours," I said to the girls. Everyone lifted up their shirts and we giggled our heads off, comparing our skinny bodies. I couldn't help but notice that they were all still flat.

"You lucky, lucky, lucky!" sang Judy. Whether I was or not, I couldn't yet tell.

I'm sitting here in the middle of the night, reminiscing about those younger years . . . and now I am getting to the place that I dread.

That summer, the Summer of '48, Daddy invited me to go with him to pick up Aunt Esther at Crescent Beach. This was going to be a long trip and we'd just gotten a new car. Well, it wasn't really new, but for us it was, a station wagon with wood paneling on the sides. Daddy was very proud of it. I wanted Mommy and Nancy to come with us, but my parents said that this was a special treat for me. Mommy promised to have everything ready for our cookout when we got home.

I was happy and sad. I wanted my sister to come so we could play on the beach, but I also liked having alone time with Daddy. I liked hearing about his adventures in New York City when he worked for the newspaper. I liked when he was nice to me.

The ride to Crescent Beach was an adventure, in my young eyes. I loved looking out the window and watching the countryside fly by. It was the trees I loved the most, the big gorgeous shadows they threw across the road, and the sunshine that dappled down through them onto the lawns and churchyards and farms with cows and horses. We saw a goat with huge horns, too. I marveled at the big white houses with front pillars and pretty flowers growing everywhere. I savored how bright it was—a perfect summer day, not too hot or sticky, the windows wide open as we rolled along through town after town toward the beach.

I gazed out the window, wondering how long it would be until we could see the ocean and suddenly Daddy's hand was on my leg. I didn't think much of it and then his hand went creeping underneath my shorts. I froze, unsure of what was happening. I pretended to not notice. This was Daddy. What could I do? Now, oh no, he's inside my underpants. The trees rushed past in a blur.

Why ? What? I couldn't turn my head away from the window to look at him. I couldn't look at him. I couldn't breathe. Everything faded to black as his fingers moved up inside me. I wanted to scream, to jump out the window. *Oh, please God make me die.*

"That was the set-up," I tell myself as I sit by the window in the glare of the village lights. I shudder at this memory. To fortify myself, I go to the kitchen and make a cup of tea, knowing that I have to continue down this thought track, no matter what, but only for a little while. As the tea steeps in my faithful mug, I return to the chair by the window and wrap my robe more tightly around my body.

Tell me, Daddy
What was on your mind
when I was born
and while you watched me grow
and on the nights you crept around,
shadowy,
issuing aberrations
onto innocence
transparent as shell
hacking a fault-line into the diamond
that was me, your own girl

Were you ashamed?
Did you sometimes want to
burn away your hands?

Seventh grade was horrible. I'd get a tummy ache every morning right before the bell rang. I was doing poorly in school since I spent so much time in a haze, staring out the window. I couldn't help it. My eyes just went there.

One day in science class, we had to bring in an insect. I found a bright green little creature, one that I'd never seen before. It wouldn't fit in a mason jar so I put it in a shoebox and punched holes in it so it could breathe. I could see its eyes and the way it stood on its hind legs. It was beautiful. I couldn't wait to bring it to school and show everyone. I was certain that Miss Knox would like it, but when she saw my insect, she screamed at me in front of the whole class.

"Take that out this minute, Marjorie!" she said. "Don't you know that it's against the law to catch a praying mantis?"

No, I didn't. I'd never heard of a praying mantis. Miss Knox made me walk to the park and let it loose. The park was a block away from school. Those were the days when a teacher would let a kid out of school and not worry about it. The sidewalks were empty with no one around. That walk took me a long time with the way my sorry legs worked. I didn't understand why I couldn't even walk from my house to the corner without stopping and now I'm on my way to the park with a praying mantis while Miss Knox, I'm sure, is wondering when I'll return.

On this bright sunny day, with the praying mantis keeping perfectly still inside the cardboard box, I remembered how that stupid pediatrician said nothing was wrong with me, and Mommy and Daddy believed him. That's when I began telling everyone that I had a heart problem, so they would stop bothering me when I couldn't keep up.

Once at the park, I opened the box and let the big green bug jump into the bushes, turned around and began my long walk back to class. When I got there, Miss Knox said I did all this on purpose to get out of science.

Around this time, I began contemplating painless ways to take my life, not just because of Miss Knox but because of Daddy and because of my slowness. I made up a game that I called, "Who would I rather be?" I would go through the names of my schoolmates, dead heroes and movies stars, and in the end I'd always pick myself. I wanted to be me, but I prayed to know who I was and why everything was so bad. Even though I had my best friends in the H.H., I was different from them and everyone else. I felt like some kind of alien living in disguise and that was not fun so for a few years I imagined ways to do it, ways to be dead.

Then I made the staff of *The Observer*, our school paper. That was a huge achievement and I was very proud because only a few brainy kids made it. I didn't write about sports or insects but I got a press pass and went to The State Theatre, where they let me in to interview the popular singer Johnny Ray. He dropped to his knees before either James Brown or Elvis ever did and I loved his song *The Little White Cloud that Cried.*

I wrote for the school newspaper but I couldn't tell my closest friends what I really needed to say. I didn't have the words. I sought answers at Hebrew School but found none. Religion was useless. The only moments I felt truly at peace were when I'd wander into the empty sanctuary of the synagogue with its tall ceilings and luminous stained glass windows, where I could stretch out on those long velvet benches, breathe in the silence and gaze into space. At those times, my "little voice" would tell me what not to do.

Whenever I'd get really into the fantasy of dying, an amazing thing would happen. A feeling would come into me that was warm and wonderful and felt like amazing love. All I wanted to do was find a way to die but whatever that was that came into my head would laugh and say, "Margie, see how much you can take today. You can always do it tomorrow." It was so matter of fact and lighthearted that it made me want to keep going, at least for another day. Where that feeling came from was a mystery because I didn't believe in that old man with the beard up in the heavens that we were supposed to be afraid of and at the same time worship. Even though we had to go to Hebrew School, I didn't believe in anything. So I talked aloud to myself, questioned, wailed and wondered. Words burst and tumbled out of me when I was alone. Sometimes I sang them and sometimes they spilled onto paper. I never expected anything. It's just what had to come out of me or I would burst and so I let it and whenever I did I felt better. I started to think that's what God might be, something nobody ever talks about, something that is warm and cozy and comes mysteriously into your head.

"The Greeks understood the mysterious power of the hidden side of things. They bequeathed to us one of the most beautiful words in our language—the word 'enthusiasm'—en theos—a god within. The grandeur of human actions is measured by the inspiration from which they spring. Happy is he who bears a god within, and who obeys it."
—Louis Pasteur

I think what saved me while growing up were the times when I'd spend beautiful hours in my grandmother's kitchen, wonderful moments in her chubby, dimpled arms, her starched, flour-dusted apron and the sweet-smelling scent of honey and flowery soap. She made me laugh and I absorbed her love of cooking. That's what she did. She just loved and as I sit here in the middle of the night by the light of the village lamps, I find myself feeling her arms around me, bathing in that sweet smell I remember so well.

But why did no one in our family ever utter a word about Gram's lost family in Poland? There was never a word about her parents, siblings or cousins. No one knew what had become of them. Questions weren't asked and tears weren't shed, at least as far as I knew.

Throughout the years, especially during holiday celebrations and Saturday morning services, it seemed that all I learned about the Jews was how persecuted we were. What was the reason for that? I wondered. And why was I personally accused of killing Jesus? And why did our parents give us a boring Jewish education when they themselves never even talked about God? What seemed important to them was getting along, fitting in and wanting us children to be something other than who we were—

smarter, less Jewish looking and more athletic. These were things we could never be.

I think my Grandmother instinctively knew something bad was going on in our house, and she'd shelter me in her tiny apartment on days when I just could not face school. Once in awhile, she'd offer me a bath in the middle of the afternoon. She bathed me clean, clean of betrayals. Strange as that may seem, it soothed my heart and soul at a time when I had begun to hate the body I was growing into. I let her love and divine scent nourish me.

Taking a sip of my tea, I'm sad for my father, and what a messed up man he was. He was like Jekyll and Hyde. I return to the kitchen, pop a croissant into the toaster oven, coat it with butter and raspberry jam to go with my now lukewarm tea, and settle back in for more miserable remembering . . . but only for a little while longer because enough is enough. But wait:

When I was a sophomore, Richie asked me to the junior prom. Of course, it was no surprise since he was my boyfriend. We had a sweet, safe and convenient relationship. I can't remember what we ever talked about, but it was always kind of nice being with him and the group of kids we hung out with. It gave me a sense of normalcy despite my inner chaos.

The next Saturday, Mom took me shopping for my gown. It was a rare occasion to be alone with her because she worked all the time. We had a lot of fun that day. Hanging on a rack in the Bluebird Shop was the perfect gown for me. It was sky blue, strapless, waltz length, and overlaid with the usual tulle that floated over all the gowns in those days. I felt as pretty as I could ever feel but like the red jacket it was a lot of money for us. Even though I wanted it really badly, I knew my parents couldn't afford it. Mom shook her head "no" and as a compensation prize, I suppose, she took me to Jensen's, a classy little restaurant where we had peppermint ice cream with hot fudge, my favorite. In a few weeks I would probably end up wearing my cousin's gown to the prom but that would be okay, I guess.

My girlfriends and I talked about the event for weeks. Then on the Friday before the Saturday of the big day, Mom came home from work with a huge smile and a Bluebird box under her arm. She had secretly put the dress on layaway and now it was here, right on time. I couldn't believe my eyes. It was even more beautiful than I remembered.

The next morning I got up early, partially from excitement and partially to do all the things that a girl does to get ready for a prom. There was to be a "coke-tail" party at a friend's house before the dance then we'd all pile into cars and merrily head for the school.

A beautiful black orchid was delivered. I had never seen such a gorgeous flower. It wasn't really black but more like purple. I loved Richie's originality and desire to be so extravagant for me. I placed it around my wrist and admired the dark flower, knowing that Richie had diligently saved up his money for this one night.

It was six o' clock. There I sat, straight as a stick in my crinolines and puffy cloud of a gown, while my family ate their usual Saturday night supper of hot dogs, baked beans, sauerkraut and potato salad. I was too excited to eat anything all day so I sat there on edge, waiting for the doorbell to ring.

When it finally did, I jumped up to let Richie in. As I ran to the door, my father said, "Tell him you're not going."

"What?" I asked in shock, thinking that I'd heard wrong.

"You're staying home tonight."

I couldn't believe what I was hearing and thought maybe my father was joking around. He sometimes did that, but sometimes he meant it, too.

"Go answer the door and tell him you're not going," he said firmly, his dark eyes magnified by the thick horn-rimmed glasses he always wore.

"Go!" he shouted. Was there some omen in the color of my corsage?

I had never gotten used to my father's irrational behavior, which would surface unexpectedly and at the worst possible moments. This time was crueler than most because he was punishing Richie, too, and for no reason that I could tell. In these situations, my mom would sit passively and wordlessly while her eyes reflected sorrow, but she had always been too frightened to start something that might lead us into a deeper hell.

The orchid soon curled up and died, and the blue gown faded in the back of my closet. Mom never took my side or comforted me about this ordeal. She didn't know how.

All childhood experience lays a foundation for who we will become. Visible and invisible scars form from any kind of abuse or neglect and the essence of the experience hides buried in the body. We have only recently begun to make the connection between childhood trauma and "dis-ease"—the essence of which manifests into not only illness but various forms of dysfunction that usually hang on right into and throughout adulthood unless we do something about it.

With me, it manifested in my being an underachiever. Which road a child takes depends on many things. I was an underachiever because nothing good was expected of me and because there were so many things I could not do but I got by because, for some reason, I always had great friends. They didn't know the real me, of course, but it sufficed that they liked me the way I was.

Elinor was brainy. She kept me facing the right direction, literally. If I was supposed to go right, I went left. She kept me as straight and narrow as possible, and we gossiped and giggled and confided many things to each other, but *not* everything. There were no words for some things. She seemed to sweep me up with the other kids walking down the street, going to the movies or the soda shop, and all the while I looked and sounded like a regular kid.

We never knew when Daddy would lash out. It could be unrelated to anything, totally out of the blue and I was usually the target. But between Elinor and Richie and my other girlfriends, I managed to get through high school. By my senior year, I was terrified about graduation. Where would I go? Who would I become? What would I possibly do with all those terrible grades? When a write-up in my yearbook said I was "sweet", I almost threw up. I didn't want to be sweet. That sweetness was not me, not really. It was just my pass to survival. I wanted to be smart, strong and interesting. All my friends were going away to the best colleges. My parents had been in such denial about my bad grades and our lack of money that they simply didn't think about my future and yet they assumed I would also be going off to college. They longed for status and thought that college was a fertile hunting ground for finding a "good" husband. I carried the utter loneliness, guilt, shame and fear of applying anywhere and everywhere, knowing the rejections would fly in like hail on a dark day. I knew I was simply not qualified and there was the added terror of having to show those rejections to my father. Yet for some reason, that didn't stop me from trying. I needed to get far away from home, if nothing else.

Fragment of Very First Painting

Following Dharma: It Began in Boston

Girl of the '50s, Loss or Gain? Cleaving Starry Skies, Off the Trampled Path

"It must have been your essay. Everything in my right mind tells me you're not a viable candidate," said Mr. McCarthy, the admissions officer at Boston University.

He was shocked by my grades, wondering how I'd even made it to an interview. Yet something in him must have known that I would do well despite my past performance. I sat at the edge of the straight-backed chair in his office and waited. He shook his head, arguing with himself, then finally gave me a nod.

"I'll place you in the junior college and see how you do. Don't let me down. If you do well, we'll move you on," he said.

Oh, my God! I was so relieved, so overjoyed! In the fall of 1955, I would be going off to college. Why do they call it *off* to college? I wondered.

I fell in love with the whole experience— the coursework, the professors, my own awakening to a whole new perspective of who I was possibly becoming as a person. Despite my mediocrity in school, being away from my father, I was discovering that I really did have a brain. Still, I was embarrassed at not being in the "real" college. Everyone in my dorm was majoring in liberal arts, education or social work. I kept my junior college status a secret from the guys I dated so, in a way, I had this good life but I still felt like an imposter.

Away from home, I began to grow into a new person, somehow smarter and more enthusiastic. At junior college, I was a solitary student among mainly older guys and Korean vets who were there on the GI Bill. My most significant conversations took place in the corridors and occasionally over coffee with my instructors, which was a legitimate privilege in those days.

I was learning how to think and question differently, to look at other cultures and ideas from the past, present and what might become the future. I was hoping all the while to make it to the art school to learn how to design clothes. It was something I had done as a pastime. I'd spent hours as a child and into my teen years drawing girls with tiny waists, long legs and glamorous outfits, while at the same time I myself was gaining pound onto pound, devouring pizzas and Dairy Queen chocolate shakes, feeding my starving heart.

When my philosophy professor learned of my career ambition as a fashion designer, he asked if I really wanted to manipulate minds, and to become a tastemaker by showing people what they needed to be wearing and not wearing in order to be in style.

"Oh, God no," I said. "I don't want to manipulate anyone."

"Well, that's what fashion is," he said. "What's good this year and bad the next. It makes people want to toss out last year's clothes and buy the latest thing, especially women."

Blond straight hair and a willowy body was the beauty standard and that's who fashion was designed for. I didn't have straight hair or a willowy body but, of course, that's what I longed for. Even I was drawing those skinny figures, which proved how brainwashed we all were and how inadequate it made so many of us feel. I had never thought about it that way and I don't think about it that way now but the conversation served a purpose as it led me in another direction.

My professors both challenged and validated me. They happily led me to believe that I had a functional brain in my head and they hinted that there was more to life than what our 1950s-American mindset had tacitly agreed to accept as reality. They started me on the path to authenticity.

Mr. McCarthy was right. I was finding myself.

My father was a political man and despite his craziness, that was the one good thing that rubbed off on me. I don't know if my support for Adlai Stevenson was simply because I wanted Daddy's approval or because I really liked Stevenson. I resonated with that famous hole in the sole of his shoe, a symbol of humility of the man who would be president. He once said, "My definition of a free society is a society where it is safe to be unpopular." I thought the world could become a better place if he got elected. He was smart and kind of lovable. "Freedom is not an ideal," he also said. "It is not even a protection, if it means nothing more than freedom to stagnate, to live without dreams, to have no greater aim than a second car and another television set."

That was a truth that spoke to me. So I stood for hours on a windy corner in some lonely suburb outside of Boston, wearing a silver pin of a shoe with a hole in it, handing out flyers to the sparse crowd of passersby. My hands froze, the flyers ruffled into fans, my ears grew red, my nose dripped, and I shifted from one foot to the other way into dusk on those cold Boston autumn days. Even though Stevenson lost badly, my efforts paid off in one unforgettable way. I was invited to a formal tea—all silver and china and delicate sweets—where Senator Jack Kennedy shook my hand with that great big smile on his face, after which I was able to stuff my own face with punch and petit fours.

One late April morning in my sophomore year at BU, as the sun sat high and bright and the sky was perfectly blue, I took myself down to the river, which seemed, on that day, to be an exaggeration of itself. It was Boston and this was The Charles. Young children tumbled in the grass with youthful parents. Older children played catch. The trees unfurled their leaves. You could almost see their dance. An occasional boat would cut through the river. Crew was at practice.

It was an underfoot pleasure to be mushing through the fine new grass. Boston University had no actual campus; dorms and classrooms were sidewalks apart. I strolled to the river's edge, as close as I could get, and settled into a deep quiet, very rare for me. My mind was always talking to itself and there were always people around. This day was different—maybe because it was Easter Sunday. Everything was unusually beautiful. I was filled with the calm of the river and the warmth of the sun above it.

I laid back, clasped my hands beneath my head and watched the cumulus clouds play tag with each other—a cow, a giraffe, a whole ocean, sweetly moving across the sky. When I finally became aware of my surroundings, I sat up and felt a genuine smile on my face. I was interrupted by the thought that if anybody saw me in that moment, they would think I was crazy. Anyway, I didn't care. I drank it in, this tingling with life and burst of spring, and when I was so full and could take in no more, I got up and left to go back to my dorm.

On the fifth floor, the elevator doors opened. Both of my roommates were there to greet me.

"Call home," they cried in grave unison. I flew into a frenzy from the seriousness of their voices (so unlike them) and dialed my parents' phone number.

Aunt Shirley answered. "Your father's in the hospital," she said. "You'd better come home."

I slammed down the receiver and like a dog after a cat, tore through my roommates' closets looking for something black. My father, I knew, was dead.

My MIT buddies sped me to the airport in their communal Oldsmobile, trying to calm and comfort me. It was hard to know what to feel. I felt every emotion at once. I was so anxious that I queued up to be the first one off the plane before it even landed. The flight attendants had to escort me back to my seat.

My sister and uncle picked me up at the airport. "He's gone," my sister said. "Gone."

When we arrived home, I leapt out of the car and ran straight to the garage. My sister had already told me what had happened. How she was in the front yard when he tugged at the cord to start the lawn mower and how right before her eyes he dropped to the ground. How our mother was in the backyard with a friend drinking lemonade and marveling at the new burst of daffodils. How the doctor from across the street had come running over to give Daddy a shot. How they took a blanket off his bed in order to cover him, all of him. How they carted him away on a stretcher after the ambulance arrived too late.

The blanket, still there on the grass, called me to it. I bunched myself into a ball, wrapping it around me, and sobbed as if my heart would never come back to my body. I was aware of my drama. I was aware of wondering if this is how people act when someone they love and hate at the same time —someone who is so big in their lives they can hardly breathe without them— dies. I didn't know, but all kinds of things were happening at once and, at the same time, this was a performance of grief. I was pissed off because how dare he get away with all that he did then just up and leave. Looking back, I've always felt that his sudden heart attack at the age of fifty was a deliberate copping out. It was no surprise to me that his heart is what gave out, so overburdened by remorse. That's what I decided was true, that he had nowhere to go from there. His business was flat. It held no passion for him and he made almost no money. He was bored, out of control, and I was convinced that he was remorseful. He just had to close up shop, so he did.

I thought, *What are we going to do now?* And I prayed, "Thank you, God."

It happened to be Passover, an important holiday, a time when Jews can't go to the mortuary or have a funeral. I grabbed a batch of photos from our album, stuffed them in my bag and ran out the door. The mourners, sympathizers, friends, neighbors and even strangers who strangely love this sort of thing packed the house as custom dictates. Some tried to stop me, but still I jumped into the family car and sped to Weinstein's Mortuary. One of the doors was unlocked, but the old men inside blocked my way.

"Where is he?" I shouted, pushing past them.

I found him in a room at the end of a dark corridor, laid out under dim golden light. He looked tenderly quiet, with a vulnerability I'd never before seen. I bent down to kiss his forehead. It felt like marble. I brushed back his course, curly hair that had grown wild from an overdue haircut. Shuffling through the photos, I chose one and tucked it along with two dimes into the breast pocket of his charcoal gray suit. It showed my mother, sister and me, sitting on a blanket by the Keney Park tennis courts, the rear side of somebody's dog in the background.

I sat in a stupor, staring at him for I don't know how long. I said some things out loud but have no idea what. The part of me that observes and criticizes told me that I was being overly dramatic, abnormal. I didn't care. I was just there being me. There was room for confusion, for my conflicting feelings. I had no clarity about who he was to me. In my state of shock, I'd gone from adrenalin overflow to total stillness.

Although my father had been bad to me, ironically, he had also been a major source of affection in a clean and loving way—exactly why that red jacket at Christmastime is so symbolic. It was as though he were two different people. When he joked with me or cuddled me or looked at me with pride, I was in heaven. I loved him beyond description. He was big and strong and sometimes handsome. Daddy was funny and smart and sometimes crazy but he talked to me as if I were the only adult in the world. Although I wondered why, I guiltily savored the attention.

When he was the other person, I was the object of his rage and his perceived source of failure. Of this, he never failed to remind me—like the times when he peered at me sitting across from him in the living room, he in his easy chair, me curled into the corner of the couch, tears running down my face, sniveling into the dishtowel I was still holding from kitchen chores, and he'd say, "How have I failed? What did I do wrong to make you like this? Your hair, your grades, your weight. Such a beautiful face and look at you. Soon we'll have to buy your clothes in the tent department."

What had he done as our father? Of course, I had no way of articulating or even knowing the impact he had on me yet, and I had so many colliding emotions it felt like the core of myself was missing, leaving a big, black hole.

Sitting in the dim room in the mortuary gazing at my father's body, I wondered about it all. I tried to review our lives together, four distinct individuals tied together by some structure called family. Neither of my parents paid much attention to my little sister. Daddy let her be. He neither touched her in a good way nor bad way. I was the attraction and the match that would ignite every explosion, and Mom and Nancy lived in dread of the scenes my father would make. Nancy moved through the house inconspicuously, and other times when she could stand the tension no longer, she'd run to Daddy and say, "Margie is sorry. She wants to apologize." Then she'd run to me and say, "Daddy is sorry. He wants to apologize." I would respond, "Why should I?" and stand in my defiance.

My mother had been absent and detached most of the time. She worked at Fox's, the same store where Daddy bought me the jacket. She fitted bras and corsets to oversized and undersized women, lacing and hooking her life away. After work, she'd trudge off to Daddy's store, which was open until nine. On the way, she would often pick up cleaning women who were waiting for buses, loaded down with bundles in the pouring rain or boiling heat, and she'd take them all the way home.

"There but for the grace of God go I," she'd say.

That was her favorite expression and the source of her kindness but, when Mom got home at night, she was too tired for us, for words or hugs or kisses. Mom never told me that I was smart or good or beautiful or that Daddy was wrong. She was either too tired, too weak or too scared to ever stand up for me and I consequently had no respect for her. Although I was the one Daddy targeted, none of us felt safe.

So I sat gazing at my dead father, asking why and I received no answer.

Back at the house after the visit to the mortuary, I snuck in the back door to avoid the mourners.

Behind her dark glasses, Mommy caught a glimpse of me and she, Nancy and I escaped upstairs. We convened around the toilet seat and bathtub, locked the door and gazed at each other in disbelief.

"He had to die for us to live," I said. It just came out of my mouth.

They nodded in sad agreement. Though we felt bereft, terrified and small, we were in some kind of strange rapture. The oppression we had lived under through the years had vanished. Even though I had escaped to Boston, it had grabbed me every time I returned for a visit but now it was really gone, just like that. We were like newly freed prisoners who did not know what to do next. The cruel tension that we might today call domestic terrorism had filled our home was now gone, and a new kind of uncertainty, a milder uncertainty, had taken its place. Still, without speaking the words, we were aware of each other's newfound ability to exhale.

Nine months later, I was stretched out on my narrow bed in my dorm, hungry as always, and waiting for my roommates so we could go down to dinner. I was relaxed and reviewing the day's events. I'd just finished a class with Miller, my sociology professor. He'd given a lecture on the Kwakiutl Indians and was so utterly impassioned over their customs that he climbed a ladder that was leaning against the classroom wall, and simply talked on and on, taking one rung at a time without missing a breath or a gesture. I'll never forget the look on his face when at the end of class, he found himself three feet off the floor. I was lying there laughing to myself about the outrageousness of it.

All of a sudden, something miraculous happened: I was shot from my bed through space as if from a cannon at great speed, cleaving starry skies, galaxies, blackness and light—brilliant, brilliant light—then pitch dark again. And there I suddenly was, perfectly still and in the presence of my father. I couldn't see or hear him, smell or touch him, but I sure felt his presence. We were in proximity, facing each other, just hanging there. I was flabbergasted that none of my senses were working and still I knew him, the essence of him, the one who had given me bear hugs as a little girl and the one who had terrorized me on Sunday mornings as I sat stuffing myself with bagels and two kinds of cheese. He was there as

love. Nothing frightening, just love. Everything was beautiful and still and there were all these lights around us. I don't know if they were stars or what.

Then, as quickly as a door slamming shut, I was back on the bed, back in my body, eyes wide open in disbelief and longing to return.

But I could not. It was as though I was stuck in concrete. I was as far from that beautiful unknown as I had ever been, but now I had unexpectedly unraveled some mystery about death.

"The fairest thing we can experience is the mysterious. It is the fundamental emotion which stands at the cradle of true art and true science."
—Albert Einstein

Is it our spirits that stay alive, our souls? I didn't know, but I definitely experienced us—my father and me—but not as we had always been. This time it was gentle, tender, loving. I definitely knew I would not share this experience with anyone. Was Daddy trying to tell me something for a second time? First by the river, as he lifted off the planet, and now, pulling me out to space? Was it for love?

That wild ride through the stars, the dark and the light, began my conscientious search for what was real yet unseen. Anything immeasurable, anything that fell outside the physical, had not been part of my education yet I knew that this was not a dream and I was *not crazy*. I started to read about esoteric topics, beginning with the books in the library and old bookstores around Boston and Cambridge. The books held a wealth of information that was not a part of anything I had ever heard of and yet, as it turned out, my experience would have seemed perfectly normal in other cultures. It felt comforting to be validated but I still had so many questions. It wasn't just the books I was reading and sometimes carried around with me —*The Tibetan Book of the Dead*, it's talk of Bardo, (the transitional place after death) and Yogananda's *Autobiography of a Yogi*. I would also meet people with an interest in these subjects. It has been said that "like attracts like." Perhaps that's what got these conversations going.

The conversations centered around things like coming into a life, where are we before we're born? Do we exist or do we come from nothing? Have we lived before? Where do the specific qualities come from that make a person unique? How does that part come into form and where does it go when it leaves? What is death? What the hell is death?

It wasn't just what I was thinking about that attracted certain types of people to me, it was also who I was becoming. A man at a bus stop would start a conversation, a woman in line somewhere. The perfect book would be lying on the only vacant table in the library where I was on a search. How did all this happen? Something opened in me that day after Miller's class. In that opening, I seemed to have become an over-focused seeker. Researching teachings from the East made it all so real and since I had already been curious from childhood, desperately searching for my true identity and my reason for being alive, I had a head start, an open mind and although I was raised Jewish, I still had no particular dogma to hold me back.

After two years in the Junior College, I was accepted into BU's School of Fine and Applied Arts but Daddy had not liked the idea of me studying something so impractical. Somehow right before he died, he gave in by saying (and I quote): "With that kind of enthusiasm, baby, how can I say no?" I was so happy I had his blessings before he died and eagerly started classes.

There was only a little bit of insurance money and somewhere in my second semester my mother informed me that there was no way I could continue with school. But I was determined to do so, one way or another. My dear Aunt Shirley and Uncle Yuddie pitched in. I took a waitressing job on Newberry Street where blue-haired ladies ate veal patties and scalloped potatoes, and I snuck cherries from under the crusts of homemade pies. My drawing instructor sold a drawing and put the proceeds on my bursar's bill without even telling me and, to my amazement, I received enough of a scholarship to allow me to continue.

So now I was out of the dorms and renting an apartment near Fenway Park with my roommate, Barbara. I had been dating Howie, a law student, pretty regularly and it was starting to look serious. Things were going well. I was in the art school and I loved my new freedom from the dorm rules and the space Barb and I shared. And then . . .

"Do you know how long it takes plaster to dry?" I asked the most intriguing person I had ever seen. He had been aloof in sculpture class. Those eyes were close to the color of morning glories and his aura of intense mystery reminded me of a picture of Sean O'Casey I had once seen on the back cover of one of his books. In it, he looked long, lean and lost in his oversized clothes, a style referred to as "shabby genteel." In his shabby corduroy jacket and baggy pants, this guy was exactly that.

"Oh," he said, slowing his gait. "Plaster dries fast. You just need to experiment to get the feel of it. You'll figure it out."

His lack of interest in me was palpable, but he was absorbed, it seemed, with other things, as he picked up his long-legged stride toward who knows where.

My obsession with the "other world" stuff had now been replaced with my growing passion for making art. Now, the minute I went into the studio, I was at home. This was what I was meant to do. My painting instructor had convinced me to become a painting major, which flattered and motivated me toward a new practice and a new dream. As it turned out, I was no longer interested in manipulating minds or becoming a taste-maker through fashion. And by the way, who was this morning-glory-blue-eyed guy named Ron?

I spent hours in the painting studio long after classes were over and then, of course, there was drawing and sculpture. But I had to know this skinny guy with the elegant hands. That was the kick-start of a chase that would continue for years to come. There was something about him that I had to have. Not him exactly but what he seemed to represent and the vibe he embodied. I was blown away by his intense dedication to his work and I wanted some of that for myself. I also wanted some of that comfort he seemed to have in his own skin, a huge contrast to this nice middle-class Jewish girl in her circular skirt and crisp white blouses with the Peter Pan collars who had been raised to marry higher than herself. I desperately needed to escape that expectation. I had been looking for change at a primal level because I was terrified of becoming lazy, pampered and ordinary. I was in the process of discarding all of society's expectations. I wanted my life to count but did not yet have a clear picture of what that meant. As it seemed to me, except for colorful cars, the fifties were beige—the clothes, the houses, the focus on status.

"When any of us meet someone who rejects dominant norms and values, we feel a little less crazy for doing the same. Any act of rebellion or non-participation, even on a very small scale, is therefore a political act."
—Charles Eisenstein, *The More Beautiful World Our Hearts Know is Possible*

I had come alive in Boston and what filled me with passion was putting color to canvas, along with this shabby, skinny guy named Ron whose still-life paintings could be taken for Cezanne's, and whose landscapes vibrated with more shades of green than I ever knew existed. This guy was in his own world doing his own business without a care about what anyone thought, older than the rest of us and on the G.I. Bill. I got some words out of him one day when we were in the same place at the same time—of course, all by design on my part.

In the U.S. Navy for four years, he had been all over the world. Maybe that worldliness made him attractive to me because—how can I say it—it was not a sexual thing. It was something beyond that.

Some afternoons after school, bursting with my own growing intensity and joy from having completed something good in art class, I'd wander over to Copley Square then into the dark cave of Storyville, sit down at a little round table and listen to the jazz greats warming up for the night's performance.

After a while, with my newfound clarity and growing confidence, I inched along the trail of the renegade artists, the Beat poets and abstract painters, and became ecstatic as I was drawn into the concept of classlessness. I was inspired by their search for an understanding of spirit, for Reality with a capital R, which seemed exemplified by my platonic attraction to Ron. Maybe I was frightened of anything else because of my father's behaviors and my self-consciousness about my body, so I managed to convince myself it was platonic. I just knew that I loved seeing him on his tall, black bike with the little leather pouch attached to the seat containing pencils, charcoal, or a sack of Gauloises, I never knew. Starting in September, he'd begin his glide over the fallen leaves of red and gold, often wet and slippery. He'd ride by snow banks black with traffic and through pollen drifts in spring looking very European.

Since it was too far for me to walk from my apartment and too expensive to take a cab to school, I decided to get a bike, too. With my crazy legs, it was truly a fantasy decision. Among a hundred posts on the bulletin board was one for a used blue Raleigh, which I decided to check out. Ron offered to meet me to look over the bike. It passed his inspection, so I handed over my twenty dollars and had a few false starts before my body remembered how to balance from when I was nine and soon I was anxiously wobbling down the street to my apartment.

The road to school was mostly flat with one little decline and after about a mile, out of breath and cheeks flushed, I'd victoriously cruise right up to the building.

One late fall afternoon, while walking the bike up the hill, I heard a pathetic little meow behind me. I stopped to find a little gray kitten trailing after me. I picked her up and she began to purr, no squiggling, no scratching, she just fell limp into my arms and purred like a little motorboat. This tiny bundle had the sweetest little moon face I had ever seen.

I thought that she must belong to someone, as she was so tame, so I put her down and begged her to go home, but she continued to follow me down the stairs into the basement where I kept my bike. When I put her back outside, she started that pathetic meow again, but I didn't want to bring her in as her person might be searching for her. Still, I thought she might be hungry so I went up and scraped some tuna off a leftover sandwich and poured her some milk, brought it down to her, and while she was lapping it up, I snuck back inside and closed the door behind me, hoping her person would come soon. In the morning, I found her curled up in a raggedy old chair in the basement. She stretched, purred and rubbed her furry self against my leg. I put her out again and decided that if she were still there after school I would take her in. And that is just what happened. So now Barbara and I had a little pink-nosed kitten to raise. We called her Moonie.

All around me, people were brazenly emerging from the sleepy mediocrity, suburban materialism and deadly conformity of the fifties in so many courageous ways. I was alive with changes that I didn't understand. I would call it turmoil or anticipation or a sense that something big was about to happen but I couldn't tell what it was.

In the midst of all of this, I had to argue hard to convince the university to let me replace some of my academic courses with more studio courses.

"But this is a university," the dean said. "We can't do that."

"I don't want the degree," I insisted. "I just want to paint. Artists don't need degrees."

"You'll never be able to teach," he cautioned.

"I don't want to teach. I want to paint," I said, and he gave in.

I immersed myself in beginning, intermediate and advanced drawing, painting and sculpture all at the same time. With my determination, Ron and I had gradually become friends. Occasionally, he'd come to Storyville with me or we'd go out for a beer. Even though I hated the taste of beer, I'd sip along, making it last throughout our conversations. Neither of us had any money so we spent most of our time at his studio—except on weekends when I did the Harvard things with Howie. Before my father's death, Howie's parents and mine had already met and they had begun to whisper about a wedding. It was the thing to do—have your daughter marry a nice Jewish lawyer. He was kind enough, smart enough, cute enough, but our relationship was all very bland and I had allowed myself to be on automatic pilot with the whole situation as it leaned unenthusiastically into the very future I disdained. But when expectation and desire are two different things, conflict arises and fate inevitably takes the time it needs.

So following my desire, I would take a bus to Roxbury where Ron was running a rooming house for old people in exchange for rent. His studio spread out into several rooms with work piled up against every available wall—still lives, those green, green landscapes, and portraits of all kinds.

One evening, we were seated on two metal stools in his studio. He had just made a pot of coffee. It was strong and bitter, but it was to be the beginning of my passion for strong coffee, among other things. Love by association. We talked about art, as usual, then it turned personal.

"What scares you?" he asked.

"Oh, I don't know," I said. "All my friends are having bridal showers, getting married, buying houses, settling down. That terrifies me. I'm having a hard time imagining it."

"Why?" he asked.

"I don't know. I want to do something more with my life. I don't want to be somebody's wife." Although I seemed to be headed in that direction. That scared me.

"What do you want to do, then?" he asked.

I was insulted. "Paint, of course. Why else am I here?"

"Well, you can't be a painter instead of doing something else. You can only be a painter if you *have* to paint, if there's nothing else in the world you want to do and if you can spend your life doing without *things*. There's no glamour in it, you know, and man, there are no guarantees."

"I know that. Of course, I do. But all I care about is to learn, to be able to make good art. I don't need a house or a wedding or kids. I don't even need recognition, I just need a studio."

"Of course, you know this culture will give you grief unless you're really good and that will probably be after you're dead. It will just be you, a pretty lonely life for a pretty girl."

That was so condescending and yet I was glad he thought I was pretty and I know he was right. I was in conflict.

"So what about you? Why are you doing it?" I asked, turning the table.

"It's just who I am," he said. "That's all. That's it."

My coffee had gotten cold and the metal stool had become hard. It was time to go. And who is this guy, anyway? I mean, deep down? I had to know. I couldn't believe that I had started fantasizing about spending my life with him in an environment that smelled of turpentine and linseed oil. Who was I kidding? What in the world did I want? Who did I think I was? In that moment, I had no idea.

"The heart has its reasons of
which reason knows nothing."
—Blaise Pascal

Then Howie landed in the infirmary with mono and when I went to visit him, he was in a large room along with many other boys wearing blue johnnies and looking very pale. I came in and sat down on the edge of the bed. He glanced over to the other boys, grinned, turned and said:

"Margie, I'm sorry, I can't do this anymore. I don't love you."

Just like that.

"Okay," I said, without any emotion. "Okay," and I rose from the bed, a little stunned, and left the infirmary. That was it. Well, I didn't blame him. He wasn't getting much from me in the way of passion or anything else for that matter. Howie

represented my conflict of destiny. This would free me from having to decide whether to settle for the norm or jump into the compelling abyss.

In that moment, everything shifted. First, I cried from being rejected. Then, in the back seat of the cab that was carrying me across the Charles River, I burst out laughing.

"Are you okay?" asked the driver.

"Oh, yes," I said. "Oh, yes. I am very okay."

And I was, despite the cab money I'd just spent to go see Howie. I was very okay with this sudden rejection. I was very okay with the fact that I suddenly felt free. I did not love Howie and never had, and now I could admit it.

I was in love with Ron! As impossible as it was, it had become clear. Yet I really couldn't imagine us actually together because of everything—our religions, his independence, and his total focus on his work and nothing or no one else. I consciously decided to take one moment at a time, expecting nothing and enjoying what we had as pals, while repressing the thought that I might be heading for disaster.

I began taking the bus to his place every night and Barbara was getting annoyed. After all, we had taken the apartment together, adopted

Moonie and now I was hardly ever home.

"What would you do if I stopped coming here?" I asked Ron.

"I'd just come to you," he replied.

One night after stretching a bunch of canvases, we went out for a beer, even though I still hated the taste.

"What do you want to do?" Ron asked.

"About what?" I replied.

"With your life, with your future."

"Didn't I already tell you? I asked. "I have no idea. Just paint. That's it, I guess."

"Where will you live?" he asked.

"I don't know. I am here now. I can't think about the future. It scares the hell out of me to think about the future. All I can do is be here. Now. In this moment."

Then out of the total blue: "Why don't we get married?" he asked. (Or, was that a proposal?)

"What?" Was I hearing right? My heart leapt across the room. We had never even kissed and here was this ascetic recluse who rarely went to class and was allowed to get away with it, who never, never socialized when there, and we had hardly even brushed against each other's bodies and here he was asking me to marry him? He was smart, talented and mysteriously inspiring. I wanted to be like that so badly.

"Well, why don't we just do it? Get married?" he repeated.

I didn't know where that came from or where it was going, but I was game. I could be just as spontaneous as anyone and my heart was jumping for joy.

"Okay!" I said, grinning from ear to ear as if I was agreeing to a first date.

On the bus, all the way home, I kept smiling and thinking to myself, I'm engaged! I'm engaged! In those days, a sparkling ring on the left finger was proof. Of course, there was no ring and neither of us would have gone that route anyway. I had never understood why girls would prance into a room and stick their hand out to show off their newly acquired wealth— or was it the commitment they were proud of? To me, a ring was meaningless, and Ron obviously felt the same way, so it was easy for me to fool myself into thinking I was engaged even though it hadn't occurred to either of us to seal this thing with a kiss.

That night, I came back to find all my stuff dumped onto the front yard. Barbara was pissed.

When I told her I was engaged, she sneered, "Not likely."

Was this some kind of fiction? I wondered.

My sister Nancy, at only seventeen, had spent that year as the caretaker of our grieving mother. She called about a week after Mom had visited me and pleaded, "How could you do this to Mother?" On that visit, I had introduced Mom to Ron as my friend, but she apparently saw more than that.

"I'm not doing anything to Mother," I said. "I'm living my life."

"You are killing Mother," she said. "You are with that guy."

Around the same time some of our instructors had been showing us work that was shaking up the status quo. New York had made it big on the international scene and Boston in contrast had become overly provincial to both Ron and me. We were all discovering that New York was where the innovation was happening. Having done close to four years at BU and hearing about the art scene in New York, where abstract expressionism was the big thing, and after spending Christmas vacation touring the museums and galleries before beginning the spring semester, I was captivated and so was Ron. We decided it was time to leave school and run to New York to pursue everything—the new arts movement, each other, everything.

I called home to tell Mom. Nancy answered the phone so I told her first. Her response: "I'm telling you, you will kill Mother by running away with a gentile 'boy', but not only that, he looks like a bum and he'll never support you with those paintings of his. And besides, how could you pour all the money everyone invested in you down the drain?"

She had a point. I painfully accepted the very heavy Jewish guilt and broke up with Ron, and he accepted the breakup all too willingly. Even to me it was somewhat of another relief, because this really did feel like some kind of fantasy that was loaded with conflict. But it was hard.

So now I was stuck in a scary place, itching to go to New York . . . but alone? This was a whole different challenge. Soon I decided that if running off to New York was good enough for the two of us, it would have to be good enough for me alone. My head was already there and I was trying to convince my body to follow. Quitting school would not be a popular thing with the faculty, either, especially after I had been given the gifts to continue. People would be pissed, but it was the only compelling thing to do.

I made some time to read. I was looking for courage and inspiration, so I began reading again about religion. Since my out-of-body meeting with my father, I had been trying to educate myself and find some validation for that experience.

One of the things I'd learned is that in Hinduism, dharma signifies behaviors that are considered to be in accord with order that makes life and the universe possible, and includes duties, rights, laws, conduct, virtues and the "right way of living." What I chose to experience right then was seminal, one of several possibilities for my "right way of living", my exploration into the wider world of New York City.

Bill Moyers once asked Joseph Campbell a very important question: "Aren't many visionaries and even leaders and heroes close to the edge of neuroticism?"

Campbell replied: "Yes, they are."

"How do you explain that?" Moyers asked.

"They've moved out of the society that would have protected them, and into the dark forest, into the world of fire, of original experience," replied Campbell. "Original experience has not been interpreted for you, and so you've got to work out your life for yourself. Either you can take it or you can't. You don't have to go far off the interpreted path to find yourself in very difficult situations. The courage to face the trials and to bring a whole new body of possibilities into the field of interpreted experience for other people to experience – that is the hero's deed."

This answer applies to so many of us lesser ones, too, those of us who've walked alone to the edge with no one holding our hands; not perceived as heroes, just seekers of something else. Apparently some part of me needed to step into the dark forest. So my heart and the little engine that could told me: "Just go. Trust yourself and go."

photo, left:
My Seventy-Four East Seventh Street apartment

Awakening

photo, right:
The Cedar Tavern

Riverside Drive and a Hundred and Forty-First Street

Uncle Morris, Refugee in New York, "Doing It" for the First Time, The Russian Baths, Cool Jazz and Beat Poets, But Where Are the Women? On the Road

I got off the train with one suitcase, and my only option was to find the YWCA. I secured a room with a shared bathroom down the hall. Old, weathered women and young, rough women were milling around the corridors and primping in the bathrooms. My little room was the loneliest place on earth.

I had no idea where Ron was and since I had broken up with him, he was probably well into his next adventure. I knew no one in New York City except Uncle Morris, who had been one of those Nazi prisoners who escaped death but turned white-haired in the moment they shot his wife and baby daughter in front of him. The story goes that they kept him alive because he could copy handwriting, so forging papers became his job. It saved his life but did not save his mind. Still, I had been so excited to meet him once more after his failed attempt to move in with my Gram back when I was still in junior high. She had been over the moon to see him again after so many years of not knowing if any of her family had survived the war. But his traumas disallowed any real relationship and so he got reabsorbed into the Jewish rescue system that existed for that purpose. Guiltily and tearfully, our family watched him being removed from Gram and Pap's tiny apartment in Hartford by one of those organizations designed to relocate survivors. He was then placed in a basement room in the Lower East Side where immigrants and bohemians came to live.

Now here I was in New York with no one to contact but him. Would Uncle Morris even remember me from when I was thirteen? The super walked me down the few steps to his tiny room and there was this beautiful ruddy faced, blue-eyed old man with a head of dazzling white hair, sitting upright in a ladder-back chair at a small table covered by a blue oilcloth and a plastic bowl of oranges. He might as well have been posing for Van Gogh the way he looked, staring into space.

Uncle Morris seemed happy to see me, or at least happy for the company, regardless of who I was. I explained as best as I could how his sister, Berche, was my grandmother. I do not know if he understood or even cared, but he seemed interested while I told him my situation and without a word he took my hand. We walked up the stairs, out of the basement into the bright street where he picked up *The Jewish Daily Forward,* the Yiddish paper of the day, leaned against the building and scanned the classifieds. I can't even remember how we communicated. Did he speak German, Polish, Russian? I knew a bit of Yiddish from Gram so together with some flamboyant gestures it seemed to work. He flagged a taxi that took us way uptown and there he brought me to a widower who had turned his once elegant apartment into a rooming house. He and the old man, M. Villeneuve, seemed to like each other at first sight so I gratefully found myself in a room with a dazzling view of the Hudson River and the foggy Jersey banks. I shared a kitchen and bathroom with a writer and his girlfriend, a Chinese cook, a Korean vet, a saleswoman at Stern's Department Store, and M. Villeneuve himself.

This was a good place. This was Riverside Drive and a Hundred and Forty-First Street. My room was my studio and also where I slept. We were a unique "family" that shared leftover

Chinese food, all drawn together Uptown in a culture that wasn't our own. This neighborhood, a part of Spanish Harlem, was just one of many enclaves that I could have ended up in. That's what I loved about New York. The whole place seemed to be made up of actual neighborhoods with their own diverse cultures permeating the city with the smell of food and the sound of music.

I don't remember how it happened but a few months later, Ron found me. I guess if things are supposed to happen, they happen. His idea was that we should periodically look at each other's work and continue the critiquing we had done before. We agreed that it would be good for both of us.

After studying the paintings and making some very welcome comments, he backed up onto the bed, the only piece of furniture in the room. Now he made his first move ever on me. I'd had the uncomfortable idea that I wanted an intimate relationship with him but when I imagined it the whole thing scared me to death. I kept denying my desire for two reasons: I didn't want to lose the connection we had, which seemed so pure, but in reality, I was scared of sex. Yet with the

afternoon sun pouring in and our proximity to the bed, all the fear faded and we were suddenly "doing it."

That first kiss was sweetly memorable, the taste and touch of it was lovely as it traveled throughout my body but what followed was something I cannot describe. Mostly because I "wasn't there." My early trauma with my father had been reignited and I was sent flying away into a disappointing disconnect. I didn't feel a thing in the frozen numbness of my body and worried at what a failure I was. Now everything was ruined. I had been a virgin and then I was not. And just like that our friendship was circling the drain—or so I thought.

"You need to come downtown," he commented. "That's where it's all happening." We need to live closer and downtown is the place to be. You will love it."

After he was gone, I raced to the mirror to see if I looked any different. It was the same face peering back at me, a little pinker but it was still me.

My room was more than an hour downtown by bus, my long but scenic means of transportation to "where it was happening." Subways, while much faster, were all about stairs, which my legs consistently refused to climb.

I soon ran out of what remained of my father's meager insurance money and hearing from my housemate that Stern's Department Store was hiring, I managed to score a pretty good job right away. My job as a shopper meant going to all of the department stores in all the boroughs to compare things such as refrigerators and TVs. First of all, I didn't know the area and had to follow complicated maps, and second, I had to ride the subway, which meant those damn stairs. So I soon quit.

Fortunately, when I left Boston for New York, I'd been given a letter of introduction by our dean to a gentleman who owned a paint factory. Even though the whole faculty was furious with both Ron and me for leaving, the dean was forgiving enough to make this introduction to his friend. I had assumed that I would never use it, but after running out of money and not being able to take the job at Stern's, I was ready to dig out that letter and make use of it. I needed a job.

Lenny Bocour was wonderful. He offered me free paint if I came at the end of the day and was willing to take what remained of the partially filled or damaged tubes. But that's not all.

Synchronistically and tragically, this man had a friend who had just suffered a devastating loss and needed a governess down on Central Park West. The seven-year-old daughter, Tiffany, was doing the interviewing and would make the hiring decision so her mother could leave for what was called a "rest cure."

"Where are you from?" Tiffany asked with a bit of condescension.

"I went to school in Boston, the art school." I told her.

"What kind of art?" she asked. "Did you dance?"

"No. I was a painting major, but we were in the same building as the dancers. Performing arts was on the second floor and the art studios were on the third floor so we only saw each other in the elevators."

"Too bad," she said. "Would you like to see me dance?"

"I would. Do you take lessons?"

"Of course," she said, stating what seemed to her as the obvious.

"What kind of dancing do you do?"

"Ballet," she said with a slight air. "We are in rehearsals now for our big performance. We're practicing 'The Fan Dance' from Don Quixote. Do you want to come and watch?"

"Yes, I would!" I said. And I really did.

"Do you want to see my fan?"

"I would like that a lot. I love fans." She took me by the hand to her all-pink, girly room and sitting on a vanity against the mirror was an intricate fan of green and gold.

"Wow," I said. "That is gorgeous."

"I know," Tiffany said. "Do you want to see my costumes?"

"I'd love to," I really did want to. After all, fashion was my original love.

She opened a closet full of tutus, all satin and tulle pastels. She grabbed a tiara from the shelf and placed it on her head. I admired how perfect it looked on her.

"Do you want to try it on?"

"Can I?" She handed it to me ever so carefully, as if it were alive. I placed it atop my massive black hair and it was way too small. I looked in the mirror and we both burst out laughing. Then Tiffany took my hand again as we waltzed back into the designer living room where her mom was perched on a white leather couch, drink in hand.

"I like Margie," she told her mom, emphatically. "She is the one."

I was already taken with Tiffany, as well. Despite her girlish arrogance she was completely adorable and what could you expect under awful circumstances, losing her daddy and her mom unable to cope.

"Good," her mom responded, then turned to me and asked, "When can you start?"

I thought I had gone to heaven. Much as I loved my tiny room with a view in Spanish Harlem, this massive apartment on Central Park West held more promise and it was closer to Ron.

With all that sudden luxury, dedicating myself to Tiffany was all that mattered. How could I comfort her, what could I do? She wasn't crying or acting out. What was worse, she acted as if everything was normal while everything in her world had collapsed. But cheerfulness and normalcy seemed to be the medicine she needed right then. Still, I kept a vigilant ear to any clue that she might want to talk or cry or get really mad. But she managed to act as though she was perfectly fine.

The apartment was vast, bright and comfortable, with a fantastic hi-fi set that filled the space with some of my favorite music of a quality I had never heard before. I could sprawl out on the white leather couch and listen to the Russians and their magnificent piano concertos, Tchaikovsky, Rachmaninoff, Prokofieff. All manner of music rang through the apartment like it was a concert hall. I was given a small studio to work in, her husband's space, which felt pretty invasive of me to be occupying at that point but I had most of the day alone there so I quickly got used to it. The view of Central Park gave me a hint of nature and my only chores during school hours were to reach into the kitchen drawer filled with cash and shop for groceries and incidentals right around the corner, then after school catch cabs to take Tiffany to her violin and ballet lessons.

As far as my art was concerned, I had become enraptured by the possibilities that abstract expressionism provided. Even though it had been breaking ground since the forties, it was new to me. I was in love with oil paint, the way it slid over canvas, allowing me to move color and blend it so softly. It was a new language and acrylics, the newest rage in paint, didn't quite do it for me.

"Color is a power which directly influences the soul. Colour is the keyboard, the eyes are the hammers, the soul is the piano with many strings. The artist is the hand which plays, touching one key or another to cause vibrations in the soul."
–Wassily Kandinsky

I was engaged in the act of painting but even more so I'd begun to see the world through sensitized eyes. That deeper way of seeing had become another layer to enjoy, an experience of living on the outside looking in, or maybe I was on the inside looking out, or both. Everything had color and light. In only three month's time, Tiffany's mom returned from her "rest cure." The reality of her situation seemed to slap her in the face the minute she walked through the door. Grief and horror took over at finding me in her husband's studio—though she had given me permission. She didn't waste a minute kicking me out, out of "the maid's" tiny room, out of the huge apartment, away from her little girl and onto the street.

Ron came to the rescue, though I don't remember how I ever managed to contact him since we had no phones. We hailed a cab, stuffed in all my belongings and the driver sped us down to the Lower East Side. Ron sat in a bar watching over everything while I rang the doorbells of supers up and down the streets from tenth to seventh. After an exhausting several hours, I found a vacancy at Seventy-Four East Seventh Street. The super took me to the third floor. It was stuffed with more than life's necessities, and was dark and claustrophobic. I couldn't possibly live there and hold onto any sanity. We climbed up two more flights and upon opening the door, light streamed out into the hall in one giant beam. Inside, it was empty of all furniture, clothes and other incidentals that had crammed the lower rooms. I knew the stairs would be a huge challenge and it pissed me off that I still didn't know why I had no strength and why everything hurt if I pushed myself and why every doctor I ever went to for help gave me a puzzled look and ended up telling me it was all in my head. I knew it wasn't but if somehow it were, I would beat it by having no choice but to climb these stairs and refuse to give into weakness. So I took the fifth floor apartment because here was a vacancy that otherwise was perfect.

Every time I got all the way upstairs, even though I had to sit on the worn marble windowsill at every landing, I felt as if I'd climbed a little mountain and I would rejoice. At the same time, I carried a combination of shame for being so incapable and anger for those damn doctors who insisted it was psychosomatic. So I was on my own to make the best of a crappy infirmity with no understanding of it whatsoever, and I would secretly rejoice when I could manage without detection from those around me.

The Lower East Side was not yet the East Village. It was still immigrant city and I, too, felt like an immigrant of sorts. If the walls could talk, they would tell stories of prejudice, persecution and poverty and Uncle Morris' story, too. For me, at that time, I thought it was luxury—not very spacious but being that high up with the windows open, it was airy and a perfect place for what I'd come to do. Okay, I had no phone but I had the crisscrossing clotheslines with their flags of colors flapping in the wind between buildings, red geraniums on fire escapes, and windows situated to give me cross-ventilation. A delightful breeze blew through my three tiny rooms in the warm season and the hiss of sizzling radiators was music to my ears in the cold season. I could lounge in my kitchen bathtub listening to an unknown neighbor's saxophone floating in on the scent of spring. The living room was my studio, furnished with a large easel, black metal stool and white porcelain table that served as a palette. I could crawl through the window onto the fire escape landing, sit with my coffee and look out at my vibrant world.

I savored this Lower East Side, still rich with small businesses owned by people from everywhere—fish markets, bakeries, butcher shops, exquisitely decorated Easter eggs, delicately embroidered blouses and babushkas from the Ukrainian shops, dairy stores, fruit-and-vegetable stands where I could buy a single egg, candy by the penny, and any newspaper. I could get anything from egg creams to magazines, and one hole-in-the-wall shop sold live chickens. This hallowed place, so crowded and mashed together, offered hope to so many from other countries—all of whom had come here with nothing but their dreams. It was hard to imagine whole families crowded into these tiny rooms with little to eat—free from the oppression of the old country but with new problems to deal with. For me, it was also a sanctuary. I, too, had arrived with a dream.

To make the rent, I got a temporary job showing the most recent immigrants how to use the Laundromat. It was broiling in there and I was bored to death waiting for people to come in with their bundles, but it kept me alive until I found my ideal job at the Jackson Square Library near the edge of Greenwich Village. The library smelled deliciously of books and old varnished wood. The lamps glowed amber and although the place was always filled with comings and goings, one could hear a pin drop. The janitor was smart and kind and born somewhere in the Alps. He invited me to visit his family if ever I went to Switzerland.

"They'll love you," he said. "They'll put you up for as long as you like." That became another fantasy for my future.

Mrs. Marsh, the head librarian, invited me to use one wall as a small exhibit space so I hung a few of Ron's ink drawings that were a perfect fit. Lucas Foss, the composer, was one of the library's recurring patrons, and after one of our animated conversations, he offered to compose a piece for me in exchange for one of the new collages I had been experimenting with. His composition ended up being something no musician could play because it was written for full orchestra, so I never got to hear it, but it was an honor just to hold it in my hands.

I walked out of my apartment one day and to my amazement, there was Howie with his fraternity brothers in tow. He had taken a job here in the city and rather than living in a fancier place working for a hot shot law firm uptown, he had taken an apartment in the building diagonally across from mine.

"I want to get back together," he confessed. "I made a huge mistake. I was sick. I had a fever. I had mono. But I'm here now."

"Oh, my God, Howie," I said, very surprised. "I'm flattered, but I'm a whole other person now. I'm not the girl you think I am. Actually, I never was."

I'll never forget the scene. I was walking down the middle of the street. There was not much traffic on the side streets in those days. Think of the iconic Bob Dylan album cover, with Dylan leaning into his girlfriend amid poetically falling snow. That's how it was, but instead of a romantic scene, it seemed funny to me. Howie's fraternity brothers spread across the road, trailing after me.

"You've got to give him a chance," they pleaded. "Please, just give him another chance."

I couldn't, although I felt a certain satisfaction that I was no longer interested.

Even though Ron and I saw each other occasionally, looked at each other's work, had long conversations and sometimes spent the night together, I felt pretty much alone. The sex was good compared to that first time in my little room on Riverside Drive so every time that key would turn in the lock on my apartment door, my heart would quicken. I was as obsessed with him as he was with his own variety of satisfactions. To make it even lonelier, I missed both the lightness and depth of intimacy that only girlfriends can give each other. I imagined that mine were living sweet, comfortable yet routine lives with their new husbands after having set up housekeeping with gifts and trinkets from their bridal showers. They were living in split-levels surrounded by maples and pines, while I was alternately blissful and anxious on the less travelled road I had chosen. They knew who they were while I remained hauntingly uncertain about my lifestyle choices and yet the excitement of the city, the little things, the ecstasies that ebbed and flowed with my work, and the random moments with Ron seemed to make it all worth it. I was living in the moment. It was a happy and unhappy time but never sad. The excitement, uncertainty and impermanence were beautiful.

Spring came to the city and then summer, as it always does. It was unbearably hot, sticky and stinky on the downtown streets of New York. I had to get out of there. Nancy was waitressing at a borsht circuit resort in Bethlehem, New Hampshire. Cool, forested New England beckoned. She said to just come up and they would give me a job. I packed my clothes, locked the door, and caught a Greyhound bus north.

Solly, the resort owner, made up a cushy job in the concessions shop selling candy, newspapers, cigarettes, cigars, and making change for the pinball machine. The guy who came weekly to empty the machine gave me whatever change didn't fit into his rolls. It was a lot of money, relatively speaking.

Sol placed me in one of the cottages with his private secretary from the New York office who wore high heels all over the lush, green grounds because she could no longer go barefoot or wear flats. She had been wearing high heels on the sidewalks of New York for so many years that her ankle tendons had shortened and it pained her to walk flat. We were super compatible roomies despite our divergent lifestyles and Solly generously let us share all the privileges of the guests, including pool access, a spacious room to ourselves and even sometimes dibs on the kitchen in the middle of the night. This was quite unlike my sister's situation and the rest of the wait staff who were stuck in hot, crowded dorms, but they seemed to be loving the wild parties like the ones in the movie *Dirty Dancing,* so it seemed just fine and fitting.

After a few actual love letters from Ron on yellow-lined paper, I tried to get him to come up. Solly had invited me to invite him and I thought it would be terrific if he would also have a chance to get out of the city. He would eat well, if nothing else, but no, he didn't come.

In the meantime, I'd met an old farmer at the store in town. We made some small talk at the register and he offered me the use of an empty barn for a studio. I spent some time cleaning out the spiders, cobwebs and horse dung, but the only light that came in was through a wide doorway and the slits between the wall boards, which cast stripes and shadows all around. So sadly after all that effort, I could make nothing happen there. I had a little fling with a sweet and handsome nineteen-year-old trumpet player from Brooklyn who was in the hotel band with four other much older guys. Their jazz was hot and sultry on those moonlit nights and Luca and I were like magnets longing to flatten our ready bodies against each other, but despite all the honey and the heat, I stayed loyal to Ron. (I later found out those guys were brothers in the mob). I couldn't wait to get back together with Ron in September, but when we saw each other again, he was, to my sorrow, his usual distant self. I knew he had been sleeping around.

The following year, I found a spacious loft further downtown on Maiden Lane near the Fulton Fish Market, close to what would become Ground Zero in 2001. This space could accommodate my ever-larger paintings but these lofts were not residential—no kitchen, bath, nighttime heat or hot water—and it was illegal to be living there. The super was reluctant to rent the space to a "girl." He felt responsible for my safety but I convinced him that I'd be fine. The thirty extra dollars in his pocket every month made it all right.

I tacked my canvasses to the walls and spread them out so I could work on several at a time. I paced the well-worn hardwood floors as I worked and savored the light streaming through huge windows. From my perch on the fire escape, I watched bankers and financiers emerge from the subway depths like amphibians breaking from the swamp into air, women clicking down the streets in their heels, and men wielding briefcases with their heads bent forward in determination for the daily hustle—while I sipped coffee with cream and thanked my lucky stars for my life.

Most nights, I chomped on bread and cheese and sipped Chilean wine straight from the bottle. I sat on the floor in front of the wooden trunk I used as a table and slept on the couch I had somehow managed to get from my parents' house in Hartford.

I took cold-water sponge baths on most days and sometimes after work, I'd treat myself to the Russian baths for a good scrub. The first time I went there, I was just desperate for some hot water. I had no idea what I was getting into. I knocked on the huge wooden door and a huge wooden-like woman answered.

"I'd just like a hot shower," I said. "How much would that be?"

"Comb in," she said, "comb in."

"How much?" I asked again.

"Comb in," she repeated.

Timidly I stepped through the enormous threshold as she stuffed a starched white sheet into my arms. *Undress*, she motioned. I was reluctant but was already on the other side of those doors and there seemed to be no escape. Besides, this looked to be an intriguing adventure, a whole different world, as if I had traveled to Russia just to take a bath.

The woman with the sheet was the only one who spoke English. The rest were Old World women with thick dialects, strong hands and watermelon breasts. I followed the woman's instructions to get undressed, take a shower and climb up on the marble table, where she proceeded to scrub my timid body with oak leaves until my skin glistened pink. It was some kind of primitive massage that was, I suspected, scarring me for life. Then I was led into the steam room where I found a handful of other women sprawled along the length of the wooden benches. Every once in awhile, one of the Russians would come in and throw a bucket of water onto the hot rocks. I'd watch it sizzle and burst into steam, fogging the room. Then came the blue-tiled, frigid pool that I was instructed to enter. I dipped my foot in and it was ice cold.

"Go!" the woman shouted and in I went from heat to icy cold.

Then I wrapped my sheet around me and was led off to a white, starched-linen-covered cot for a rest. I paid my two dollars, and walked out of there shiny and refreshed. It was so rich that I continued with this hidden ritual every week behind those massive doors.

In the building practically touching mine, I befriended another painter. He made these geometric things that I severely judged as rigid and boring. There was nothing free or open about them but he, too, was as young and dedicated as myself. We climbed over the fire escapes, and in and out of each other's windows just for company in that dark, empty neighborhood. Later, he became very famous as an exquisite painter. In fact, just the other day, as I wrote this, I walked into the Kreeger Museum in Washington, DC and there in the entrance were two of his beautiful, very non-geometric paintings. I was thrilled to see them. When I got home, I Googled him just for fun. Of course, he's an old man now and no matter what, it's always a shock to see someone decades older than when you last saw them and remember that I am that much older, too.

Those downtown lofts made perfect studios and not yet legal living spaces in the cramped city. Ron, too, had found one on Vesey then Chambers Street, both of them even more primitive than mine. We continued to visit each other off and on as friends but also as lovers.

Eventually the real estate tycoons saw the potential of those large spaces and they soon became legal, gentrified, beautifully renovated and way too pricy for people like us.

When I left Boston University, I was determined to believe that an artist did not need a degree. Rational or not, the journey to New York without one had been my choice and my dharma. I had been so sheltered in terms of culture, and limited in my activities because of my physical weakness, that all of this was a breakthrough for me—becoming strong (my primary goal in life) and pulling away from the middle class into my liberated state of classlessness. My work hours at the library were from afternoon through early evening, leaving me free time to go to the Cedar Tavern in the Village, a place where all the artists hung out.

From my beginnings in Hartford, the land of my personal oppression, until this time in New York, I was driven to be free, free to stay out 'til all hours, free to sleep late, free to eat what I wanted, and hang out with whom I wanted and where I wanted, and free to answer to no one but myself.

So it was always a fun time at the Cedar. We crowded into booths, downed glasses of beer, and chatted endlessly about what we loved the most. Who was showing where? Did the new work have the power of the old? What was going on in the galleries Uptown, the museums? Who wanted to split a roll of canvas? Who could afford a roll of linen? We sat around the tables gossiping and sharing stories:

"Last night I heard Franz say Lester Young is the most brilliant saxophonist who ever lived and David Smith said something I couldn't hear about Coleman Hawkins and John Coltrane."

"Speaking of David Smith, he's over there,"

my friend Marty said. "This is what I read that he said when asked what art is: 'A very big question of all time,' he said. 'We ought to, very simply, let it be what the artist says it is.' Do you agree?"

"Yeah, I definitely agree. I hate all these pretentious reviews where the reviewer analyzes what he thinks every artist is trying to say."

We'd argue well into the wee hours about everything we deemed relevant to our passions and our survival. Some of us had also taken an interest in religions from the East—particularly Zen Buddhism, which as far as I knew had only recently reached the West in the books of D.T. Suzuki and *The Four Pillars of Zen* by Alan Watts, as well as the California Beats who were now making their mark.

Since I had already begun to investigate some of this eastern stuff so I could understand the rendezvous with my father in that other world, I had found this little book by Suzuki. I remember a quote from it that convinced me it is all about possibility because I think there is just so much we don't know. Suzuki says something like, "Emptiness is not nothingness—it's possibility."

I think that's true—not only for life, but for art. With emptiness we are open to something new,

anything, and from there comes our innovations, from the stillness, the emptiness.

"Yeah, this Zen thing makes sense," my friend Edward added. "Suzuki also says that Zen, even just a little bit of it, turns life into art, filled with creativity. It turns one's humdrum life, a life of monotonous, uninspiring commonplaceness, into one of art, full of genuine inner creativity. That sounds like what you're talking about. I dig that."

"Yeah, but what's 'just a little bit of Zen'?" I asked.

"I guess just having a sense of it as a beginning, an opening to something larger, a way of looking at things with a kind of detachment that allows all possibility, not clinging to what you believe but letting other things come in. And also it seems to make a connection with nature and beauty and gives it meaning. You don't walk down the street without noticing the beauty and significance of a dandelion or an ant. It's about appreciation, too, maybe even a religious experience. Is that it? Something that is everything and everything that is something?"

"Sounds like a riddle," someone at our table said.

"In terms of art," Ron chimed in, "part of

the emptiness they talk about is transcending technique, too. You can't have art with pure dedication to technique. That's too mental, like from the top of the mind. You have to let the unconscious do the work."

"But we are so conditioned," I countered. "How do we even get to the unconscious? That is the work, I guess."

Ron got up to order another beer and the rest of us sat for a bit in silence, enjoying being in the company of likeminded friends, relishing the exploration. The clatter of dishes and glasses and the chatter of voices in the background in this packed space were always alive with enthusiasm and positivity but also with cynicism about how things were in the larger world around us. I loved it.

As Ron returned with his beer, Edward sat forward in his chair and proclaimed emphatically, "Religion makes me puke. All this bullshit about a God in the sky looming over everyone, judging, scaring everyone with this fire and brimstone crap."

"Yeah, but that's not all religions," someone added. "The Jews don't think that and certainly not the Buddhists."

"Well," I said, "the Jews do. They also have a scary God, a jealous God. Why would God need to be jealous? Makes no sense to me."

"I like Watts' take on it," Ron continued. "God's not a being you find out there looking up in the sky. God is something you find by looking inside."

"Do they even call it God?" I asked. "Blasphemous!" Marty remarked, laughingly. These conversations were sweet nourishment to me because we all came from different backgrounds and we had a lot to debate, discover and argue about.

We were also enamored by the romantic lifestyle of bohemian Paris before our time. I think every artist is influenced by someone or someplace or something. We fall in love with the thoughts and visions of others. They inspire and mingle with our own and out of that comes something new. I think maybe nothing is really original. Some of what we think of as original may come from what I always thought to be a sort of an unlimited cosmic warehouse you could tap into. All of the thoughts and imaginings of others from anywhere in the galaxies, just lingering in the atmosphere, floating around out there as an idea, invention or creation. There it lingers waiting for some alert person to pluck it and bring it forth through their own unique selves. Then when some rare thing is brought forth, it's laughed at, scoffed at and dismissed before it gains interest then trust and then traction.

Movements are inspired, too. How do we have access to that inspiration? Many would call it inner guidance that brings it to us. We follow it consciously or not. It probably doesn't matter. Movements may begin small, always originating from fearless innovators or those with unbridled passion who bring it to the people. Movements can happen after a gradual build-up of need in the hearts and minds of some and then what seems to be all of a sudden it explodes into mainstream visibility. From there it may become significant enough to change the world. Such were the musings we engaged in at these crowded booths in this crowded bar.

> *"All things are implicated with one another,*
> *and the bond is holy;*
> *and there is hardly anything unconnected*
> *with any other things."*
> —Marcus Aurelius, The Meditations (7.9)

Despite my occasional sips of Chilean wine with my baguettes and cheese, and my occasional beers with Ron, I wasn't really a drinker, but I got high from the clinking glasses, the buzz and hum of conversation, the smokiness, and the hustle and boisterous chatter that filled the Cedar Tavern. When that door swung open and we heard the stamping of snow off of boots, heads always turned to see who had just come in. In the summer, it was a dark, cool cave.

One night, rumor had it that Elizabeth Taylor was in a booth in the back with Paddy Chayefsky. I had to see. When I walked past her on the pretense of going to the rest room, I got a good look. It was true. In person, she was even more beautiful than on the screen. She was downright exquisite. I wished I could stand there and just stare for a while.

The food at the Cedar was good, too. John, the owner, had also been bartering for paintings and he loved to chew the fat with his patrons, hanging over the bar, leaning on one elbow, discussing Yogi Berra, Mickey Mantle and the Yankees' latest win. In the process, he might have been accumulating what was becoming a monumental collection of contemporary masters. As for me, I paid my cash and was able to eat well (something besides bread and cheese). It was all thrilling yet still I remained inwardly quite isolated in the uncertainty of my future—which, by fits and starts, I was ambiguous about.

One day while working at the library, I had the good fortune to wait on what turned out to be the friend of my favorite painter, who I would never dare to approach at the Cedar. Embarrassed as I am to say, I took the liberty of sneaking his address and phone number from his library card—the card she was using—and stuck it in my pocket. Then one brave day, like a run-of-the-mill groupie, I walked to the corner phone booth between the library and his studio and breathlessly made my call. " I'm a painter," I told him. "A huge admirer of yours. I know this is presumptuous but I was hoping I could meet you for just a minute."

"Sure, come on up," he said. Within minutes, I was at his door. "Come in," he shouted from the far end of long, open space.

Sprawled across the floor were a slew of his drawings. My foot could not find an empty space and no matter where it landed, I was going to step on one of them. They were simple drawings on newsprint. I wanted to scoop one up and stick it

in my bag. How could I not have wanted that? Leaning against the walls were a series of small paintings in color. He was famous for large black-and-whites so I had never seen anything of his work in color.

"What do you think?" he asked.

"I think they're beautiful," I replied in all honesty.

"Do you want a beer?" he asked, motioning for me to sit.

"No, thanks."

We chatted a bit then I blurted out, "I would love for you to come down to my studio sometime. I would love your opinion."

"Well, I would love your opinion about these," he said. He was preparing for a show that would debut his color. They were beautiful, but I didn't know what to think. After all, everyone expected large, bold black-and-whites, which, by now, were very valuable. Great artists have no fear of departing from what has given them fame. They just keep breaking through their own paradigms, no matter about the money or what anyone thinks.

"I love them," I said, pointing to my favorite of the bunch.

After a few more attempts at conversation, I sensed it was time to leave. "So will you come?"

"Sure," he said. "Just let me know when."

I was dumbfounded but then figured he was just being nice.

Then one night at the Cedar, I saw him at the bar with a bunch of his cronies. I took a deep breath, walked over into their midst and boldly invited him down to my loft. He gulped what was left in his glass, grabbed his coat and said, "Okay, let's go." Again, I was dumbfounded. He hailed a cab, had the cabbie stop while he ducked into a liquor store, came back with a bottle, and off we went to Maiden Lane. He had definitely been putting down the beers, and at the top of the stairs, he surprised me with a big bear hug. He wasn't very tall but his hug was quite powerful and seductive. Naively, I had not anticipated this but there was nothing ungentle about this man and I had no fear of any weirdness that might develop.

"No," I said, shaking loose from his embrace. "This isn't why you're here."

In a flash, he was sober. He dropped his hands and faced my wall lined with canvasses tacked to Masonite and studied the work for what seemed like an eternity.

"Good, good," he said. "These are very strong. Do you have more I can see?"

I showed him two others that had been leaning against the wall on the other side of the studio and again he looked for what seemed a long while.

"Good, good," he repeated. "I like these. Keep painting."

That's all he said then he turned and immediately lost his sobriety, grabbing onto me again but this time I think only for support. I had never seen anyone turn it off and on like that. Arm in arm, I escorted him down the stairs and up the dark avenue to find a cab. In his inebriated state, he spoke sadly and deeply of his beloved wife. For a few moments, I was privy to this deeper layer into who he was and the beauty of what made him tick, but I didn't know his story and, of course, I didn't ask.

For the rest of the evening, I was flying high from his response and the time he took to study my paintings. I could tell that he sincerely thought I had something. Still, with all my enthusiasm and independence, beneath it all was hidden a river of dread. What trick was I playing on myself? Would I ever make it as a painter? Would I ever get married? Did I want to? Would I ever have children? Did I want to?

"Probably not" was the answer to all of the above. So what then was I doing with Ron? What was I doing, in general? I didn't want to think about it. I wanted to just keep doing what I was doing.

Recalling this now, it may seem like I had a vigorous social life, the neighborhood bar and my artist friends and all, but it was very impersonal, with very little intimacy and no real depth of friendship. Yes, it was a lifestyle that defied the status quo, that shunned anything smacking of "the bourgeois" and was made up largely of idealists all looking for meaning, whether through painting or music or spiritual seeking, all doing their own thing, but for me something was missing. . . they were mostly all male and we were all operating from our heads.

So where were the women? There was Toby, another woman who often went to the Cedar and we'd often find ourselves crammed into the same booth. I should have been friends with her but wasn't. It just didn't happen. If I could write her a letter, I would say:

Dear Toby,

whose last name I never knew, I apologize that we didn't become friends, both of us painters, not artist's models or easy lays. We were both serious young women striving for acceptance with our art, equal to any one of the guys.

We had no women's movement yet and I don't know about you, but I never signed my first name to the work. We were also not of the Hartigan, Mitchell, DeKooning or Frankenthaler brilliance or fame—not yet, anyway.

Can you imagine how great it would have been if we were buddies, sisters in that sacred world, living for the moment, two isolated women gorgeously alive in our perseverance with our work?

We competed with each other, it seems, each of us distancing ourselves from the beauties, those flamboyant models who giggled and squirmed around the guys. We distanced ourselves from each other, too, I suppose vying for credibility. So sad.

So here's to you, my belated friend and oh, how I wish we could compare notes.

I was emotionally overinvested in Ron for what I was getting in return so out of self-defense, I suggested he go to California, something he had been talking about for a while. We were all enticed by Kerouac's *On the Road* and this would be a good adventure for him and give me time and space to get over him. Besides, he was footloose. So one winter night, three of his friends got together and left for the West Coast. After plowing through several storms and a few breakdowns, they made it to San Francisco, which had its own brand of happenings.

Although I missed him, I was relieved he was gone. I didn't have to listen for his key in the lock anymore. I could settle in with myself and started dating again. I had met a beautiful man who was in New York from France. Julien was a survivor of the war, about five years older than me. His entire Jewish family had been wiped out when he was a child but he never told me the story of his survival. He was in the United States getting settled with an international law firm. I liked him a lot. He seemed a lot older then me, very European in a lovely way, and he was looking for true love, having lost everyone in the war. But again, there was no chemistry between us. He didn't care. He wanted to marry me on the faith that chemistry would grow with time. I was tempted. I would have an attentive, sweet husband and all the luxuries I could want. Did I still not want luxuries? Did I still not want to settle down? My twenty-fourth birthday was coming, which meant I was getting older. In those days it was older, not like today. Would my paintings ever sell? Was I about to cop out on myself? Give up my dream? Did I really just want to be with Ron?

Three months went by. I called him in San Francisco. He was staying with some painter friends he had met. I told him about Julien.

"What should I do?" I asked.

He didn't say, "No, no, don't you dare marry anyone. Come here at once." No, he didn't say that, but that is exactly what I did, despite my mother's continued protests and the accusation that I was killing her and making a fool of myself. None of that mattered. I got on a plane and flew out to San Francisco determined, once and for all, to make it work or break it up for good.

"... it's the too-huge world vaulting us,
and it's good-bye.
But we lean forward to the next crazy
venture beneath the skies."
— Jack Kerouac, *On the Road*

Two Realities

The Wedding

Should I Stay or Should I Go?

Trailing Ron to California: The Willing Rabbi

Wildflowers and Rosemary, The Houseboat, Two Realities, The Baby, On the Road Again

Ron met me at the airport with the same miserable distance that I felt when I returned at the end of summer from New Hampshire. I knew this was absurd but now what was I supposed to do? It wasn't like he had insisted that I come so I hated myself for being here.

"Let's go make love," he said. "Then we'll connect again."

I was hot and tired from the trip but soon found myself at the "Hotel California"—well, not really, but it was a seedy little place with shadowy comings and goings somewhere near the hip part of town that I was told was the famous North Beach.

Afterward, he took me back to where he was living, in the basement of a house rented by a couple with four little kids. The couple and Ron seemed to be passing their days and nights drinking Gallo wine and smoking dope. Where was that intensity I loved? Where was the painter? The wife clearly resented my presence in her home. I could see and feel something secret transpiring between Ron and her that gave me a bad feeling but what did I expect? Really?

"We have to get out of here," I said to Ron. "You're losing yourself with these people."

"No, everything's cool," He balked. "You're just tired. You need to relax. Maybe go take a nap."

I was not about to spend another hour there, even if I had to go back to New York. I had come to feel out the situation, hoping this would be it, that he would agree to setting up a life together here in this beautiful city, so different and open from New York.

He agreed. We immediately found our own little place on Potrero Hill and Ron continued his work at a music store where he had started to build shelving for record albums. That job became the beginnings of an eventual career. While he was building this career, I ended up stuck in "our own little place" alone without a car, and no ability to walk the hills. I hung around in the backyard, reading and keeping a sketchbook and trying to practice my drawing, but the hours dragged. There was no phone, no television, and Ron had

no particular schedule. I worried that he was in North Beach carrying on with the likes of those he had been living with when I arrived.

My mother worried about me living in sin. It wasn't about what God would think but rather about what people would think. I used this as an excuse to bring up the concept of marriage. My feelings for him were hopeless. There was no one else I wanted to be with. Ron was surprisingly agreeable, not enthusiastic but agreeable. Somehow I felt even if we lasted only a year, I needed to pursue this crazy, possibly tentative relationship. Though I had no idea what it was, I knew there was something that made me so obsessed about all this but I just couldn't name it.

So Ron readily agreed. I went on a lengthy search to find a rabbi who would marry us. Mixed marriages (meaning, couples from different religions) were taboo in those days, but I found one rabbi who was willing.

When my mom flew over for the ceremony, the first thing she asked was, "What are you going to wear?" I hadn't thought about that and I didn't even own a dress. I ended up wearing her straight-skirted, navy blue faille dress that clung somewhere below my chubby knees. My mother's dress made me look like an oversized pear as my hips were "out to there." But it was a dress, and it seemed that jeans would not have worked, even in San Francisco in 1960 at a progressive synagogue with the only clergy in town who would marry a Methodist and a Jew. It didn't matter much because there were only three people in attendance and the ritual was mainly for my mom, or so I told myself. We didn't tell Ron's parents about it, as they were out of the country and we wanted to just do it before we changed our minds. I'm sure there were some bitter feelings about that, but we also knew they would have disapproved of their oldest boy marrying a Jew with wild black hair and paint under her fingernails, who they had met just once with an unwelcome chill that had not surprised me.

The friends we had made in the short time we were there refused to come to our wedding because to them weddings were just some piece of paper that meant nothing. Even our friends George and Louise didn't come, as they thought it was too bourgeois for their sensibilities.

After the so-called ceremony, our two cars caravanned down to Fisherman's Wharf, where we devoured a lobster dinner. My mom secretly fantasized about a new life with the only guest, our gay doctor friend who traded art for services and kept a menagerie of animals wandering freely around his home and office. In his cuteness and aloofness, he had not paid the slightest bit of attention to my mother, much to her disappointment.

So now Ron and I were married in the least sacred ceremony I had ever attended. There was nothing beautiful about it and I didn't feel cherished the way I would imagine a groom should feel about his bride. What did either of us know, anyway? It was all so unconscious except for one thing: I knew that to step into a life with Ron, I would have to become strong, my primary goal since the beginning of my life. I knew with this marriage that I would have to stand on my own two feet, shaky as they were. I had always been emotionally invested and he had always been emotionally detached. I wanted some of that detachment for myself and I guess that had been part of the attraction. Despite the insecurities I felt, I was where I needed to be.

So there we were in a San Francisco duplex and nowhere near the water. One of the most beautiful cities in the world and we were stuck in no-where-ville.

Someone had given us a faded, 1940 red Ford coupe with a missing gear. We decided to take a drive along the bay looking for a prettier place to rent. Industry was everywhere along the water's edge, until we spotted a little cove populated by a few funky houseboats and shacks. As we turned onto the dirt road, we were ambushed by a pack of barking dogs. A man came out of his house with a shotgun and asked what we wanted. His wife sat heavily on the sagging porch. We were startled to come upon such a scene right there in the city. It was a small cove, part of a place called Hunter's Point, originally a busy shrimping harbor but now across the road, home to The Projects and discarded marine parts.

"Who owns this place?" Ron asked, referring to a violated houseboat covered in graffiti and smashed windows.

"Who wants to know?" said the guy with the gun.

"Just us. We're looking for a place on the water and it's nice here. We could probably fix this thing up."

"The ol' fella out on the barge. Name is Hienie," the guy said, lowering his gun and pointing to one of the wrecks out on the bay.

"How do I get there?" Ron asked.

"Dunno. I guess you can walk out on the planks when the tide shifts in about an hour. People been known to sink in that mud, never seen again," he said with a grin. "Here, take this pole." He put the gun down and handed Ron a broom handle for navigation. We walked around the edge of the structure, surveying the disaster, kicking bits of glass and parts of pipe. We were sure that we could make it work, though. The surroundings were beautiful. Wild roses, rosemary bushes, sparse little buildings scattered around and bay and sky. When the water receded, Ron headed out.

"Don't go," I yelled, suddenly panicking about the depth of that mud shifting to water, but he was determined and slowly made his way out there, getting tinier and tinier as he went, continually shoving the broomstick down into the mud to measure its depth. After a short while, he made his way back and when he touched the shore he couldn't stop laughing.

"You won't believe this," he said. "I had to walk past all these dead boats, half sunk in mud, and way out there, Santa Claus just sitting there watching me slip and slide while I made my way out to him. He invited me to climb in and have a seat. He has an actual room with a couch and chairs and a wood stove and TV. He's living there happy as a clam with half that thing underwater.

"So what did he say," I asked.

"For fifty dollars, it's ours!"

We took it right away, knowing we could fix it up, and we did. It was so beautiful there on the Bay when the tide was in, slapping peacefully against the shore.

Wildflowers and rosemary grew all around the place. To one side was the guy with the gun and his porch-sitting wife, and on the other side was a pristine houseboat owned by some transplants from Greenwich Village who brought their printing business across country. Around the corner was an old sea captain who told us his claim to fame was that he had no belly button. We humored him and he insisted on showing us. Sure enough, surgery had made it seem so but he insisted he was born that way and when we accepted his story, he gratefully offered us some green gage plums that he had plucked from his tree. There were a few other characters in the tiny

diverse community . . . and now us, all lovers of the bay.

After painting inside and out and fixing the windows, we put in a wood cook stove, one of those green enamel ones with ornate pie shelves. Inside was a bathtub hooked up to nothing. We found a set of tables and chairs on the street, painted them a milky blue, set up one of the rooms for a shared studio and fished in the bay for our suppers. At midnight, we'd listen to Rockin' Lucky, a wailin' DJ who introduced us to Ray Charles. He opened every night by singing out "It's Midnight!" and we began to dream our beautiful dreams. We were making friends and our life together was becoming sweet as we gradually grew into being a real couple.

Secretly, I felt there was something romantic about living so close to the bone, about surviving with the minimum at a time when America was diligently consuming everything it could. These days we would call our way making a "small footprint." But after awhile, the hardship novelty was wearing off. Depending on fish was getting tired and we felt we needed more.

I took a job at the post office for the second shift. I'd take the bus going and a bus coming back. On lucky nights, a co-worker would give me a ride. We no longer had to fish in the bay for supper.

I had mornings and some of the afternoons free, but I couldn't immerse myself in the studio with the post office job hanging over my head. So we just hung out together when we could and took care of our new German Shepherd puppy that we named Fritz.

Sometimes we had lazy lunches in North Beach, hopped around to galleries, coffee shops and Ferlinghetti's Bookstore. Once I was off to work, Ron settled into the studio to draw.

At midnight, we'd sit at our little blue table and savor a glass of wine with an exotic dinner straight out of *The Joy of Cooking,* a wedding present from my library friends in New York. Ron was learning to cook, and his wonder meals and the music was almost enough for me. Yet without realizing it, we were looking for meaning, reinventing our lives, and we weren't the only ones. San Francisco was alive with seekers, poets, innovators and rebels. Although Ron and I arrived at the end time of the Beat Generation, it was a new beginning for us. Meanwhile, *Time* and *Life* magazines spread their words of negativity about the Beats focusing on the shadow that was simultaneously emerging.

Norman Podhoretz in the likes of the *Partisan Review* raged about the worthlessness of the Bohemianism of the fifties: "This is a revolt of the spiritually underprivileged and the crippled soul." But Michael McClure, the poet, spoke for many when he argued that the Beat movement was a "spiritual occasion." Those walking the path knew it to be true and I agree that "the Beats were significant not only in terms of their literary legacy but also in terms of their spiritual legacy."

I think we were all searching for something more beautiful from within and without, and in our zeal we shined the light on the superficiality of the culture, an age-old job of the artist. Life was expanding for us through the wisdom and beauty of a few of our own, and especially the wisdom and beauty coming from all over Asia. There was a simultaneous fullness and emptiness flooding our souls.

Just a few months after the loveliness of midnight music and sumptuous dining, Ron started back as a carpenter in North Beach, continuing to learn on the job at the record store just a few hours a day. The rest of the time he hung out with friends while we women worked our regular jobs. That seemed to be the way back then—a laid-back California lifestyle, except for us women.

Then after a year, that, too, got old. A boring job sorting mail on my feet for sometimes nine or ten hours a day and struggling up those San Francisco hills got to be too much. Ron, too, was ready to leave. California had a different rhythm than the rhythm on the East Coast. I had wished I was born in California so I could adapt more easily but the quicker pace of the Northeast was still in my blood. I had begun to dream of green fields and maple trees, autumn leaves and falling snow. It was time to hit the road again.

A couple that we met through a notice on a bulletin board had been looking for companions to help deliver a car back east, which was a cheap way for us to get home, so we decided to take the chance.

We had gotten the doc to tranquilize Fritz, who slept soundly cuddled up in the back seat as we took turns driving the spanking new Lincoln back home. We drove night and day, eating on the road and washing up in gas stations. My hair was unwieldy, too thick and always out of

control. I was not one of those Nordic beauties whose thin, straight, blonde hair looked good no matter what, and the heat and humidity made it worse. Somewhere in the Midwest we found a public pool, hauled out our suits, changed and cheerfully headed to the water. I swear it became a *tableaux*, a diorama. Everyone stopped mid-stroke and all heads turned to us. Our driver's girlfriend was outfitted in the first bikini most Americans had ever seen. We must have been perceived as a threat because the hostility was palpable so we managed to just get wet and out of there immediately.

On the Pennsylvania Turnpike, we got pulled over by the state police, who must have been thinking, *What are these longhairs doing driving that brand new Lincoln?* After an hour of searching the car for drugs, phone calls to several states, and much shuffling of papers, they let us go. Through the rear window we watched them standing in the road, legs apart, hands on hips and frowns on their faces that seemed to say, *We know we've missed something.* The girlfriend was young and giddy and laughed out loud for several miles, but we hadn't known they were carrying pot and we didn't think it was one bit funny.

We decided to part from them before reaching the city and go to Ron's grandparents, who had a dairy farm in New York State, then onto some cousins of mine in Buffalo. It seemed perfect for family introductions, a hot bath, a few good meals, and lying down flat, as we eased our way back to the East Coast.

Our first stop was that sprawling New York dairy farm, where I would meet the grandparents for the first time. We quickened to the green, lush land and towering shade trees. The house was formal yet comfortable, filled with antiques and old charm. Grandfather needed a tractor picked up from town before the evening meal so he sent Ron out with one of his workers to pick it up. While they were gone, he offered me a tour of the farm and down we went to the silo. Once in the small dark cylinder, like a robot on speed, he shot his hand out and grabbed my breast. I ducked in shock and scooted out of there, dragged myself up the hill and waited for Ron with grandmother, as she stuffed sprigs of dill into pickle jars. When it was time to leave, I pushed a resistant Ron into the middle of the front seat so I wouldn't have to sit next to grandfather on the way to catch the Greyhound into New York City.

We stopped by our old stomping grounds in New York and all of our friends said that affordable housing was now a thing of the past. The place to go was across the river to Hoboken, New Jersey, only twelve minutes from Times Square by tubes. So after a quick stint in an unfurnished railroad apartment on Hudson Street, we found an empty store for rent right across the river from Manhattan. God, I love rivers. Rivers and bays. It was the perfect setting. We wasted no time securing the place and moving in was easy since we had no furnishings.

The first thing that Ron did was cobble together a kitchen from salvage shops and junk store parts. We had lots of open space for a bedroom and studios, and we kept it heated with coal. On one side was a string of bars facing the river; on the other was a beautiful brownstone rooming house. Our neighbors in the bar had rooms upstairs that would house seamen off the Holland America Line when it came in to dock. Paddy and Delia became as doting to us as our own grandparents might have been.

Ron continued his "career" by finding a job across the river building shelving for a paperback bookstore to be housed on the street level of Carnegie Hall. Later, the same people would expand their stores to other neighborhoods. Paperbacks were just coming into the market so it was pretty innovative. Who would ever have dreamed of a Kindle or other type of reader book back then? When the store was almost ready to open, Ron crafted a special stool for the person who'd be at the register. That was the first of many stools he was to build, always getting better and better in function and design. That turned out to be the seed of his coming career.

The bookstore owners gave me the job at that very register so Ron and I had an adequate income. There was even time for me to continue experimenting with collage, like the one I made for Lucas Foss. Ron had found piles of old postcards with photos of Carnegie Hall in some cranny in the building and brought them home for me to play with. We set up a door on saw horses for me to work on and we were thoroughly nestled in. Things were good. We were making art and we were making money.

Then one day, we discovered that we were also making a baby. Both of us were thrilled and began making whatever preparations we knew how. It was just the two of us, nowhere near family, and we were naïve about all that lay ahead. Something shifted in us both, though, and not only were we excited, we were also committed to doing whatever it took for our new baby, whom we already loved. I began reading voraciously about pregnancy and birth and babies, their care and feeding and sleeping and gooing. But so much could go wrong, especially with my unreliable body that couldn't even walk up stairs without stopping every few minutes. So I made a promise to myself that I would not think of that. I would have no fear and I would nurture only positive thoughts and images. It was a frightening thing to be pregnant for the first time with a body that doesn't obey, a body with legs that don't do what they're meant to do like run, jump, hop and walk from one point to another without having to stop, a body with arms that couldn't lift anymore than a baby-sized bundle for any length of time, and who knew what the rest of me would be able to do when the time came? It was a scary prospect because no doctor was ever able to help. I did not know then and would not know until my fifties that I was suffering from a very rare muscular dystrophy condition.

So I vowed, with all my heart, that I would be vigilant in my thoughts and imaginings for the eight months remaining and that perhaps there would come a miracle to allow me to do what needed to be done to care for a little child.

The pregnancy was good—no morning sickness—and I was very proud and looking fine moving around with this growing belly. Then, one September day in my eighth month (because, as usual, I didn't want to deal with the subway stairs) I had taken the bus home from work. The summer of 1961 was a steamy one and racially charged. On that broiling day, New York and New Jersey felt worlds apart, even though the Hudson River was the only thing separating them. The talk among some of the passengers and the driver was getting ugly. There was name calling and racial slurs darting back and forth and I was relieved to finally reach my stop.

With one armful of delicacies from Ninth Avenue and the other arm grasping the pole, I stepped down the big step and wasn't yet off the little step when the driver abruptly revved up, tossing both my feet into the air. He didn't catch sight of me, still hanging onto the pole, my toes now scraping along the road. Some people on the sidewalk screamed, shouted, and ran after the bus until the driver finally saw what was happening. He stopped just as abruptly as he had started, while my round body rolled with the groceries to the curb.

Ron found a note on the door when he came home from wherever he had been: "Marge got run over by a bus and she's at St. Mary's." But I had not been run over by a bus, thank God. I merely rolled away into the gutter.

Meanwhile, lying on a gurney in shock or delirium or some crazed state that I was unaccustomed to, I found myself in two places at once: the past and the unfortunate present, where I was all alone in this tiny white room.

The dim memory of my own experience in my own mother's womb had been vaguely with me my whole life on some back burner of my subtle self. In fact, it's impossible to describe in words that feeling of knowing and how it brushed against my life every once in awhile, and particularly now, at the moment I lay on my back in this "twilight zone." It was a double awareness. Not only was I acutely conscious of the precious baby that had been growing inside of me for eight months but, strangely enough,

I was also remembering my own gestation as a growing fetus in my mother's womb. It seemed as though the essence of me, perhaps the soul of me, had drifted in and out of that fetus, testing the waters of the life that awaited me while I tried to decide whether or not to fulfill this birth that I

knew would come with my first breath.

This painting is a picture of my mom's belly carrying the little fetus, the developing baby-body that would be me after nine months when my soul would nestle in, after I'd squeezed through the birth canal and taken that first breath when I would become a full fledged person. This painting does not show the fetus that is growing or the soul that is deliberating because that is impossible to show.

This is what I, the pregnant one, experienced as I waited for someone to come into this tiny white room and talk to me:

1936:

What feels true to me is this: I am inside my mother's womb, testing the waters to see if I want to really go through with this birth, take on a body and walk the earth again. (Oh, my God, is this

what my baby is doing right now, I wondered? Is it trying to make that same decision?)

As the fetus is developing into the little baby, I, the soul, have the ability to move in and out of that bundle of material and even the physical world itself because I am not tethered to it, not yet. As all of this is going on, this me, this soul, comes and goes out of my mother's body, floating around outside and back and forth from where I came from. Checking out this family and this environment, I see they are not very easygoing people and I begin to have second thoughts.

Do I really want to go through with this? Do I have the courage? I'm beginning to remember how hard it is to work with gravity and how hard it is having a physical body in a place that is so full of discord and pain. So, I have a dilemma before me. Will I be brave enough to get born?

Well evidently, I was because here I am a grown woman with a baby inside of me and I hope he or she is not having the second thoughts I had about coming into this world.

On the other side, in the so-called Spirit world, before I came into this developing body,

I had been warned. I knew that once I was here I wouldn't remember a thing about why I came or even where I came from. So what I think happened and although I can't be sure if this is true, I do believe it is. I think we all have buddies on the other side up there that are either angels, masters, ancestors, aspects of ourselves or some other kind of agent of God, whoever they are, however that works; they helped me take the plunge toward my destination (my "destiny nation") smack into this woman's body, into the beginning of a human baby, in the heart of New England, America, and then into the dependency of people who would take care of me for the younger part of this life.

Lying there on that gurney, I couldn't believe I'd made the choice to come into that family and go through all that I did, but I had done just that. Will this baby do just that?

And now I wondered why I had been left alone in this room for so long. Where were the nurses? Where was the doctor? How long had I been lying there? And where was Ron? So back I slid into that other reality.

Dimly I remembered that I knew we had been given nine months to prepare, the three of us: this mother, that father, and me. In those nine months, I had wondered if the earth was really changing as I had been hearing, if people were really becoming more compassionate, if all the science fiction was preparing this world for the coming reality of a leap in consciousness, technology, a shattering of the existing paradigm and if women were taking their turn to lead. As I slid in and out of the little baby-body that was growing every day, what became clear was that I would have to evolve, never mind the world. I would have to founder, find my way, solve puzzles, recognize clues, witness and experience triumphs and tragedies, and open my heart wider and wider. I had to stay awake. I had to hold this memory and then maybe I could become part of the evolutionary shift that was a promise of the Divine.

In this tiny space within my mother, I developed into a cute little girl. Off and on I looked forward to my birth so I could get started. But as the months dragged by, I began to have increasing trepidations about this mother and father. I travelled in and out of the womb to see what everything was like on the outside. Often I wondered if I was making a scary and horrible mistake. And what were they doing to prepare for my arrival?

What far outweighed the doubts and fears was the knowledge that this was truly the right place to learn new lessons and to burn off the karma I was anxious to get rid of. I was trying to obey universal law, yet the sound of their voices, their fights and their anxieties seemed to be getting closer and closer as the time in there dragged along.

I slowly opened my eyes and squinted into the stark white room, felt my round tummy, the hard gurney beneath me and began to remember the accident. I couldn't help but think that this accident had shaken me into remembering some reality that I had long ago forgotten. A beam of light was streaming into me and as I watched it, something in me expanded and I suddenly realized that I did have a larger purpose. But no, we were not evolving into a compassionate society—not yet, anyway—and I had a long way to go to be of use to anyone. Along with this mothering thing there were more things I had to learn, see, and do.

I wondered how all of this could be happening as I cherished, more than ever, the baby almost grown inside of me. That's all I cared about. Nothing else mattered at this point and I only hoped he or she was okay and that Ron and I would be good parents. I only hoped and prayed that we would be able to take good care of this little baby and that nothing bad had happened at the curb.

Then Ron was beside me, all out of breath and terrified.

"I'm all right," I tried to say, but no words would come out of my mouth. I felt so bad for him because he didn't know that I was okay and aware of what was going on. I just couldn't move my lips or any of my parts to let him know. But after awhile I began to come back to myself. I could think straight and my body seemed to move okay. Soon they dismissed me and, holding onto Ron, we walked back home.

The very next day two suited men from the bus company paid us a visit. I was still in bed recovering from the shock and very minor bruises. They towered over me as I lay there and offered to pay me off. I would not be paid off no matter how badly we could have used that money.

All I wanted was for my baby to be born safe and healthy. Even though Ron and I made ourselves trust that everything would be fine, I told them straight out that if anything went wrong they would hear from us.

So we went about our business as if it never happened. No negative thinking and no worries were allowed as I was holding tight to my vows.

We had a great time getting the crib and the carriage and all that was needed from Pappy, who had a toy and baby shop in Hartford and was thrilled to be furnishing us with the goods for his first great-grandchild. Everything, of course, was new. Now we were ready and happy with the sweet space we had created and we waited patiently for our child to come.

It was dawn on a cold and blustery October morning. I was snuggled up against my husband as I was awakened by my first contraction. Yikes. The day had arrived.

I hobbled into the bathroom, looked into the mirror and convinced myself that this was real, no longer a dream, and that all was definitely going to be fine. I gave my body a much needed pep talk, rummaged through my bag, threw on some clothes, then woke Ron, who reluctantly rose out of bed, still drowsy with sleep. He threw some coal into the stove, jumped into yesterday's clothes, and off he ran to find Carl.

Carl was the vender who sold steaming coffee and sticky buns to the longshoreman on the docks. With almost a sacred dedication to his own role of fatherhood and his eleven kids, he'd earnestly promised to drive us to the hospital whenever my time came. He abandoned his truck and the customers waiting in line, piled us into his van and off we went to the hospital.

Margaret Hague Memorial was an enormous Catholic maternity clinic where I had been trekking regularly for prenatal care in Jersey City, the closest place for me to deliver. I had mentioned that I was interested in natural childbirth and even though a part of me wanted to do it, another part of me was reluctant, as this was my first child and I'd never met anyone who had gone through it. Still, it sounded cool and seemed pioneering in 1961, and I was all for as natural and pioneering as I could be. The response I got at the maternity clinic was an emphatic "no", as no one could anticipate which doctor would be on call when I went into labor and, as far as they knew, no doctor would have been happy with the arrangement anyway. I was secretly relieved.

When the time came, I was wheeled into a small room with another woman in labor who was moaning and wailing through the walls, floors and ceilings. I vowed to this baby that I would not make a sound. I willed myself to focus on the clock on the opposite wall and prayed that my body would behave once and for all. By some miracle, I managed to doze between contractions. I did this for seven hours, tuning out the wailing woman and falling asleep every three minutes. Every time the nurse came in to check on me, my contractions stopped and she said it would be many more hours before I would deliver. As soon as she left the room, they would begin again. I felt that I was ready to push, but she wouldn't believe me. Finally, I demanded that she check me out and suddenly we were in a state of emergency. I was almost crowning when they forcibly placed a mask over my face and poured in the ether, telling me to count backwards from ten to one.

"No, no," I said. "Not now. Please, I want to be awake."

At that point, I'd endured almost a day's labor with no drugs, no screams . . . and now they were slapping this mask on my face? I reached up to pull it off and the nurse shoved my wrists into restraints. Now I was furious. In this most sacred moment of my life, and in my frustration, flailing around, I kicked the redheaded nurse in the stomach (my only available form of communication). She still wouldn't remove the mask and reprimanded me like a naughty child.

Later, when I heard all the babies' little cribs rattling down the corridors like supermarket carts in a parking lot, I could barely contain my excitement. But no one brought my baby.

"Well, you held your baby, Mrs. Curtis," the redhead said, getting me back for kicking her in the belly, I presume. But at the time, I had just enough ether in me to have registered nothing, only a vague impression of a doll covered in what looked to me like oatmeal.

When she finally brought Adam to me, along with a bottle of sugar water and a bottle of formula, I took one look at that little face and those tiny fingers and toes and fell excruciating and ecstatically in love. My baby was fine and my body had come through. I told the nurse I didn't need formula because I was going to nurse. In 1961 in the US, this was almost anarchy. For the four or five days I was in the hospital, they kept bringing me formula and sugar water and when they saw me nursing they disdainfully drew the curtain around my bed so the other three women in the ward wouldn't be embarrassed.

"This is 1961," the doctor told me. "No one nurses anymore. We have way better ways to start a healthy child."

Before I was gone from that hospital, all three of the other women had switched from bottles to breast.

Once home in our cozy storefront on River Street, we snuggled in as one little happy family, inexperienced but confident. Then within a week, Ron's carpentry job suddenly ended and that was the end of that.

During the last month of my pregnancy, my job at the bookstore had been eliminated. A recession had hit and people weren't buying so jobs were getting lost; but I needed to find one so during Adam's naps, I clipped ads from *The New York Times*.

While wandering up and down Forty-Second Street through the late November wind, referring to the ads in my ungloved hands, I passed a storefront window where a young man knocked on the glass and beckoned me inside. I was only too happy to have a reprieve from the cold. There we stood in the middle of a futuristic gym packed with equipment that appeared to be designed for torture.

"Looking for a job?" he asked.

"Well," I said and then right away he offered me one.

I, of course, was still nursing, and I guess my fullness must have attracted him because my job would be to stand in the window wrapped within a bear-sized machine while the metal bars of this contraption would glide over my body, up and down. These things were a few generations before the Nautilus machines that came into the gyms later on. I felt that I had no choice but to accept the offer. For the next few months, I spent my lunch breaks sequestered in the restroom stall, fiddling with my breast pump so I could keep my baby well fed. It was humiliating, as well, to be playing a window mannequin.

Christmas shopping season had come and passersby ogled me. I disappeared from my mind and sailed out of my body into Never-land as the machine went calump, calump, calump, up and down and up and down and up and down my body.

Since Ron had lost his job, he'd begun painting again, and despite my humiliating work, I was flowering with motherhood. We had our precious son and I had begun my new role as nurturer. Little did I know at the time that it would be many years before I would put brush to canvas.

I was mad at Ron for not looking for work. In those days, though, men needed what they called a "work record" (a resume by today's standards) and as a dedicated artist he had no such thing. It was easier for me to find work because I would take anything and a woman's labor came cheap.

Among the tourists that flooded into New York at Christmastime, planting themselves in front of my Forty-Second Street window, was a young man with a lovely, sexy French accent.

"What is someone like you doing this for?" he asked.

He could see me. He could actually see that I didn't belong there and the look of compassion and understanding got to me. I burst into tears, ran to the owner's office and quit on the spot.

It was a struggle from then on, at least until we received a handmade postcard from Topanga Canyon. It was from our dear friends George and Louise from San Francisco beckoning us to come back to California but this time, Southern. They, too, had moved. We loved these guys and had thought we'd never see them again because they were Californians and destined to remain so. By now we had purchased a funky 1951 Chevy pick-up truck and impulsively decided to pack it up and go. Why not? What did we have to lose? Before long, with baby in tow, we were getting on the road again.

The longshoremen across the street who worked on the ships had hated us. They had been like a cluster of big red states surrounding us, a tiny blue one. We were longhairs and slept late compared to them. They were out front at the crack of dawn gloved and booted and ready to begin unloading. Word had gotten out in our neighborhood that we were leaving for California. It must have been Patty and Delia. Most of these guys had never even been into Manhattan. They were born in Jersey and remained in Jersey. On that day, as usual, they spent their break shuffling around Carl's lunch truck blowing smoke and watching as we loaded up our truck.

By three o'clock, just as they were trailing

out from a hard day on the docks, Ron was loading the dinghy he and his brothers had built with their Dad when they were kids. It fit perfectly over our belongings, creating a sheltering roof. A few of the workers walked across the street and told us to wait one minute. What in the world did they want?

Up drove another truck and, to our astonishment, they opened the back of the truck and unloaded four tires.

"You'll never make it out of the state on those things," one said, kicking the front tire.

So the gang got to work and helped Ron switch tires. With our one-year-old boy and no reclining seat, we took off for a warmer, dreamier place. About thirty guys stood around singing "California, here we come" and waved at us as we disappeared from sight. It was a rush of love. We began to realize they were just hard working guys doing their best, just being themselves and never even having an interest to see New York City. (Think Brando in *On the Waterfront*.) They couldn't understand folks like us as we couldn't understand folks like them but we were all humans. All the animosity had melted away with their amazing gift and we felt they may have

wanted us to take their own dreams down the road with us. Or were we projecting?

We later learned from Patty and Delia that a bunch of them had played the lottery, betting on 306, our address, and the number came in, making them all winners. That made us chuckle in gratitude for them and the fact that you can never really judge the hearts of anyone.

Changes

Cowboy Hats and Inlaid Boots: It's a Wide Country

April Babies, The Loft, Buying the Farm, Much too Dangerous, Do I Even Believe in Ghosts?

We finally reached California and the Mojave Desert four days later and celebrated by getting out, touching the sacred ground, and admiring the vast and beautiful landscape, so foreign to our East Coast eyes. It had been only three years since we were in the houseboat. Now we were headed south.

After stopping and asking for directions along the way, we managed to find Topanga Canyon and then George and Louise's house. Of course, we didn't have mobile phones then, so it was bound to be a surprise visit.

Their house was empty except for a mob of fleas that had attached itself to Ron's ankles the minute he stepped through the doorway. *Oh, shit!* Now what?

People around there all knew each other and it didn't take long for word of our arrival to get out. Friends of our friends heard about our arrival and came looking for us eventually finding us wandering around like lost pups. We followed them through the canyon to George and Louise's new home, a one-story log cabin with roses all around and lizards the size of small cats sunning themselves in the yard.

Of course, our friends were overjoyed to see us and after many hugs and much laughter we all sat down to a dinner of vegetarian lasagna, homemade garlic bread, salad with flowers in it and a jug of red wine. A couple of joints were passed and when their other friends finally left, we three crawled into our sleeping bags and snuggled each other to sleep, tired, full and happy.

The next morning after a breakfast of oranges, more homemade bread, cheese and several cups of strong coffee, it was time to look for a place of our own. We caravanned out of Topanga and up into a neighboring canyon, bumping over unpaved roads until we got to the most surreal place I'd seen yet, a place they knew about that had been abandoned, hidden away at the top of the canyon.

Strangely, it was an unfinished miniature theme park, a replica of everyone's image of the Wild West, owned by a man who had loads of land in Cornell and who lived not far from

there. We convinced him to let us rent the tiny house, all made of rocks with one round stone shower, a third of the size of the whole house. Down below was an aviary perpetually flapping with exotic birds.

Ron in the doorway of the rock house in Cornell, California

The tiny house was furnished with a kitchenette, a place for one crib and a mattress on the floor, plus a small radio. Three donkeys meandered nearby and a Nubian goat named

Margaret visited us often. It was a beautiful piece of land yet as dry and tan as sand. To get there, you had to wind your way up the famous Mulholland Drive, which was still undeveloped, unpopulated and not yet famous. The whole area was soon to be luxuriously lived in by major movie stars and wealthy politicians. Ronald Reagan, the only neighbor, relatively speaking, already owned the ranch below us called *Yearling Row* but it would be years before he was president. We'd pass that fancy iron gate as we wound our way up but, of course, we couldn't see anything but rolling land.

I had heard that there was a horse ranch up beyond our place, so one crisp day I began to inch Adam in his stroller up the road until a cruiser stopped me.

"You can't walk this road," the policeman informed me. "Get in. I'll take you to your destination."

The hospitable cop put the stroller in the back seat, Adam on my lap, and off we cruised the rest of the way. The ranch was owned by an old rodeo guy who had broken every bone in every limb of his body. When I first saw Jim, he was bent over a wheelbarrow full of horse dung—the image that I would keep of him forever. He was an appealing combination of sweetness and roughness, and when I pleaded to exchange chores for riding lessons, Jim agreed. It was another attempt to find something physical that I might be able to do. After all—just sitting there on top of a horse.

So Ron and I moved onto the ranch and into an even tinier shack-like place. This one had a dirt floor that was a real challenge to sweep. Ron put in windows and a sink, though we had to haul water. A sculptor friend of ours built me a wood stove out of a steel drum and if I kept my knees from touching and burning myself, the thing worked great. We put in a garden and Ron built an addition to the "shack", which became his pottery. We dressed all up in Western gear, inlaid leather boots that I'd gotten from Jim, several sizes too big with a steer head embroidered on the front, and my U-Roll-It cowboy hat and off we went to our new jobs as trail guides. Weren't we the coolest? We'd line up the horses while the few people who knew about this dusty old place would bravely circle up the rutted road to the top of the canyon in their fancy cars. How they ever came upon The Circle JR all the way out there I never did know. Then off we'd all go, Ron and me leading the string out on the trails through the woods and fields. It was so much fun to be up on my high horse doing something physical.

I actually thought I had learned how to ride until a neighbor asked me to take her Arabian out for her. She had hurt her back and the horse was getting "barn sour." That flattery soon turned to horror as the sleek black filly got the bit between her teeth and like a shot out of the blue galloped away with me hanging onto her mane for dear life, hoofs thundering in my ears like a cartoon of an old Spaghetti Western. Way ahead of us was a chain link fence directly in our path and I had no idea what she was going to do. I had the mistaken notion that this ride was like driving a car. If I didn't put on the "brakes" before we got to the fence, we'd run right into it. Crazy thinking. Why would an animal run into a fence? That was my aberrated instinct and I was terrified. All I could feel was that pounding through my ears. I threw my feet out of the stirrups so I wouldn't be dragged if I fell off, which it seemed I was about to do.

Later, I was found unconscious in a field while the horse, which was tied up properly to the fence, waited patiently. Jim had drilled into us the importance of tying up a horse the right way or they would choke themselves to death, so since I had not been found until then, everyone figured I had obediently gotten up, did the deed, and passed out again. I couldn't remember anything for days and soon learned that in order to ride properly, I had to use leg muscles, not just sit there looking great. I had only gotten this far in my riding experience because Jim's string horses were well trained and skilled, and not me.

One sun-drenched day, the firefighters came around to tell us to trim all the dry grass down to nothing. They said that when the fires come, there is no way out because the road would be blocked by fire and rescue trucks. As much as I loved it there and loved our friends, I was not a Californian. Again I missed the green of New England, and dreamed in all four seasons many nights. This was the wake-up call telling me it was time to go home once more. But where was home? Back east, in general, was all I could be sure of.

Only a year later and after four days and three nights on a Greyhound bus with a two-year-old baby and shopping bags with the remains of salami, cheese, baguettes, apples, Fig Newtons, pretzels, a gallon jug of apple juice and baby sundries, as well as my sorely cramping legs, we finally, finally pulled into the Port Authority dock in New York City.

But we had become so countrified from romantic but rugged life in California that we couldn't bear to enter the rush of NYC so we made a detour, catching the bus to Hartford, Connecticut. The first order of business before going home to my family was to find a store that sold bras. My mom would have been horrified to see that I had given up on those tortuous pieces of apparel, especially since fitting other women into these things was her daily occupation.

We surprised them with our appearance and Gram took enormous pleasure in cooking for the three of us. We savored the comfort of central heat and the humor and kindness of my jolly grandfather who delighted in our little Adam in the way only great-grandparents can.

Then after studying the classifieds for two weeks, we found an affordable country place about an hour away above a roadside dive with a scraggly little field in back. Ron returned to his old job in the bookstores in New York and I took care of my boy, made peach pies, jellies and jams and on one of Ron's weekend commutes, became pregnant again.

On one particular weekend, Ron left the city early Friday morning. For no reason that either of us could figure, we found ourselves in a bitter argument, both of us screaming about I don't know what. I ran downstairs to the little restaurant to pacify myself with a bag of potato chips. The radio was on and a sudden hush came over the place. It was November 22, 1963. President Kennedy had just been shot. He was dead. That president whose strong hand I had once held in mine was gone. I raced upstairs to tell Ron. We fell into each other's arms, hanging onto each other in shock and sorrow, with the awareness that everything as we had known it to be had suddenly changed. The western worlds' optimism had vanished in a flash.

The recession over, the bookstore guys from Carnegie Hall were expanding and they had lots more work for Ron. He was becoming really skilled with his woodworking but the commute was becoming too much. We needed to be together more, especially with this pregnancy happening; so once again it was time for us to relocate. These relocations were more exciting than a nuisance. We liked the idea of being nomads, not stuck in any rut. We were becoming closer all the time in these adventures and our optimism with this job. Our new baby was looking good and we knew we couldn't keep up this lifestyle for much longer.

We found one of those dark little apartments on the Lower East Side exactly like the one the super first showed me on East Seventh Street. This brick building was about a foot from the brick building next to it, allowing no light in and it was not in any way a charming neighborhood like over at Seventh Street. But the mom-and-pop stores were still a delight to shop in.

I was getting bigger and bigger with child and had decided to have this baby naturally, finally and hopefully without the meanness of Margaret Hague Hospital two years before. New York Hospital was giving lessons in the Lamaze method but I couldn't get up there with a two-year-old, so I practiced the relaxation techniques at home. I had read over some of the literature and received permission from the hospital for Ron to be present at the birth. We figured we'd be able to wing the rest and we were excited.

On April 10, 1964, the time came. A nurse gave Ron some scrubs and tied a mask over his mouth and we headed to the elevator, me in a wheelchair, him walking beside me.

"Where is your letter?" The guard asked as we started to board the elevator.

"What letter?"

"From the president of the hospital. You can't go in there without your letter," said he to Ron. "But we had this all planned ahead of time," I said. "The doctor was in agreement. In fact, he loved the idea."

"Sorry," said the guard.

I was shifting now from excitement to rage, much angrier than I should have been for the task at hand.

"Hurry, Ron," I yelled, "Run up the stairs. Just come."

"No. No. It's okay," he said. "Be calm. I'll stay right here sending good vibes. You need to relax now."

The elevator doors were already shutting and as it climbed I kept yelling until I realized it was useless. So I switched gears and focused on my breathing. I breathed myself into a sweet and peaceful state. By the time the doors opened onto the maternity floor, I had practiced the relaxation technique that Lamaze had taught me and I was transformed. The intercepting nurses marveled at my calm, none of the screaming they were used to from women in labor. Their surprise and encouragement, their delight in my demeanor gave me the confidence I usually didn't have in my body. They hadn't heard my rants downstairs and had never seen the Lamaze technique before so they were impressed. I actually began to enjoy the rhythm, the painlessness, and the expectation. It was a short labor and the nurses scurried around to adjust the mirror so I could see the actual birth. One more breath and easy as could be, out slid my new baby girl. I knew right away she wasn't an Olivia, a Michaela or a Gabrielle, any of our chosen names. We didn't know who she was yet but the nurses dubbed her "frosty" because her hair was streaked with red and white gold.

The thing was, this little, so-far-nameless one wasn't a calm baby like Adam and she didn't latch on like he did once I started nursing her. She didn't sleep soundly like Adam and, in fact, she cried incessantly. No matter how I tried, I was unable to sooth her by nursing, rocking or singing.

Ron had built a cradle with the female symbol carved into it. (How could he have known she'd be a girl?) I got very little sleep those first few months, trying to stop her crying by rocking the cradle with my foot throughout the night, but she had gotten a rough start on the way down the birth canal hearing my abrasive voice in the elevator and no doubt feeling my anger traveling through my body, making her fearful of her journey into the unknown. The calm that followed the elevator scene apparently wasn't in time to calm her little self so no wonder she came out so fast. The whole thing only took an hour from the first contraction to her arrival, which I was able to witness through the mirror. It was amazing to watch my body perform this miracle. When she was first placed ever so lightly into my arms, her ecstatic new mom, she didn't like it one bit. I agonized over this for many years. It was bad and I was heartbroken that we didn't bond right then, that my baby didn't respond to my love in one of the holiest moments of our lives.

But she was bright and beautiful even so, and we named her Jennifer Day after the light that she brought in on that very early morning. Jennifer actually remained aloof with me through her earlier years, which bewildered and saddened me. Then at age seven, she told me a dream. It was remarkable, poetic and a prophecy of a lifetime of vegetarianism but most of all it proved her love for me. I was so relieved to know that after seven years, my guilt and sorrow began to vanish, though I still didn't understand.

Jenn eventually discovered, through regression therapy, that indeed my yelling for Ron right before her entrance into the world had been traumatizing and she unconsciously carried that association with her for a long time. I had been the very source of her fear, a birthing mother yelling for her helpless father to defiantly run up the stairs. It must have been a violent experience for this tiny one just as she was to begin her journey into this world.

On the heels of that therapy, Jennifer called me from California where she was at school studying to become a chiropractor. "Mom, now you can be my mommy. I can be the baby you wish you could have had when I was born. You can buy me a doll to symbolize our union." We both cried over the phone as the mystery of those earlier years were solved and the hole that had been so long in my heart was healed.

What fun I had shopping for the right doll that would symbolize what we had missed over twenty years before! Today, Jennifer has come full circle. She is a pediatric chiropractor and, among other things, knows exactly how to soothe other people's babies, getting them to latch on, to bond with their moms, to sleep well and to dream sweetly.

One year after Jenn was born I was pregnant again. The birth control New York Hospital had provided hadn't worked. The doctor botched the procedure of inserting an IUD and now we were in a bind. How were we going to pay for three children? How was I going to physically carry two babies—an infant and a one year old? We had no idea and immediately committed to doing so. When it came time to deliver, I did the Lamaze breathing again and felt no pain. I couldn't get over how miraculously this technique worked, so I experimented with it during my labor; I'd start to breathe normally and whammo! There it was.

Ouch! This Lamaze guy was a genius. Lizzie was gracefully long and narrow, her skin was like velvet and she had none of the difficulties that Jenn had. She slept like a baby and nursed like a baby.

With Lizzie's birth on April 27, 1965, the British rock and roll invasion had come into full swing—new music, new styles and great joy. That was the year we moved out of our tiny apartment on Fifth Street into a loft on Avenue D, still the Lower East Side, and I was and once again into a wide-open space. The best gift of all was the elevator, the big freight kind that I could wheel the carriage into, close the gate, grab the crank and hold it until we were level with the top floor. No more lugging everything up flights of stairs.

The loft had two skylights and twenty-two van-sized windows. The space replicated the supermarket below. In the front were Ron's saws and drill presses, rolls of canvas and paper, and all the rest of the supplies for making art, which is what he did a good deal of the time. With three little kids, Ron and I couldn't go out at night so we threw our own parties. We had partitioned off this area from our living area and the rest of the loft was empty space, perfect for parties—dance parties—and on many weekends that's what we did. We served no food or booze. Folks brought their own or smoked their own, and we danced through the night, maybe a hundred of us squeezed together, pounding away to The Stones, The Beatles, and Motown beats all while the babies slept.

Oh, how we danced! It was no longer girl following boy in ballroom style; it was wild and free and the best part was one could dance alone. It was something I could actually do in my own way at my own pace and having watched dance evolve on television, I knew how to go wild. One downstairs neighbor claimed that he couldn't believe that I—this person who he saw scouring pots and pans, scrubbing baby poop from under my nails, and dropping onto the couch at the end of the day—was the same woman he saw with turquoise eyeliner, hot pink lips, and hair piled high into a beehive on Saturday nights. I did transform myself on those nights—backless, braless, bright prints, and flared bottoms—not because they were in style but because they flowed when I moved they gave the illusion that I was dancing better than I actually was. I knew all the tricks to hide my physical limitation, that perpetual mystery that hindered my every move. But how could I have danced? It was a mystery to me that I could dance through the night yet not be able to walk two city blocks without stopping to rest. Years later, I figured out that my body with a mind of its own allowed the muscles to take over to the beat of the music and when they gave out I'd stand still, planted on the floor, legs locked still while flailing my arms around, never missing a beat. Then once my arms gave out, my legs were ready to take over again. Free-style was made for me. I never could have followed anyone in a two-step, a polka, or a waltz.

Those parties took place before we were so impacted by the war in Viet Nam, the war that made no sense. Adam was four when I first felt its significance. In fourteen years, he would be eligible for the draft. I could hardly picture it. My heart broke for the mothers of young sons who were draft age, sons who were trekking into the jungle so far from home and into the depths of ugliness, violence and death. How could these mothers bear it?

Word of our parties got out and people would come from uptown and downtown, all kinds of artists, collectors and producers, people in stained jeans and leather jackets, fur coats and even tuxes, sometimes even strangers from off the street. We didn't care. Everyone was welcome then. People were free and innocent. Everyone uptown and downtown was looking for a scene, art was big news and there was trust in the world. For that short time, everything felt safe. Everything was alive with color and sound.

Liz and me in the studio.

During Lizzie's first winter in 1965, I carried her snug against my body, buttoned inside a yellow velvet coat that I found at what everyone called the Gravediggers, a grungy secondhand store that sold assorted treasures; but this coat was not grungy. It was elegant. I'd tuck her in with one hand and push the carriage with the other, with Jenn snuggled under piles of quilts and Adam holding onto the side of the carriage.

I was proud to be the mother of these three adorable children all under the age of four and was pleased with my body for doing the job. My dreams of being a painter had become insignificant and had faded into the background, while the fullness of motherhood took center stage. My job description was clear.

Winter and summer, we moms sat on benches rocking babies, knitting mittens and stringing beads in Thompkin's Square Park while the kids played in the sandbox together or scrambled after each other in circles. We were wives of artists who were trying to make it in the city while we were trying to keep it all together. Despite all that we loved about being moms, we had plenty to worry about. Money was always in short supply. We had let go of our own aspirations as artists or whatever our dreams had been and sometimes we didn't feel much appreciated by our guys. But we figured you can't have it all, at least not all at once, and we had love. Genuine happiness and frustration was a thickly woven tapestry we were all willing to accept. We had that in common and so we talked about schools and recipes and paying the rent. Sometimes we strolled over to a neighborhood bar and had a beer and a ton of peanuts, which were free in their shells. We were women—black, white and brown in a class of our own—cooking, cleaning, bargaining with the butcher or the fish man, squeezing every dollar for a better deal, dragging laundry and groceries through the streets, taking care of the babies around the clock without time for a bath or an uninterrupted moment on the toilet. Our situations as women seemed to be the same.

When my legs were working well, they took me across town to Washington Square Park in Greenwich Village where there was always someone entertaining, juggling, miming or simply making music. On the days where they weren't working so well, I wondered why and pushed the carriage just the few blocks into Thompkin's Square.

Then one day I was surprised to find the black moms squeezed onto the benches on one side and the white moms at the other end. The young Civil Rights Movement had reached our neighborhood. Suddenly, we were segregated and our camaraderie appeared to be over.

First, I was pissed. Then hurt. Then I became confused and I began paying attention differently. Watching and listening I soon began to realize there were much larger issues then paying the rent or not being appreciated enough by our guys. There were deeper issues and I began to understand that we did not all have the same dreams. We had different battles to fight, different sets of priorities. I began to pick up on the fact that it was about time and that this was actually progress. So much had to change in America; opportunities had to open up for everyone. Although I had felt, at first, betrayed by my black sisters for segregating themselves—I did feel we were sisters— I realized that despite our unconventional appearances we white women did not get stopped and searched. We were not scrutinized with suspicion when we'd walk into a store. So I came to know where the loyalties needed to belong. Although we all had

the same dreams for our children and we all struggled as women, the only way that would change is if the Black Power Movement took its rightful place in history.

I finally realized that we were living separate realities and, in truth, no matter how I viewed it, how on the edge I was living, it was by choice and by being born in white skin I was of a privileged class to be able to make that choice. All of this new awareness was opening to a new way of being, a new way of thinking and a surge of energy focused on truth and meaning.

Most everyone was searching for balance during these extraordinary times. The Civil Rights Movement, then the Women's Movement, the unbearable assassinations that seemed to happen one after the other (John Kennedy, Malcolm X, Martin Luther King, Jr., and Bobby Kennedy), the war, the damn war, the drugs and the constant booming soundtrack that played behind it all, a cacophony of influences making profound statements and searching for profound answers, all of it expressing everything the counterculture was feeling. A new morality was emerging that was creating wide and deep polarities. Everyone knew someone being drafted or someone trying to avoid the draft and the image of body bags coming home continually marched across our TV screens during the nightly news. Those images permeated our lives and made us sick. Some took comfort in staying stoned. Others got onto the streets to protest in many ways. The country had split apart and there was no more dancing.

The times they were a changin' because of many heroes: Martin Luther King, Jr., the Kennedys and Malcolm X, Betty Friedan, Bella Abzug, Letty Cottin Pogrebin, Robin Morgan, Andrea Dworkin, Kate Millet, Gloria Steinem, Billy Jean King, the folk, blues, rock and Motown musicians all writing songs to bring in a new and powerful consciousness.

During that summer of miserable heat, Ron and I just needed to get away from the physical, mental, emotional and spiritual boil of the city. We packed up our kids and fled to the fields and forests of Maine where the weather was cool. Ron was intent on showing me two cherished things: the color of the light in Maine, which he described as blue, and the art school he had attended before we met. So we were off in our Chevy Greenbrier with the babies safe in the playpen (way before car seats) for the journey into cool, blue light.

A Maine ranger found us camping in a field and guided us to an empty hunting lodge with no electricity. Beautiful oil lamps encouraged us to follow the schedule of the sun and moon, and bedtime stories took on added atmosphere in the glow of the lamp and the moon shining in.

At the art school, we were met by an older couple who took us under their wing. They were acquaintances of Ron's from when he had been a student there. Among other things, they were plein air painters and had raved to us about a spot in a town up the road where they often went to paint. It was a great old cape with loads of character and mountain and valley views. They hinted that we should buy it. Of course we were not in any position to buy a house but they insisted that we take a look. We learned that the house had been abandoned years prior by an eighty-year-old hermit who had taken ill and one winter's day just up and left. He walked to a relative's home in town, leaving everything behind. (Eighty seemed so old to us then but here I am now in my own eightieth year. Amazing.)

We went along with the fantasy of being homeowners, practicing the "as if" principle ("as if" we could afford it). The townspeople had been reluctant to tell us who owned the place because we were "outsiders" and with my hair out to here and Ron's down to his shoulders, we were not ordinary looking people. After much asking around, one day a fire truck stopped us at the main intersection. The driver said that although he had been fire chief for twenty-seven years, he was still considered an outsider so he would tell us who owned the property, and where in town he now lived.

I rang the bell of that address to inquire.

"I'd rather let the ground take it," said the old man in a faded blue suit who stood a foot behind the screen door where the sun bleached out his face. He wanted nothing to do with us but I could not leave it alone and on my third attempt he gave in, I suspect, because his relatives convinced him to show the old place and take what money he could get. We agreed on a time to pick him up and take him back to the homestead.

His eighty-year-old self wiggled his way headfirst, feet kicking behind him, into the wood box from the shed to the kitchen, went around and ceremoniously unlocked the door. (At the time, we thought it amazing that such an old person could move like that, and now we are 80 and we're still doing everything that we always did. Funny how one's perception changes.) The house was two hundred years old and in serious disrepair but still beautiful and functional. Once this Mr. Baines let us in, we were greeted by a hoarder's paradise—everything from coffee cans stuffed with wishbones to high-end antiques. He had to make a path through the rooms to show us around. As we stood in one of the bedrooms around a hole in the floor that went clear down to the cellar, he announced: "Fifteen hundred takes it all." Fifteen hundred dollars for two buildings and twenty acres! The tour included the barn and a trip through the scruffy field. To the west was a view of the mountains and at the very top of the field we could see straight down into New Hampshire. This was beyond what we would ever have imagined. The two older artists who had been encouraging all of this despite our cries of poverty amazingly offered to help us buy the property. They wanted someone they liked to take it over before the harsh winters would take it down as had happened with many lovely structures in that same area. These folks we barely knew must have felt safe taking their chances with us.

So we made all the arrangements with the help of our mentors and that sweet aunt and uncle who had helped me go back to school after my father died, and there we were—property owners with much beauty and much labor facing us.

But we weren't ready to make that major move . . . not just yet..

Maybe this was an investment. Something for our future because how could we not do this for $1,500 and the support of these new friends? In the meanwhile, Adam was now ready for school. Did we want him in the city? Would he walk the streets of New York to get there? That's what other school-aged kids were doing. The idea terrified me and we jumped at the chance to move once again. The decision was made when our friend's mom had a friend who had a house in the small, sheltered town of Roosevelt, New Jersey. She said she would love to have a family of artists stay in her house and simply pay the water bill.

We got to our new home just in time for kindergarten. The house was just right for us. The yard was flat with scraggly tan stalks showing evidence of a neglected garden but holding real promise of a sweet spring. As the girls grew into toddlers, I was domestically inspired by this one-story house surrounded by low growing shrubs. This was luxury, a step from the yard to the kitchen door. We could walk outside barefoot, cook in a real kitchen and live in actual rooms divided by walls. The Maine house would have to wait for us until a later date. We didn't know when but loved having it available to us for summer vacations and the security it provided.

Turns out this little town was founded by President Roosevelt, who had a vision during the Great Depression to provide sanctuary and opportunity for Jewish and other immigrant garment workers who were then crammed into factories and those same tenements on the Lower East Side where we had just been. Only for us it had been by choice; for them it had been necessity.

Roosevelt had been designed as an independent farming community, which was developed with socialist principles and the belief that nature and fresh air would benefit these working-class people who had been through so much. It had become a mini-utopia, a respite from anti-Semitism and unbearably long working hours under stifling conditions. Everything felt like milk and honey, as the saying goes, but this didn't last long. Human pettiness and competition was the undoing of the community. By the time we arrived a generation later, however, there were still remnants of the original utopia, a sense of ease and cooperation. Although it was a progressive town with many artists, proportionately, there were factions like anywhere else. This was a human experiment and it proved the beauty and flaws of humans; still, everyone was civil.

In our zeal to recapture the camaraderie of our loft parties (and I suppose in our arrogance to show off our "hipness"), Ron and I decided to throw one of our parties in order to introduce ourselves to the little town. The excited talk going around was who would be invited but there was no need because we invited everyone. We were aware of the factions but we felt the party was bound to loosen folks up and bring everyone together.

We scoured the nearby farms and markets for enough artichokes to go around with pounds of butter and lemons, nothing else. We felt no one could stay aloof with lemon butter dripping down their chins and we enjoyed planning this silly plot. It turned out to be the best party we'd ever given and so began a vibrant social life for us in this comfortable town.

Roosevelt was a flowering, wooded town where everyone watched over everyone's kids and Adam could walk the gentle sidewalk path to school.

By now, the war was in full wreckage. Body bags and burning villages were still visible every night on the news. Many of us protested in various ways and sex, drugs and rock and roll seemed to amplify the heartbreak in many ways. The movements from just a few years earlier were intensifying and different forms of escape were the norm.

The Roosevelt artists, as a group, were invited to exhibit our work in a special show at the Summit Museum, a charming but traditional museum a few towns away. I would love to have entered but I had nothing to show. What was I making? Nothing. I was now a housewife raising my three babies all under the age of four. I was busy and very tired and it made me sad that I had no art to submit to the show.

Then I had an idea. I could do a self-portrait in the form of an installation. I could bring our round oak table and five chairs. I could litter it with three empty milk glasses, two empty coffee cups, and three cereal bowls with a few soggy Fruit Loops in them and a half-eaten piece of toast. I would tip the box haphazardly on its side with a half-gallon carton of milk partially spilled across the table and a smear of jam at the edge. In my sky-blue, 1940s housedress printed with clusters of cherries, purchased for a dollar from the Salvation Army and my hair out to there, I would pose legs up on the table, drinking coffee and reading the *Sunday Times*. I would stay that way, appearing oblivious to the activities around me, a harried housewife stuck in time and space. And that is what I did.

Most viewers kept a self-conscious distance studying the paintings surrounding me as they made their way around the room. Only a few brave people, after circling a few times, approached to ask if I was part of the show. This sort of installation art was happening in New York but apparently the concept had not yet reached New Jersey. The reviews for the art were positive but we laughed disappointedly that there was no mention of my installation, the elephant in the room.

Ron had started building chairs and benches for some of our neighbors and spent many hours making paintings in a small building that a friend had let him use while the nation was once again in a recession. Since Ron was trying to build a career as painter, I needed to find a job. There was nothing in the classifieds that I could actually do so out of desperation, I answered an ad for a mathematician. Math had always been my worst subject but I seemed to have no choice.

Turns out I actually got a second shift job at the Forrestal Nuclear Reactor at Princeton measuring the distance between bombarded atomic particles. Here were the first computers. These were almost unheard of, a true phenomenon and a glimpse into the future. What I did, along with a few others in my position, was sit a table with a black screen measuring tiny white dots as they moved like stars across a black ground. The scariest thing was that every few feet, it seemed, there were these glass cases housing protective gear in case of a nuclear accident in the building. The reactor itself was terrifyingly immense and took up what seemed, though I wasn't sure, several stories high and an acre wide. By the time I drove home from Princeton to Roosevelt, sometimes in the falling snow, I was exhausted and when I got home I'd curl up against Ron and fall into a deep sleep.

Around four o' clock one morning, I woke up to an empty space beside me. Where could he be? I began to panic with suspicion. When I asked Ron later where he had been, I discovered that while I had been going to work every evening, he had fallen crazy in love with a beautiful younger woman who was in the throes of divorce, had three young children herself, and had taken sanctuary in the welcoming arms of my husband. His studio, it turned out, had been serving as their little love nest for months. I was devastated. I was livid. Here I was with three little children, paying for and driving a baby sitter back and forth so I could go to work and he could paint. My despair was so devastating that it caused me to temporarily lose my mind enough to do something outrageously dumb. Stupidly, I just didn't care. It was frustration, revenge and I guess some kind of self-destructive tendency that was driving me.

Out of total abandon and a need to throw caution to the wind, I left the kids with him, drove to the Greyhound Station and jumped on a bus to Manhattan with the intention of lying down with any fool who whistled, gestured or cat-called to me as I strolled down the avenue. I wanted to get even. I didn't care what he looked like, spoke like or acted like.

So there I was on this boiling hot day, walking down Third Avenue in a red mini-dress with navy-blue piping, tossing out pheromones like a cat in heat when a young man overloaded with camera equipment struggled by. No sooner had he passed me that he turned around and blurted out, "I'd like to know you, I really would."

"But what will you do with those cameras?" I laughed.

"Uh, oh, uh, uh, just wait. I'll put them somewhere," he said, and he scrambled into a doorway down the block, taking an awful gamble with that expensive equipment, I assumed. Maybe he lived there. I never knew.

"I'll be in the coffee shop across the street," I shouted, needing to prepare my head for whatever was about to happen and needing some fortification, I ordered an egg cream. My adrenalin rushed like a wild river through my body, temporarily obliterating the anger and fear of losing Ron and at the same time laughing with disbelief about what I was about to do.

My handsome young lover found my booth and took a seat. Laughing, we agreed right away to not ask each other's names but we could ask other questions. He was an NYU political science student from Argentina with dark handsome looks—the Hollywood image of a Latin romantic—and was very soft spoken. He ordered an egg cream to join me, slurped it down and off we went.

It took some effort to keep up with him on the walk to his apartment and I worried about how many stairs there'd be to climb once we got there. I tried to remain cool in the city heat and the situation, and I might have if my legs hadn't started to give out. The last thing I wanted was to have to stop and "rest" or look into some store window on the pretense of fascination with some mundane object for sale. I needed to give my stubborn legs a break. Was I crazy? What was I doing here? How could I turn back? No, I couldn't. I was too invested. So as we walked, I stopped to gaze from time to time into a store window as if there was something intriguing there . . . and I prayed.

We turned the corner and finally reached his building but his darned apartment was on the third floor. I made some excuse about the need to stop and rummage through my purse, taking the time I needed before facing the stairs. After finally reaching the third landing, huffing and puffing, he suggested we continue on up to the roof to catch a breeze. By the time we got up there, I was shaking and nauseous and feeling all of my usual debilitating symptoms from this hideous plague of mine. My humor and charm had vanished and the last thing I wanted was a kiss on the roof with a stranger. But he was gracious enough to pick up on my vibes and turn away from what might have been sweet romance beneath the stars. He nevertheless walked me back down to what turned out to be an empty apartment with cans of paint clustered on a tarp in the middle of the floor. By then I was coming back to normal as I usually do after the crisis subsides.

The floor and drop cloth served us well as we proceeded with our original intention to have pure, erotic but emotionless sex. When we were satisfied, he asked if I would like him to bathe me. Was that a Latin touch? I was thrilled that I hadn't disappointed him with all of my angst. As the electricity had not yet been turned on, he lit about a million candles while I soaked in the cool, clean water. While soaping me up and rinsing me off with the kindest of hands, we laughed and laughed about how this was all happening. He knew I wasn't *that* kind of girl and he happily walked me back down to the street, caught a cab to the place where he had ditched his equipment, and I sped off to the Port Authority. With a huge grin on my face, I caught my bus back to Jersey. He was a lucky, fine young man and I was a lucky gambler, finding a guy with intelligence and sensitivity. Someone was watching over me.

I got back home safe and satisfied. I found our young neighbor dozing on the couch while the kids remained in bed, fast asleep. I paid the boy and let him go then collapsed into a chair. There was no doubt where my husband was and with whom. I was desperate to gather the kids and leave home but where would I go and how would we live?

Okay, that's the way it was, sad but true, and I didn't know what to do. Truth was I could do nothing and was so frightened about the possibility of being abandoned with my three little kids and this skimpy job that I began to fall apart. I refused to have a nervous breakdown and

felt I was coming close so I decided to go away by myself in order to think, gain strength and plan my next step. Ron and his *girlfriend* could handle the kids for a little while. Screw them.

A friend drove me the endless hours to the house in Maine that we had not yet ever occupied. It still had shabby, antique patchwork quilts and dusty afghans on the beds. The house was there in the same beautiful spot except for the dust, looking like a sanctuary just waiting for me, waiting to be occupied, waiting to be loved. I stripped off the bedding, shook everything out and spread it over the grass in the back. The fresh air and morning dew should help. I slapped down my sleeping bag, scooted down into it and cried myself to sleep.

The next day was spent in a ladderback chair, staring at the wall. After I had my first pity party, I popped up, gathered my tools and began drawing. I wasn't sure how to fix my marriage, but I did know how to climb ladders to hang some curtains that I found packed away in an antique blanket chest. The blackness coming in the windows had reflected my sorry image and exaggerated my emptiness. So curtains were a must. I began digging through the closed-off rooms filled with antiques and junk, and gathered what I wanted to surround myself with in the kitchen, where I'd spend my time reading, writing and drawing. I gathered up some sea green bottles, ironstone dishes and crocks, a rocking chair, some pictures and curios. A kind of peace fell over me when I stepped outside and saw the beauty of the orchard, the field of flowers and the mountain views. I picked some purple asters, Queen Anne's lace and a bit of milkweed that smelled like honey and tucked them into crocks in the kitchen. Then I began to hum and sing and I started to remember myself—not as a mom, not as a wife, but just me.

The next day, the neighbors from the farm down the road brought me up an apple pie. They knew we had bought the house and saw that the lights had been turned on and that someone was there. They seemed to have accepted us. Their dairy farm was diagonally across the road down a long and winding driveway. Mary invited me down the following day to meet the family and have the first of the corn and their own butter, which was as sweet as candy. Afterwards, she graciously brought me into the formal parlor and showed me an album. In it were pictures of the family who had lived in the house before the

hermit. The old woman in her black dress sat in the rocking chair I had been using. The stoneware crock with the same combination of wild flowers was in the same corner of the kitchen just as I had arranged them. Of course. It was the same field sowing those same wildflower seeds and weaving their roots in the same places for all these years. It gave me a welcome sense of groundedness. In the photo, the glass bottles were on the windowsills in exactly the same order as I had placed them.

"Can you believe it?" I asked Mary laughingly, feeling kind of magical for having replicated all of that.

"I don't like it," she said with alarm. "That's wrong that you would know that, like the devil is talking to you."

"It's just a coincidence," I told her. I didn't believe in coincidences, but I had to say something. I went back to the house, sat down at the table and began writing to my sister about what had just happened. I described to Nancy how I had placed all of the objects back into the room exactly where they had been a century ago and as I was writing these things, the atmosphere in the room changed. I had never thought much about ghosts, but in a sudden thrust of constriction, I realized that across from me sat one in the rocker. I could sense the presence of an old woman who had lived there long, long ago and had come back to haunt me. It was clear she was unhappy about my presence in her kitchen and with her things in their rightful places, too. I could feel her hostility, sharp as a whip, and I dared not look up. With my head bent down, I turned around, grabbed a match, lit the letter on fire and dropped it into the stove. The room cleared instantly and there was peace in the kitchen once more.

Over the following two weeks, I did a lot to clear my head as I explored the field and orchard and connected back with my writing and drawing. Although I wondered about my babes, I wasn't a mom right then. I was just me. I knew they were safe and probably getting an abundance of treats just to keep them happy. I wasn't worried about them even though I didn't know what would happen with Ron when the two weeks were up. But I was starting to feel centered as if a core of trust had gathered itself within me and given me some necessary strength to keep my family together with or without their cheating father.

Ron took the Trailways up to Maine to drive me back to New Jersey. I was chicken about driving long distances by myself, terrified of highway traffic and trailer trucks, so I was sadly dependent on him in that respect. That night, while in bed, he revealed to me that he had decided to leave us and go with the girlfriend. I was shaken. I rapidly lost that core of trust and barely slept through the night, wishing he were elsewhere and not right beside me like this; but there was nowhere else to be.

The trip from Maine to Jersey was a long one and I had time to re-gather myself. Eventually, I said, "Okay, I deserve more from my life anyway." I didn't know what we would do but I trusted somehow we would be okay. Though it made no sense to me, my little voice told me so and it felt good to believe in that.

When we got back to Roosevelt, I told him to pack up and leave. He didn't go. For a full week, I begged him to get the hell out of the house and move in with her so I could get on with my life, so I could find a way without his presence crowding my mind and breaking my heart. He wouldn't budge.

Then suddenly he was in pain. He was never in pain, at least that I knew about, and I had to drive him to the hospital. He had been so conflicted about us and the affair that he had stressed himself into a knot, which caused him to spend some time in traction. When I went to get him a few days later, he said, "I want to stay with you and the kids. I'll break up with her tomorrow."

After his pleading and tears and sighs and words, I responded, "Only on one condition: that you stop painting and get a job. It's time you start to support the family. It's your turn."

I had faith in him as a painter and hated to take that away from him but he had to start acting like a father, an age-old conflict, I suppose, for artists with families without inherited wealth. He agreed to put his efforts into designing and building furniture, an expansion from the shelves and stools he had built for the bookstores and those few neighbors.

He set up a shop in an abandoned chicken coop that sat at the far side of our yard. It was a big space, low ceilinged but very long and he started to design and build some beautiful things even in those primitive surroundings. But it was hard. The girlfriend had lived in that town before we moved in and was loved by the people there. She had friends and allies. I dreaded bumping into her or, worse yet, Ron running into her. We needed to get away from Roosevelt, all of it—the dinner parties, the angst about the war and all the sex. We had been there for three years. It had given us a community of good people who enjoyed getting together, sharing child care, hosting scrumptious dinners, engaging in good conversation but it was the sixties and the sexual revolution was driving everyone's fantasies and Ron could not resist turning his into reality.

We needed to go to Maine. Our very own house and barn were waiting for us and since we owned it outright, there was no rent or mortgage to worry about. We could start over in a peaceful environment, somewhat isolated and that, I thought, was bound to bring us closer together again.

Fire in the Heart, Heart in the Fire

Random Snapshots I Carry of a Family in Flux

Maine, the feel in my palm of plaid flannel,
warm off the line
and the rippling, smoky heat
as I stir beans, stuffing yellow birch into the
stove.
Then Hartford: I cruise the schoolyard at recess
to
sneak a peak at my girls, my young ones with
red-brown hair, bent in whisper
their backs to me
against the wind
All of us
far from apple orchards
onto urban streets

gone from the open door onto a second floor
And in my soul I carry Ron
I carry feathers and stones,
laughter and weeping

and on this skin and in these bones
Adam, Jenn and Liz always in my keeping
I carry the river and know
no matter what
the river carries me

and all four of them
slowly, methodically,
brilliantly, into the golden field.

Mommy-ing is not simple in its big joys and little sorrows but complex and beautiful. And like the elements of sacred geometry, the potential is immense and never ending.

118

This Used to Be Us

Foreign to Me as Mars, Captured by the Magic, Invoking Amelia, Kidnapping the Baby, Conversation with My Sister and Woman Power

So now I was "back to the land" in Maine, though I'd never really lived on the land in the first place. I had pushed to come to the beauty of the North Country, determined to bring my family back together, find time for art making, and maybe even to explore that mystical experience I had back in college—that meeting I had in my dorm when I flew out of one reality into another, where I unsuspectingly met my dead father amongst the stars. Maybe I could finally start to think about

that again, maybe even find someone who would know what that was all about.

The North Country was ruggedly beautiful but as foreign to me as Mars. This, though, was our potential. Would this forever be our home? We lived sweetly, happily, even ecstatically for awhile, with me in my clear-cut role as Mommy, cooking and baking and heating the house all with the generosity of our big wooden cook stove and Ron diving in and embracing all the hard work, all the fixing up and the work in the gardens.

That first summer, we discovered other "refugees" from the cities. We spotted each other at auctions, at the laundries and the country store. We were all relatively young and idealistic, purposeful, opinionated, self-righteous, confident and very naïve. Despite the plan to get away from all the social, political and sexual turmoil of the cities that we had moved from in exchange for the stillness of the wilder country, it seemed that there was no way to really do that. Unrest was there, too. It was in us all. But it was less, much less.

Despite our resolve to remove ourselves from all the distraction, we were still part of society. It continued to be a time when war, truth telling through the music, and the sexual revolution permeated everyone's lives in some way even up here. I proudly slapped my *Another Mother for Peace* bumper sticker on my car and drove around with clipboards and petitions against the war. Naturally, that aroused suspicion about us long-haired outsiders up there in the country, which was revealing itself to be as conservative as the south. Some of the locals called me a pinko, some a commie, and some a Jew, even though they had no idea I really am a Jew, a fact

I kept hidden for the sake of my children because up there Jews were suspect and often hated even though most people had never even met one of us. My kids didn't need that on top of our outsider status so we were able to "pass."

Ron and I were desperately hanging on financially, trying to pull ourselves through the coming winter to keep warm and make ends meet.

I spent the winter feeding the stoves and running thirty feet across the snow to the outhouse. I contracted a bladder infection from the wind whipping up through the hole in the bench, a kidney infection, a lump on my breast, and pneumonia. For the bladder infection, I had been prescribed antibiotics and was told to get a douche bag. I had never owned one of those things so I drove the long road to the drug store, picked out this bright yellow rubber piece of equipment, brought it into the outhouse, hung it on a rusty nail and did my business. As I sat there in the cold, looking through the cracks between the boards of the outhouse into the coziness of our domain, light glowing warmly, I burst out laughing at the absurdity of what I was doing and how it must look if anyone were to see.

As for the lump, it was nothing . . . not then.

Ron had sold a large painting to the Newark Museum and a couple of his chairs before we came to Maine but that money had run out. There had been much to buy to set up a home and a shop, so that winter, Ron took the second shift at a mill, which was hard labor under dangerous conditions. This was not exactly an artist's dream. What kind of a corner had we painted ourselves into? How could we have been so naive? I guess artists follow their muses into whatever maze it takes them through and that is called the journey.

Coming home through ice and snow in the middle of every night that winter must have been trying for Ron, for he soon found refuge with a co-worker at the mill, a young divorcee with four young children who always seemed to need help with a door hinge or a water pipe or something. She had created a honey-do list for him to take care of on some of those dark nights on his way home and he would oblige. But he wasn't her honey. Or was he? She was a little scraggly, lonely, girl-like woman and it didn't take long before the second affair of our marriage had begun.

Ron had originally agreed to stop painting in order to get paid work and had committed to the family in a brand new way by coming up to Maine with a new dream. Now this. We fought and he insisted that she meant nothing to him. He said that he felt sorry for her and was just helping out a single mom who was doing a man's job and dealing with four little kids at the same time. How could he not help? So we fought and that was all I saw that I could do. Although he had sworn off ever having another affair, there he was again having one and I could find no way to claim any leverage. If I left or kicked him out then I would be the single mom dealing with three little kids and what for an income? There was war on two fronts.

Vietnam was an ongoing concern while the Women's Movement was making its appearance in my life just when I needed it. It had not grabbed me in any conscious way until Robin Morgan's book, *Sisterhood is Powerful,* fell into my hands. It promptly awakened me to all the injustices in the world toward women in general, in my own life, in the things I had encountered and had not thought much about but had nonetheless been affected by. I hadn't yet read Betty Friedan's *The Feminine Mystique* but with Morgan's book, I was shaken awake and overnight became an angry woman with newfound clarity of history, both personal and political. That book addressed many specific issues I had been repressing in my own life. So many of the women's stories within it touched a nerve in me by clarifying feelings I had not yet identified.

It began early. When we were in sixth grade, I remember, we girls would sit around playing "Fortune", fantasizing the kind of man we wanted to marry, how many kids, what kind of house we would live in and where. I distinctly remember wanting a man that was just a little bit smarter than me, a little bit taller than me, and just a little bit better than me in every way. That would be the ideal. We had been programmed to hold lower expectations for ourselves because our value was perceived by who we would marry and one of the many myths of the day was guys don't like a smarty pants. We hadn't even realized the ramifications of the amount of psychological damage, intimidation, physical and emotional abuse and economic injustice we were facing.

Except for the goddess worship in Paleolithic times and in other cultures at other times when anthropologists speculated that the first "God" or gods of the peoples were feminine . . . except for then, the crazy beginnings of all this injustice and prejudice can perhaps be traced to religion. Women were seen as distractions. Men couldn't keep their focus on prayer if their eyes were wandering and their bodies were lusting. That seems to have started the whole thing. Women had to be moved out of sight and out of proximity in houses of worship. Women were the threat. Just as an example, it is believed that Eve was the cause of the ills in the world because she ate of the tree of knowledge, and worse, she influenced Adam to do the same. What a bad girl, what a bad influence. How much angst we must have caused men all those centuries ago and we're still paying for it today.

After all this time it lingers. The sexual objectification of women is perpetually portrayed on the streets and in the media. The images of women's bodies are used to sell everything from alcohol to athletic shoes to automobile parts and everything in between. After all the awareness that came about in the Women's Movement and all that we did to counter it, today, we are still inundated with popular music that is saturated with sexism and even violence, and the worst part is many women are participating in it. They sing and dance to the songs that victimize them and call them names. That is happening now in 2016.

In our awakening during the sixties and seventies, all we had to do was look around our own workplaces, inside our own bedrooms and to the world at large to see that women have been targets of violence throughout history. Our professional lives have been affected by sexism as leadership roles and elected offices were closed to us. And worse, in our country, our biased justice system still rarely convicts rapists when there is no witness; or when it does, even if there are witnesses, the punishment is never enough to fit the crime, the effects of which last a lifetime. Does anyone really believe that rape takes place in front of people? Even now in this 21st Century, there is enormous effort to repeal Rowe vs. Wade, an attempt to once again take away from us control over our own bodies. I sometimes wish pro-choice voices would also talk about the consequences of bringing unwanted children into the world and the neglect and abuse that so often comes from that. Don't we all pay the price for the results of so many un-nurtured kids both in time and money? Doesn't this restriction affect whole families, as well as the size of the population in relationship to planetary resources? Yes, it's about the rights to our own bodies but it seems it is also a responsibility to our planet and the civilization that inhabits it.

This same discriminatory thinking lies behind the continuing gender gap in pay. No matter how often it comes up in politics, it still has not become resolved. Outrageous.

After reading Robin Morgan's book, I conducted my own experiment. I stopped wearing lipstick and eyeliner, and began wearing Ron's black leather jacket. I wanted to remove any feminine appeal I had and look as tough as I could. I wanted to be androgynous. I wanted no more cat calls or disgusting sucking sounds when I passed a work zone, and I wanted to look like "no one better mess with *this* woman."

With that image change, I was instantly treated differently by men and women. Women were condescending and I was invisible to men. It was a very foreign feeling but my new image had nothing to do with my love for cooking and baking and raising my babies. I was totally into the mommy role. I was grateful to be making stews atop the crackling stove, which I was able to do only because Ron was out in the cold splitting wood. So it was a double-edged sword and it provided a lot of grist for reflection. I often wondered, If I were physically fit, would I have enjoyed working up a sweat in the cold outdoors?

Soon I found a consciousness-raising group, a concept Gloria Steinem had borrowed from indigenous people that she had sat with and listened to in her travels. She brought the concept to the Women's Movement and it was a format that spread all over the country. Women would meet in circles to tell their stories. The circle was important because it kept everyone on equal footing and it seemed a natural thing for us to have no hierarchy. There were no rows and no leader up front. Women felt safe enough to share very personal stories, and through listening to each other would themselves become aware and empowered.

It was validating realizing we were not alone in all of our inner discontents. We supported each other in trying to make changes within our families, attempting to enlighten our husbands and raise awareness in our kids, and also to recognize how competitive we were with each other without really owning it. As a result, my girls got no Barbie dolls and my boy got no G.I. Joe. The question being: are these preferences inherent in children or are they taught through conditioning? Most of us were acting from frustration, a sense of discovery and the expectation that we might be able to help empower our girls and sensitize our boys. Why does every girl have to grow up to be gorgeous and why does every boy have to grow up to be a soldier?

Although we were doing our best from the bottom of our passionate hearts, we collectively were building a somewhat flawed movement. First of all, we couldn't create change from anger. Second of all, we were women but still different from each other with differing priorities and approaches. Change comes hard and educating ourselves as we went was an awesome task. We did what we could from who we were at the time and I do believe that despite all the complexities, we definitely made many inroads in the long run. By the end of the sixties, for example, more than 80 percent of wives of childbearing age were using contraception, allowing more women to enter the workforce. With that came the persistent struggle for equal pay for equal work, and later in the eighties during the Clarence Thomas hearings for Supreme Court and the Anita Hill challenge, the discussion of sexual harassment was born. The consciousness-raising groups brought everything out in the open. It was now safe to share the most intimate of complaints and we became friends with each other on a much deeper level.

Back in Roosevelt, I had sought some means of creative expression other than painting. That would have required more time and space than I had, so I taught myself how to weave from a library book. I'd always loved fabric and the little loom Ron had built for me was portable, which meant that I could use it on the kitchen table and stash it away when I was done, something I couldn't do with paint.

So now I had the chance to really get into weaving. With the kids at school, Ron gone at work and basic chores done, I settled in at my new antique loom that we'd found in a dealer's attic and purchased at a great price. It was a four-harness, overhead, counterbalance loom in glowing worn pine that took up the whole parlor. I focused on rugs and tapestries because I could change colors randomly. I was not disciplined enough to place the pattern in the warp where the weft would simply go back and forth for hours on end to create a predetermined pattern. Oh, no.

I had to create it and build it at the same time, a spontaneous and exciting act. What emerged was always a surprise in texture, color and design, sometimes even function. If I had the patience to figure out warp patterns, I may have tried that but I had no tolerance for working out details such as how to string a warp for a predetermined design. That was limiting and would have bored me to tears. In a way, it was a metaphor for my life. Living the way we were, in the moment, I just wasn't a planner.

The rug I was working on was beginning to look beautiful with its hand spun, hand dyed yarn and vibrant colors. I began to cherish the remaining days I could spend on it. When spring came, there was garden planting and things seemed to move into high gear all at once.

Besides, I hated touching wool when the weather was hot. But now it was March, and March in Maine is still deep winter. As I worked furiously to finish that rug, I had no idea that it was the final winter before Grandma Berche would leave the planet.

Ode to You, Gram

The Last time I saw you
Your eyes were closed.
I laid my hands on your belly
Like petals on water
(You were in coma)

I remembered your waist long hair
Now cropped ear high
I'd stand behind you in the mirror,
The two of us looking back at ourselves and
each other
Your flowers springing bright
Off quilts from their scrubbing in Oxydol

You'd hand me the jade colored bakelite brush,
motioning,
Knowing I longed for a mane like that

Instead of the frizz I got

Once I placed the brush down on your tray
The same green jade made an oval frame
Around glued-down butterflies
On linen under glass.

This was a sacred thing for a girl of twelve
Who was bearing a dangerous sin
Maybe you knew,
Because every time I went to your house
You asked if I wanted a bath.
And I always said yes, and you gave me one.

The last time I saw you
It was my hands offering love
Sailing lightly over your body,
Now thin under your hospital gown,
Smoothing you in place,
Printing the text of your form in my hand,
Your forehead, so cool, in my palm.

The freezing temperatures, Ron's affair with the little waif, short-lived as it was, Gram's dying and my ills almost overcame me that winter, but on we went. As far as making friends, we had the

128

most in common with Rhea and Peter, who lived a somewhat long and rocky drive from us. We had been artists in New York, and Peter had also turned into a furniture maker. They had two girls and the same goals as us so there was much to share—including woman talk with Rhea, who was a pertinent part of our consciousness-raising group.

On one muddy Sunday afternoon, I was sitting at Rhea's kitchen table amongst five adults and three small children. It was a round table with a Formica top that allowed constant drawing and wiping away so there were always designs, doodles and kid's drawings scattered here and there, and often underneath was sprawled a white lab named Albion. There were glasses of red wine and mugs of cocoa, and while we were savoring chunks of bread and homemade cheese from their own cow, a blue Jeep bolted into the driveway and screeched to a stop. A stocky man in a red-and-black hunting jacket walked up the drive toward the house and, curiously, my hands began to sweat.

With the approaching footsteps, the children and dog vanished and backs stiffened. The guy came boldly through the door, scraping mud from green rubber boots. He was not an attractive man. In fact, he was kind of scary with a coldness that emanated from ice blue eyes. Besides the hunting jacket, he was wearing work pants and a knitted cap scarcely covering a salt-and-pepper buzz cut. He hunkered through the door, nodded, and settled against the sink, arms crossed over his chest.

Rhea's voice broke the silence: "Marge Curtis, this is Harlan Tripp. Harlan . . . Marge."

Harlan rubbed his hands together and crossed the room to the stove saying nothing, but squinting at me with those cold eyes as he moved. He rested a leg up on the rim of the stove, and one by one, everyone in the room found a reason to leave.

I had nowhere to go since I was waiting for Ron to come back from the lumberyard. Avoiding the man's eyes, I began to methodically wrap cheese and wipe away crumbs. I could have followed Peter to his shop, but I seemed glued to the kitchen chair. With nothing else to do there, I managed to plant myself in front of the skinny bookcase between the windows facing the woods. I knew I couldn't actually read right then, but I pulled a book from the shelf, and with my back to him, I tried to look absorbed.

I knew the man's eyes were still fixed on me. I took a deep but quiet breath in an attempt to prepare myself for leaving the kitchen to anywhere, but somehow I was pinned there. Finally, I turned and looked straight into his eyes. Hoping to break the tension, I made some inane comment:

"Where did everybody go, I wonder."

He immediately broke into laughter—not genuine laughter, but diabolical laughter.

I turned back and continued to flip the pages of the book, seeing nothing, one page after another, until I landed on a color photograph of a Japanese garden, serene and lush with mosses and rocks of many shapes. It became the Zen moment I was looking for.

"If you're looking for something, you won't find it in a book," said the deep and sullen voice by the stove.

The page blurred.

"What do you mean?" I asked.

"You heard me. What you're looking for is not in any book."

Do I want to pursue this comment? I debate with myself. Then I was saved by the rumble of our truck coming up the driveway. I slammed the book shut and shoved it back in place.

"Nice meeting you, Harlan," I lied, threw on my coat and dashed out, slamming the door behind me and nestling in next to Ron.

"What did you think of Harlan?" Rhea asked me when I bumped into her at the general store the next day.

"Pretty bizarre," I said.

"Yeah, I'd be careful if I were you. Sometimes he's just a regular guy coming around carrying on about his truck or how high the riverbanks are, but other times he can get into some weird stuff."

"What kind of weird stuff?" I asked.

"Oh, I don't know, *energy*, he calls it. He talks about energy a lot and doesn't believe in book knowledge. He says anyone can know anything with their own mind. They don't have to read it in a book."

"Yuk. What kind of work does he do?"

"Cuts trees, has his own woodlots all around here. He's no dummy, though. I wouldn't fool around with him if I were you. He just comes by to hang out with Pete. He's a neighbor and a local so that's nice. Doesn't bother us. But it's best not to engage him on any real level."

In the weeks that followed, Harlan proved

his weird abilities by mysteriously finding our house then making ill-timed appearances. At first, he was a curiosity. I got over that initial strangeness and was intrigued, if not challenged, by him even though I had been warned. He could always tell when I was home and Ron was either at the mill or in the shop, which was most of the time. He also seemed to drop in when Ron had saws running and couldn't hear a train if it pulled into the driveway, let alone a Jeep. Or if we had company he'd never met before, we could count on him to happen by, but most of the time it was just us, cozy and domestic and serene.

Meanwhile, garden catalogues had been coming for a month and the pictures of peas and peppers and tomatoes were thrilling to consider. It set me to dreaming. That's one thing about weaving; it allows for a lot of dreaming.

I went to the shed for more wood to feed the studio stove, and I swore I could smell spring rising from the earth. I could taste it. I vowed to get outside before the kids got home, and then . . . *damn, surprise, surprise:* I saw that Jeep slow down for the turn. My stomach turned to knots for a second and I went through five different emotions before he got to the door. How did he always know? *Careful. Just be careful.* He pulled right up to the house, leaving the motor running.

"Come for a ride," Harlan said. "I want to show you something."

"No, I've got to keep working on this," I told him, and I didn't want him to come through that door.

"C'mon," he said. "It's warm out."
Oh, shit, there was no refusing. It was beautiful out. Even though there was something strange about him, I wouldn't acknowledge it to myself because there was also something intriguing about him. I wondered what discovery lay before me that might bring me some answers to my many questions.

I pulled on my boots, threw on my jacket and walked out into the sun, which reflected blindingly off the melting snow. It was delicious. I savored the sounds of dripping icicles and the sudden crash as they broke and fell onto the packed snow, water running free beneath the crust. Folks told us that the snow wouldn't be gone in the woods until May, sometimes June. With this February thaw, though, and the glaring sun, I was awakened to a new state of alertness after sitting so long at the loom, breathing in the dryness of wood heat.

"Where are you going?" I asked.

"*We* are going for a ride."

What the hell. The lure of a ride through the country on a day like today was irresistible. We traveled over the gentle ups and downs of DeCourcey Hill Road and took a right on the main road going north. After a while, the atmosphere seemed to change, but I couldn't put my finger on it. It was as if my vision was blurring and we were in a kind of slow motion.

"Do you hear that?" he asked, as he turned onto a dirt road toward Moore, a nearby town.

"What?"

"Listen."

Then I heard it. Very quiet but high-pitched. It sounded like the hideous squeal of a dental drill, but it was coming from a ditch and there was no one there. It got louder and shriller yet I knew it really wasn't being heard by my ordinary ears. Maybe it was being heard by my imagination. I was skeptical, but there was no escaping the fact that I really heard this sound.

"What is it?" I asked.

"A car crash," he said. "There was an accident here once and the energy is still trapped. Let's neutralize it," he said, looking at me as if to watch my surprise.

I was stupefied but I wouldn't show it. I acted as if he was showing me how to fish instead of how to hear inaudible sounds or neutralize bad energy.

I sat still as the noise subsided and eventually stopped.

"Now, there's that much less negativity in the world," he said, all full of himself.

This is good stuff, I was thinking, but didn't dare say.

"C'mon," said Harlan, "let's go find some more."

It was a crazy thing but it made me feel powerful and helpful, learning how to rid the roads of inaudible but dangerous sounds. Were we really hearing what we thought we were hearing or was this like the *Emperor's New Clothes?*

We drove around and soon it was me who would first notice a place that seemed to call from the side of the road. Other times, we would both hear it at once. We spent the afternoon eradicating bad vibrations from our little part of the world, the road between Covington and

Moore. I thought it was amazing to be secretly making the roads safer for people by doing whatever it was we were doing. Harlan had told me that fear lingers in the place where something violent happened and can act as a magnet for other bad things. Maybe . . . maybe not.

Maybe that's why some people put crosses at the site of an accident, or flowers, not only to create a memorial to their loved ones, but also to neutralize the site and act as a warning to people driving fast. Still, I had to admit, I couldn't get rid of this creepy feeling that we were messing with something that was not in our hands.

The trip back to the house was without conversation. The sun had dropped down behind the trees and I felt suddenly chilled sitting there next to this strange man in his blue Jeep. Harlan broke the silence.

"You can go all the way," he said. "You know that, don't you? I can take you all the way."

"All the way to what?" I asked sarcastically, not sure what he was getting at.

"Knowledge," he said, almost in a whisper. "Knowledge."

I climbed out of the Jeep wondering if he knew anything about meeting dead loved ones in the void, or things like that.

The words *all* the way hummed in my brain as I felt for the driveway under foot, slippery again, the sun already below the horizon. I didn't know what that meant but it sounded to me like *all the way* to my potential, to unknown things. This had always been an underlying longing. I wasn't enough of a person the way I was. I needed to be more. My parents always said so. I believed them and that belief was still haunting me. So a*ll the way* meant he could take me further and that was a great prospect. What did I have to learn from him? What was it that was keeping me even bothering with this guy? What was it I couldn't find on my own?

The kids were all home and it felt late, like I was stepping into a room where things had been completed without me. Ron was in the house stuffing birch logs into the fire. I felt delinquent and guilty. Even though Ron knew I had been gallivanting with Harlan, it didn't seem to bother him. He knew I was always itching for understanding. There was nothing to say about this, no way to explain what I didn't understand myself.

The kitchen was warm. Jelly and toast crumbs

were evident on the counter and Sam Cat was flipping a pretzel around on the floor.

The February thaw didn't last long. Things had frozen up again and near the end of that cold and windy season while picking up our allotment of surplus food from the delivery bus, I heard about a meeting that was coming up. The Federal Government was organizing advisory committees for those of us on the roles for these so-called handouts and that meant us that first year. I wanted to check it out. There was something pulling me and without knowing why, I needed to be there.

The morning of the meeting, school was canceled due to inclement weather but having no phone, I could only hope that the event was still on. It was one of those surprise blizzards where the sky suddenly opens and drops its load of heavy whiteness. I jumped out of bed and got dressed. Snow was piling up and blindingly coming down in clusters.

Though I was terrified of driving our ancient truck through the storm, I had to take my chances and tackle those seventeen miles. There were no windshield wipers on the old Dodge so I had to stick my head out the open window every few seconds in order to see the road ahead. My hand only reached over half the windshield. Fortunately, hardly anyone else was out. My legs jumped with fear, but I kept telling myself that Amelia Earhart went through much worse and much further but this trip was plenty long enough. I imagined Amelia up in the dangerous and lonely sky and spent the entire drive talking to her as if she was driving and I was her passenger.

That trip turned out to be worth everything. The meeting had not been canceled. I made a point to meet the man in charge. He would interview me in a few days for a community organizer position in President Johnson's Great Society Program, his War on Poverty. Johnson had created an Office of Economic Opportunity and I was offered the opportunity to interview for that job for two of the counties in Central Maine. One week later, I put on my most respectable clothes and went for the interview. My life, our lives, would change for the better, once again.

Ron was able to quit the mill and begin to design and build really interesting furniture: tall, beautiful, comfortable, hand-shaved, nine-spoke chairs from local walnut, cherry and maple, as well as long-backed benches. Their raw-edged planks were largely influenced by George Nakashima, the famous furniture maker who uniquely and gracefully left natural raw edges on his benches. Ron loved his work and I took inspiration from him. He also began making inkle looms, like the one he originally made for me. They were simple, primitive looms for narrow weavings like belts or panels for other wearables, and he made all heights and shapes of stools from local fruitwoods. That began to attract attention.

We started to bring in some money and were finally able to get off the surplus food, that horrible spam-like substance, the endless bottles of corn syrup we never used, the bland orangey cheese and powdered milk. Whatever was left over we fed to the piggy, who, through his short, sweet life, remained nameless for obvious reasons. Although we were amazed to discover how smart pigs are, he was not to be a pet. We were bent on becoming self-sufficient and now we could start our own tiny farm, the garden, the apple, pear and cherry trees, the high-bush cranberries, the blackberry grove, the chickens and their eggs and, of course, piggy, our experiment in what we thought of as authentic Maine living. We had the belief that aside from the money we saved, we should be aware of where our food came from. In those days, packaged meat on a grocery shelf was no longer appealing, as we wanted to be conscious of what we were eating. We wanted to honor the food we ate.

Our lifestyle in Maine had gotten better and better as we acquired more conveniences, like plumbing, propane to augment the wood and a spacious bathroom that held a tiny woodstove. Ron made a fitting for the pipe to go outdoors and we fired up that baby to turn the space into a sauna, which became our pleasure palace on frigid winter nights. He had taken down walls and opened everything up. The Mystic Maine, my cherished cook stove, kept us cozy and helped me make great meals, bake biscuits, challah and whole grain breads to eat with the honey from our own hives, maple syrup from our own trees, and jams from our own berries. Life was sweet.

And yet I couldn't shake the feeling that there was something more. I remained hauntingly intrigued by Harlan's offer to take me "all the way." I had in my head the notion of some kind of initiation into something mysterious, something possibly even sacred, as I had always been driven toward the mysterious and it seemed this odd person was holding a key.

Up on Robbins Hill

1.

The road is dirt, winding over rocks and roots.
We wildly climb in this grumpy truck, up, up.
He comes to a clearing and stops, a flat place,
no lights,

He says, "Before we get out, make friends with
the land, the house,
All the inhabitants and guardians of the yard.
They're watching us."

"Why am I here?"
We sit still as frightened mice under a crescent
moon
Harlan shouts out the window, "We mean no
harm."

We wait.

And when the tension lifts and silence falls we
open the doors

And step out. Standing here is, I suppose, like
standing on the moon.

We scope it out, my stomach grumbles as we
approach the stairs,
"This is a test," Harlan says "Calm down."

A test for what? I cry inside with memory of
some Aztec rite
But there's no turning back and to save myself I
lower my fear.
We creak up the stairs, some without risers,
some totally gone.

I follow.

In here the silence is a thunder of moths around
the lights we hold.
"You have to be bold," he says, "you'll find
some treasures here,
Don't belong to nobody no more."

On the old plank floor a floral woven carpet lies,
thin as a sheet,
Reversible, red and yellow, a fur coat that might
reach my ankles, fitted and silky with a collar

136

Of darker fur. It hangs off a rack looking like a
lady in shadow.

"Let's go," I say, already sneaking downstairs,
a common thief, the coat over my arm and the
Growing fear of being ensnared by this silence,
or culture of ghosts.
I have my trophy.

Mockingly, he takes his time, I wanted to speed
away
Down over the bumps under the moon,
Coat or no coat, far from this dark forgotten
road to town.

Instead I'm pleased I passed the test.
But why?
Why did I follow this guy to this place?
What was the test anyway?
I know I had to prove to myself I was brave,
That I was strong, afraid of nothing,
Always ready for an initiation of some kind,
Another naïve attempt at power,
another foolish scheme that comes from
Longing to be strong.

2.

It was an eerie-old and lonely place.
But I had to go back
Today, the sunshine dappling through the trees.
Bees and butterflies darting from bloom to bloom.
"Welcome to the light," they say.
I climb the rise to the tiny cemetery,
A miniature monument against the sky
All fenced in and overgrown.
There's goldenrod, aster, and blackberry stalks
leaning over.
I pluck the juiciest of berries.
My mouth rejoices.
With blue-stained hands I stroke the granite
stones.
That engraved with names like Sarah, Olin,
Albert, Kathryn.
Seven of them, all dead before they were ten,
How it was for mothers then, I dare not think,
But even now it is the same, yet different.
I say a little prayer for children, all the possible
catastrophes,
Climb down through clover, Indian paintbrush,
Not in any rush, don't need to prove a thing with
any test.
The ghosts were kind and let me keep the coat.

Ron was sporadically selling his work and I loved my job. It involved driving around the two counties looking for people in need and there were plenty of them. I loved creating job corps, convincing our doctor to offer "family planning", finding little tikes for Head Start, and soliciting women for the Manpower Training Programs. I wore a button that said, "Ask Me About Contraception." Surprisingly, it was the boys who asked. They told me the girls didn't want to plan sex, they just wanted to be carried away by it. I liked the opportunity to bring something to these isolated single moms and married moms, the poorer farmers, lumber workers, mill workers, and the many people with disabilities and illnesses.

I wanted to expand educational opportunities for the kids, set up co-ops and register the women to vote. Our own kids were rapidly outgrowing their boots and snowsuits so I thought, *Why not have a boot exchange?* Kids could never wear them out before their feet got big. Berkeley had come up with the concept of a Free Store and I thought, *Why not here?* We had an extra room, the small part of our 1760s Cape Cod that had its own entrance so folks could come and go. It was that part of the house I had lived in during those two runaway weeks when I encountered the old lady in the rocking chair but now the space was empty.

I collected clothing, books and toys, and everything was free. Whole families would walk through the door on a weekend afternoon, pick up what they liked, perhaps leave something else or drop some coins into a can I kept by the door. I didn't see who came or went because I was either on the road or in the main part of the house doing my own thing.

The women loved my visits because they welcomed some company into their houses and it gave them an opportunity to gripe about their conditions. Still, in general, they were so obedient to their husbands that they wouldn't venture out at town meetings to vote for their own interests. They stayed at home cooking hot meals for the guys who spent all day arguing for big boy toys and the policies that would affect us all. I couldn't make a dent in that mindset. I eventually learned that we can't bring democracy to a home any more than we can bring it to a country. I learned that people change only when they are ready and that's probably a good thing because what did I really know about this culture, anyway? Maybe these simple coffee klatches were enough.

But there was one client I will always remember. The story has it that she was brought here from New York as the mistress of one of the workers employed to help build the Wyman Dam. When the dam was finished, he went home, leaving her here to fend for herself. Now, years later she was my client. This poem written for her, a woman I occasionally drove to the doctor, or to whom I snuck a can of beer, some candy bars, or a couple of cans of cat food.

My Client
You ask me about Gladys.
The last time I saw her
I found her slumped on a car seat
In her front yard,
A bag of Hershey kisses in her lap
Crinkled silver balls dotting the spotty grass.
Her hair was out to here.
She wore red,
A housedress crazy with flowers.
Roy Orbison crooned from her kitchen window
Clear across the yard.

Gladys I called,
Her head turned slowly toward me.
Her eyes were flat and black.

"Margie, she gasped,
Laughing her way out of reverie,
Lugging her way out of the seat
One hand smoothing her hair,
The other reaching for me

Where have you been?
Come in to the house, come in.

Torn, I readied myself to hear her yarn,
Dreaded a visit that would be too long
In this place of solitude, smells and disarray,
Magazines moldering in stacks
And the evidence of too many cats.

Her crooked hands stroked mine
And she began
My boys never visit,
Never, not one of them
Come around anymore.
Pinkie needs a visit to the vet
And Fluffy, too.

The town wants to get me out of here
To a nursing home somewhere.

They're scared I'll burn the place down
I know they want to do it themselves,
Haul them trucks out here
And what will happen to my girls,
You know, my cats.

I'll run away, I swear I will
Straight down the interstate.
They'll have to tie me down or I'll be gone.

Can't keep an ol' broad like me locked up.
I'd rather be dead, I would.
So what can you do for me, Margie?

I am clueless, biting back tears.
What can I do?

My babies were already reaching the middle of childhood, which meant they were growing into the beginnings of independence. That also meant that I, too, was gaining back some independence. Now, it was a whole different way of being a mom from when they were little.

So when I became pregnant again because the darn contraceptive failed to do its job, I knew I had to do something about it. We did not have the finances or the energy for another child and we needed to keep moving forward with our lives, staying focused on the growing children we already had. Ron and I both believed that life begins with the first breath just as it ends with the last. I know many people who agree with that and many others who don't. But without a doubt, I had to do what I had to do, and I did it with conviction and with Ron's support.

Abortion was still illegal in most states and, even though we were working, money was always tight. We had just enough for me to go to New York and as we waited for the bus in the dim morning light, we froze and we prayed. Ron was dropping me off to face the challenge of a long, long trip and the gamble that all would work out.

I had expected that it would be free because they were offering free abortions in New York, but when I got to the clinic, the quotas had been filled for the month. I had only a small amount of money with me so I walked from one clinic to the next to locate a doctor who would perform the procedure. My legs could barely carry me around in the cold and the last doctor I went to see had the same story. His quota had also been filled. Hopeless and helpless, I sat in the waiting room and told the receptionist that I could not go back home pregnant and I would sit there until someone agreed to take me in. When they saw that I was serious, they called a doctor out in the boonies who agreed to see me. I took the train to what seemed to be another world from Manhattan. When I finally got there, I was greeted with a smile by the receptionist. It was a relief to be warm and welcomed.

Five of us were gathered together for the same reason and individually were called in for a chat, counseled and questioned to be sure we wanted to go through with it. All of us had good reasons, including a sixteen-year-old Catholic girl who was brought in by her mother. Her doctor had told her she would probably die if she went through childbirth (something about her heart), but she argued with her mother right there in the waiting room, insisting that she did not want to go to hell and would rather die than have an abortion. They both left crying much to the sorrow of the rest of us. One of the women had come all the way from Chicago, leaving her daughter with a neighbor for the day. It turned out she was too far along and had to go into the hospital, hoping and praying her neighbor would take care of her little girl. We all supported each other in this sisterhood that had briefly formed over a common dilemma.

I felt so confident when the time came and when asked if I wanted someone to hold my hand I said, "No thank you." But during the procedure, all by itself my hand reached out for comfort. They were compassionate people and I was so relieved to have the whole thing over with. I was no longer pregnant and did my own inner celebration as I waited in the Port Authority for my bus. This, I knew, was not murder, as some believe, because the soul lives on and chooses a different baby-body to enter. Still, on the long ride home, I couldn't help but imagine how it would have been to bring another child into the world. No doubt it would have been adored by us all but it would have been an enormous strain on the family in so many ways. I still cannot completely describe the relief I felt at that time and my gratitude for this opportunity. I arrived home safely and on we went with our lives.

I thought very little of it after that until

about eight months later. I was fast asleep in our king-sized bed under our blue-and-violet quilt when I was awakened by an incredibly warm feeling that permeated my whole body. A flood of compassionate love entered my heart with a sweetness too beautiful to describe. Then I heard—not with my ears, but from somewhere deep inside me—a voice introduce itself as the soul of the one I had aborted.

"It's okay," this soul presence said. "We just needed a very short time together and everything now is as it should be."

I was astounded by the depth and clarity of the message and lay there for hours after, glowing and grateful for the kindness and the knowledge, the sacredness of the moment and the way I had been awakened. I didn't mention it to anyone until months later when I finally told Ron. He gasped with amazement.

"The same thing happened to me," he said. "I couldn't talk about it. It was so private."

We fell into each other's arms and cried. Grace without form had paid us a visit.

Though sometimes discouraging, my job with the Office of Economic Opportunity was often stimulating, frustrating, satisfying and challenging as I continued to drive the back roads looking for people to help. I had buddied up with the community organizer from the next county who (an aside) later went to New York and became a rock star. To protect his privacy, I'll call him Ted.

We saw that so many people had old cars with no place to fix them in the frigid months so we rented a space, put in some heat, collected donated tools and created a garage co-op. There was never enough money for all that we needed and the director actually laughed when I proposed a place for women in emergencies, something we now call shelters for battered women. Despite the Women's Movement and all the new revelations of bad behaviors, the powers-that-be didn't think there was a need for such a thing, but I had met too many moms who had been sneaking away at night to hide themselves and their children in reluctant relatives' homes while the husbands slept off drunken nights. Still, the concept of a shelter was premature and stood no chance of getting funded; no matter how we begged and pleaded, they chose to hand out surplus food while refusing to provide garden seeds, which most everyone requested. I gave talks at the Fireman's Hall and the PTA about the program and our resources. There were those who didn't trust government programs and didn't like what we were doing. Maybe that's why there was a lack of trust although we were helping lots of folks despite some archaic attitudes, or maybe they were simply political influences of some kind. I don't know.

One day, I went to check on a client in the small hospital seventeen miles from town. This woman was due to have her eleventh baby and they were trying to convince her to have her tubes tied. When I walked in, I heard a loud commotion in a side room. I recognized Mrs. Vight's voice and peeked in. Her baby had already been born and was in a precarious condition. She needed a blood transfusion if she were to live. Some of the doctors didn't have much sympathy because Mrs. Vight already had so many children and very little resources. Her baby lay at the brink and they would not perform the transfusion unless they could get her husband's permission. Her permission as the mom was not enough.

Mrs. Vight kept pleading for them to make the transfusion, but they were never able to contact her husband because on that scorching summer day, he was in the field and out of reach. The doctors and nurses argued around Mrs. Vight's bed as the baby lay dying in her arms. She searched my face, silently begging me to help.

One of the nurses apologetically told me that they could do it in the big hospital twenty-eight miles away but they definitely could not deliver the baby without the father's permission—and even if they had permission to get her to the other hospital, the trip would probably be too long for this emergency.

"I'm taking the baby," I said, lifting the swaddled infant from his pleading mother's arms.

"That will be kidnapping," they informed me.

I tightened his wrappings and dashed with him out the door. The collection of doctors and nurses were horrified and warned me that the baby might die, but Mrs. Vight kept motioning for me to go. I couldn't think. I just fled. A nurse came running out with a carrier for the baby and off I sped.

With my nervous legs jumping and shaking on the gas pedal, I made the twenty-eight miles to the hospital where they were already waiting for us.

Mrs. Vight agreed to have her tubes tied and the baby lived.

In those five years in Maine, I knew who I was and had a clear job description as a mom first and as an earner second. My disability (which was much greater than my family ever knew) got in the way, mostly with play. I could manage my work since it was in the car or sitting in someone's kitchen much of the time. Sitting in the car and at the loom was not very strenuous, and cooking and baking only had me walking a few feet back and forth from stove to pantry, so how could they know the severity of my limitations when I hid them so well? I just didn't do certain things like hop on the toboggan going downhill because I wouldn't be able to get back up the hill. I couldn't risk that shame in front of my children and certainly Ron didn't understand. How could he when I made myself look perfectly normal? There was no explanation for these limitations and no doctor could ever find anything wrong with me, so everyone concurred when I couldn't do more, that it was all in my head or I was just being lazy. All I could say was, "I'm too tired" when I really meant, "I am hurting like hell" so Ron was the one who provided the physical

adventures for the kids.

At work, I wanted to do more than the Feds would let me do. They decided that I was too radical in my talks. I couldn't believe there was such a thing called an Overseer of the Poor. This man owned the only grocery store in town. It was small and expensive *because* it could be and he was the one who determined who was qualified to get money that could then be spent in his small store. To me this system was almost criminal and as I went about speaking of the benefits of our program, people like him got mad.

After three years of this work, I was "invited" to just stay home and keep the free store open. No more work in the counties. No more driving around delivering clients to medical facilities, finding lawyers for poor people, organizing car pools for Head Start, driving kids to their job corps work, drumming up audiences for my educational talks, chauffeuring housewives to their job interviews or helping girls keep from getting pregnant in their teens. No more of that. So I accepted their offer for two paychecks and then I quit. It was impossible to take money for doing nothing.

In 1964, President Johnson was the first

president ever to launch an aggressive program to eliminate poverty. We did accomplish a lot in terms of much needed opportunity but not enough. Because of political pressure our program was not allotted enough funds to grow nor was it maintained. The opposition from local governments and politicians was adamantly resistant to helping the previously silenced and invisible black, white and native peoples, both in the cities and counties. However, although Community Action was not as effective as Johnson had intended, there was an amazing growth in nonprofits and new agencies formed to address the needs of these same people but in time they were systematically dismantled. Now in 2016, there is a dire need for a resurgence of such programs.

Meanwhile, I had fallen in love with the patchwork quilts and colorful afghans I had seen in some of these homes and at the auctions we attended. I had an idea. Some of these beauties had very formal geometric patterns and some were haphazard. They were called Crazy Quilts and they were warm. We'd find all kinds of things at auctions, from colored glass jugs and labeled tin cans to wire egg baskets and vintage clothing. My idea was to see if the area's elders were interested in bringing back some of their traditional crafts through workshops for the younger generations.

Polyester and acrylic were rapidly replacing natural fabric, as manufactured baked goods were also replacing the homemade goodies that these rural folks were so skilled at making. Most of us from the cities tried to make a living with pottery, woodworking, spinning, dying, jewelry making and weaving and we had started to sell our handmade products at the craft fairs throughout the state.

I thought it would be great to talk to the owner of the inn on the crossroads of town right on the main route to Quebec to see if he'd be interested in renting me a room for a store. He loved the idea and was generous enough to let me set up on the wraparound porch, come summer. He thought it would also be an attraction for his inn.

Many of us were also missing the natural and organic foods available in the urban areas but they had not yet caught on this far north and now there were those of us planting organic gardens and baking with whole grains. I decided to add natural foods to the inventory and placed an order for bulk peanut butter, brown rice, beans and other foods from Erewhon, the natural foods distributer at the time. I got local honey from an established beekeeper, homemade jams and jellies, pickles and local maple syrup. All along the porch railing, I featured baked goods made by newcomers.

I figured that if I could create an environment that would carry quality goods by honoring the locals and the newcomers, it would close the culture gap while bringing the riches from both generations together. Also, it could be a stopping place for those driving through to Canada and even bring revenue to the general store across the street owned by our "friend", the Overseer of the Poor.

Folks out in the woods brought in beautiful handmade sweaters, baby clothes and blankets, jewelry, pottery, wooden bowls and benches. Ron made a colorful wooden sign and we called the store Northern Lights.

I set up my frame loom on the porch of the red-and-white historic landmark, began weaving and waited for the truck to come with the goods while hoping customers would stop and shop. Maybe our little community within the community would be able to find a little income from the tourists driving through and maybe the locals would get turned back onto natural products. Day in and day out that summer, I woke up early, drove to town, sometimes with the kids, sat at the loom and waited for customers. The kids worked on crafts of their own. I got plenty of visitors, lots of compliments but very few sales. The locals were happier with Wonder Bread and other processed foods from across the street. It turned out they were sick of all that "old-fashioned stuff" like dry beans instead of canned, white bread instead of brown; most had already made the switch from good farm food to processed food. So the only thing that really happened was that my freezer got overstuffed with date, nut and banana breads. Come fall, I thanked Mr. Boucher and closed the shop.

I think about all of this today and can see how sanctimonious I was, how I seemed to think I knew it all; but this was all a part of my own growth and personal evolution. It was also a part of some form of what I might call a cultural (r)evolution. By seemingly living a backward life, we were all trying to move forward and there was so much work to be done, personally and collectively, with each of us a little microcosm in the thick of a complex macrocosm.

One day while driving back from somewhere over July's hot hills, I passed a man hitchhiking. There was no such thing as public transportation and it was high noon so I pulled over and picked him up. He was Native American and so tall that he had to bend way down to squeeze himself and his cowboy hat into my little car. Once on our way, he began to say things like, "No girl ever picked me up before." This was said in a voice that spelled danger. I was horrified because up until then I had felt so privileged to be sitting with a *real* Native American who I automatically felt so indebted to because of our American history (typical of white guilt). But he got instantly creepy and as he reached for my knee some instinct kicked in— something Harlan had taught me about energy. I found myself expanding. I seemed to be making myself bigger and bigger with each breath. Soon, I was Alice in Wonderland pushing against the boundaries of the car until it felt like the car would burst apart. The guy blurted out in panic, "I'll get out here, miss. Stop! Stop!"

I pulled over, and he got out and continued his walk over the hill. I felt so stupid for my assumptions and stereotyping and, at the same time, I was grateful for what I had learned from crazy Harlan about "mind over matter."

One winter night when I arrived home from a meeting, I found that my sister had called for help. She had just had her second baby and seemed like she desperately needed some support. I wouldn't dare drive that distance in our old car and the bus trip would be endless. While pondering this situation, there came the blue Jeep up the driveway. It was inevitable. Harlan always knew when there was a dilemma.

"I'll take you," he said, without even hearing what the problem was. He just came in and said, "I'll take you."

Well, that was something, I thought it was pretty psychic of him, and I was relieved to have a way to get there and happy that he would be able to actually help us for a change. I wanted to be there for Nancy so I took Harlan's offer as a sign that she truly needed me to be there. But would it be unbearable to be in a car with him that long? After some deliberation, I decided that I needed to go even if this was the only way.

Right after supper, Harlan came back to pick me up. I slipped and slid across the driveway to the Jeep. Ice was rapidly forming on the streets but the momentum had already begun for this journey and it seemed like there was no turning back.

"It's not freezing further south," he said. "We'll be fine in the four-wheel drive."

The Jeep was warm and cozy inside. He drove with ease for a while but as we climbed the hill it must have gotten worse because he suddenly yelled, "Stop thinking negative thoughts!" I wasn't aware that I was doing that, but because of the panic in his voice I tried to shut my mind down tight.

Then there we were careening off the road in slow motion and then to a shuddering stop. The front end was now stuck in the bank of a stream with rushing water below and the chassis was precariously perched on the edge of something, leaving the rear end up in the air. Neither of us was hurt but my heart sank to the pit of my stomach and there it stayed. It was the worst possible scenario, stuck in this car with Harlan, not getting to my sister and no way to find help. *How did Harlan know what was going on with our family? Why did he come over tonight in this miserable weather? So now what?* I was worried about Nancy, and Ron would assume that we were well on our way so he wouldn't come looking for us. I had Gram's seal jacket on so I was not cold and decided that Gram (looking down on me from above) and her jacket would keep me warm through what promised to be a long wait until morning when someone was bound to drive over the hill and find us.

I had never been touched by Harlan, not even a handshake. I felt his energy ominously shifting. He was coming at me and here I was trapped in this tiny crooked space. I would not panic. He grinned that diabolical grin and disgustingly reached for my breast. My arm flew up in self-defense and fear turned into fierceness. I found myself glaring at him the way I had seen him glare at other people to intimidate them. I did the same. I had drawn my power up. He backed down, rolled over and went to sleep.

I opened the door, tightened my jacket around me, and stepped down into the soft freezing rain. I was Jack racing down the beanstalk while the giant slept.

What else could I do? I held onto the Jeep's

hood as I maneuvered around it and back onto the ice-covered road. I found that if I could stay on the edge, the grasses poking through the snow and ice would provide some traction.

Rhea had warned me about Harlan, but no, I didn't listen. I was just too curious and, as always without realizing it, I was testing my resolve.

Every few minutes I looked over my shoulder into the glistening chill as I headed darkly home.

I had never paid attention to the distance from there to our house whenever I'd driven by. But I knew this walk would be the longest one ever and if I died on the way I'd be better off than staying in that Jeep.

I focused only on where I placed my feet and grabbed onto twigs and branches as I made my way down the long steep hill. The road was desolate. There was no one to pick me up and I had no sense of time. After awhile, it began to get light. The mist at dawn made the trees and rocks take the form of bears but I knew it was a mirage and I just kept moving.

I must have been walking in a trance for hours and wondered how this was possible, unaware of how slowly I was traveling.

Finally, with the sun high in the sky reflecting blindingly off the ice, I was home. Ron was astonished to see me walk in with my eyes glazed over, nose and cheeks red as pomegranates and no car in sight.

"Don't ask," I said, as I ran to the bathroom to fill the tub with the hottest water I could stand.

How could I have been so stupid? I asked myself over and over again. I just wanted to get to my sister and Ron had been relieved that I had a ride. That's all I could think about and although I knew Harlan was stranger than a two-headed goat, I hadn't realized all the danger I was stepping into. I told Ron the story and we vowed to get him out of our lives.

After dinner he made his dreaded appearance. I hid in the bedroom and told Ron to get rid of him, to tell him to never come back. I could hear muffled conversation but it didn't stop. Then I heard laughter and knew Ron now was caught in his web. I came out of the bedroom screaming for him to get out of the house and to never step foot on our property again.

Harlan laughed one of those grotesque laughs like the carnival lady in the booth and Ron could not demand that Harlan leave. I was furious with him but the truth is, he had been just as manipulated as me. Harlan was the devil incarnate.

Something came over me again and I was able to pull courage from somewhere (or maybe it was divine intervention) but my fear vanished and my fierceness came back. I glared at him again and slowly, calmly, determinedly told him to leave our house.

"You will never get away from me," he grimaced. Then he left.

That night I jerked awake with what felt like a wrench tearing at my brain, a hundred times worse then any migraine. It was so excruciating that I staggered to the bathroom mirror to look into my eyes and see if I was still in there. My hair was wild. My eyes were unrecognizable. He had a hold of me from somewhere beyond the physical.

In the quiet of dawn, I sat stiffly by the kitchen stove fighting the pain. The house was asleep except for the hum of the refrigerator and logs shifting in the firebox. I couldn't think straight. I sat there bouncing my feet against the floor and staring into the fire. I didn't know what to do.

I don't remember how I got there but the next thing I knew, I was up on my favorite rock in our field, praying, chanting, humming, pleading, sitting cross-legged like a yogi, trying to be holy, chanting OM, chanting the Sh'ma, chanting Hu, asking why and begging God. But the longer I sat on the rock, the weaker I got. I could feel the life force draining out of me. I knew I was dying.

I wondered if my legs could carry me down the hill to the barn. By now, Ron would be already running machines and he'd never hear me. I slid down off the rock and prayed my way down through the field. Thank God Ron miraculously appeared at the window, took one look at me and raced downstairs. He gathered me up as if I was a rag doll and walking me to the house, he placed two fingers on my right temple. Immediately the life force began streaming back into me. I could feel it coming in. Then he gently laid me down on the bed, where I slept for a day.

Recently, when I asked him how he knew what to do, he said, "I don't know why I went over to the window but I remember seeing you down there. You looked white as a ghost and well, really scary. I ran downstairs as fast as I could and in my head I kept asking for help. To whom, I don't know. Then I fell into a kind of trance and I knew what to do. It just came into me."

Sometimes we clearly know what to do,

especially if we ask. Then it comes into us in mysterious ways and miraculously we sometimes hear it and get it right. If we try to figure it out, our minds would probably be racing around in panic and confusion. Thank goodness Ron asked, listened and acted without a moment of doubt. I had been under psychic attack by a master of such things but it was not yet my time and Ron was there to save me.

After that we never saw Harlan again.

Since I had not yet been in therapy of any kind, I had not been aware of myself as vulnerable or naive but my original abuse had made me susceptible to these errors in judgment. I was always stubborn in my curiosity for the mysterious. I should have listened to Reah when she warned me not to get involved with this guy but I was intrigued by the mysterious and was unaware of any inner warnings I may have been given. Because I was hungry to know about immeasurable realities and I wondered about miracles, I had put myself in jeopardy. I had no idea to the degree of manipulation some people are capable of. I had no idea about mind control and I had blindly stepped off a cliff. But I heard years later that Harlan inevitably got his dues.

Every experience has a hidden gift, however, and I had learned a few things. During that same year, Ron and I had some errands to do in town. It was a nice day so we did not check the weather. Well on our way, we noticed that what little traffic there usually was had thinned out to nothing. No one was out on the roads and it had begun to snow. Now it was piling up fast, but we were too far along to turn around. Halfway into town, we noticed a car that had slid off the road and was stuck in a ditch. Ron stopped to see if he could help. An elderly woman was out there in just sneakers, no socks, slushing around in the deepening snow trying to push her car back onto the road. We got out to help her and no matter how hard we pushed, we couldn't get that old car out of the ditch. Then like a distant light emerging out of the whiteness came an oil truck chugging up the hill. When he got to us he, too, stopped and climbed down out of his truck. Together, we got the woman on her way. Then he climbed back into his truck, but now he could go nowhere. He kept spinning his wheels without gaining traction. We stood on the side of the road watching him slip back, start again and slip back, over and over again. This was a very long and steep hill and we were smack in the middle of it, halfway up and halfway down. It was a hopeless situation except for one cross road we thought he could have turned around in but he seemed determined to be on his way strait up that hill.

With the snow icing over and the driver getting nowhere, I decided to try one of Harlan's techniques by planting a powerful focus on the truck with might and determination. It wasn't effortless. I had to focus with pinpoint energy. It was like pushing down in childbirth, breathing and focusing and then like magic, suddenly he found his traction and went whizzing right by us with a look of astonishment on his face. I held my focus until he was out of sight and then breathed victorious. I knew what I had done and it felt really good to have the ability to do something like that. I don't know what something like that is called but I do know I felt powerful and that felt great. I would later learn that that, too, could have had consequences. Was there a difference between trying to help someone and interfering with what's supposed to be?

Nancy was over her crisis that had called me to her and that summer she and her husband, Joel, invited Ron down to Connecticut to design furniture for their Plexiglass factory in Hartford. Plexiglass was the hot trend at the time and they knew we could use the money while they employed Ron's creativity. We thought this would give us the funds to create a showroom that would attract more customers that would help us participate in what would be the "Made in Maine" movement that so many of us in the community were trying to expand. Just setting up at the craft shows scattered around the state was a difficult way to make a living so Ron went and I stayed home with the kids that summer.

Things worked out so well with Ron and Joel that Joel asked him to stay on. I didn't want to leave my life in Maine but staying was not in the cards. We were lucky to find a nice second-floor flat in the West End of Hartford, a sweet neighborhood but with no easy access to the puny yard—which was dry and brown, as opposed to the milkweed-laden fields with its butterflies and bees. I felt totally ungrounded, which seems to me to come with new beginnings.

The kids happily made friends and rode their bikes all over the neighborhood. Ron was working across town and I was well, adrift without my many chores and dependencies of the kids. Nancy was my saving grace because she knew everyone in town. She had a swimming pool, which was a social magnet for many of her friends during the summer, whether she was there or not. Nancy always had many places to go and many people to see. Feeling restless at home and like the epitome of obsolescence after my life in Maine, I drove over to Nancy's place once in awhile but I always felt that I needed to be somewhere else. I just didn't know where.

One afternoon, Nancy introduced me to a television producer who, after seeing some of my work, invited me to be on a program called "Women in the Arts." Beth came over to plan the event. But during the actual taping, I was just as disconnected from my art-making as I was from myself. As I wove the beginnings of a tapestry under the eyes of the camera, the visual was on the yarn in my hands and the audio was recording my rambling voice, surprisingly expounding on how my children had always been my art form. And it was true. In that moment, I was sadly uninspired and feeling like an imposter as an artist while my role as a mom. My identity was shaken in this city of sad childhood memories.

I had felt humbled to be chosen for the show, however, and Nancy wanted to give me a start in Hartford but I missed the warm nurturing of my wood stove and all the things that occupied my rural living—including my passion for cooking, which had fizzled out over the skinny electric stove that occupied this otherwise barren kitchen. I was indeed displaced and needed something to capture my imagination, something relevant and concrete. I applied for an artist-in-residence grant to the State of Connecticut. I needed to work, I needed the structure and I wanted a monetary justification to keep creative. If I could get the grant, it would be an impetus to immerse myself in the weaving, or bring me back to painting and, at the same time, unleash some sparks of seventies thinking onto the students I would meet. So much had been changing and there were so many ideas to be explored. I wanted the opportunity to teach in a progressive school where exploration was valued and women's roles could be seriously studied as part of the curriculum.

For some reason, this TV stint had become a measure of success to Nancy and my mom, who seemed to have different ways to find meaning than I did, so it was a little rough relating to each other at that time. It's like they had no idea what I had been up to all these years, and finally someone important was giving me recognition and that made them almost giddy. It was nice that they cared but they certainly didn't understand. Paradoxically, Nancy, for some reason, had idealized our New York and Maine lifestyles and had raved about us to everyone, so by the time we got to Hartford, we were already a legend we could never live up to. It was annoying to have to contend with the mythology already preceding our family. Nancy had talked us up as if we were righteous minimalists and I was expected to be "very cool" but I was very far from that. So now

Sign of the times.

that I was in her territory, she had good intentions and a hundred ideas for what I should do with my life. The best thing was that our two families enjoyed time together when it was all of us, eating and dipping in the pool and dressing up to hit the town.

We tried to be friends because we adored each other, but we were worlds apart. She was trying to drag me into the spotlight and I was trying to "find myself in the shadows."

We had always been opposite in so many ways. Since she is often the eye of a hurricane of activity, she's hard to pin down. Even when she's away there are friends and acquaintances

At Nancy's pool.

lying around sunning themselves like turtles on flat rocks. Some days, though, I would drive over there to take a dip, to lounge in the hot tub with the main intent to catch her alone so we could talk without interruption. Because of our love and despite our differences, I was always hoping to find common ground. On this day it would happen. We would talk. We would discuss what we had both known but had never before talked about. There was never the time and space. On this day, though, there was a chill in the air. I found her stretched out on a towel, in a small spot of hot sun, tanning the length of her long, lean body. She jumped up with glee, we hugged and, holding hands, slipped into the icy pool; but the hot tub seemed a better choice so with little discussion we climbed out of the cold into the steaming water. Rapturous in the contrast of the outside chill and the heat of the tub, eyes closed and wordless, we mellowed under a cerulean sky. Then the talk began:

"We are so different, Babe," I said contemplating the moment. (We all called each other Babe in those days.)

"What do you mean?" she asked.

"Well, I've been thinking. We had such different childhoods. You know. And it made us such different people."

"I know, but how are we different?"

We dance wildly and exactly alike, which is surprising since we never even danced in the same town together, never mind the same room. How does that happen? And then when we first saw each other sleeping exactly alike knees up, hands under chin, head bent to the right, we thought what was that about? We laughed and agreed that our mother's womb shaped us that way.

"So how are we so different?" Nancy asked.

"Babe, you know you love the spotlight. I don't. You love having people around you. You're at your best when surrounded by lots of people and you usually are."

"Well, not always. I like to be alone sometimes."

"But you never are."

"I know. There's always something going on."

"Okay, but I prefer one on one, alone, or with close friends. It's just that now my close friends aren't close anymore. They're all over the place—New York, Maine, New Jersey, even California. And you have a million friends right here in town. You are lots more fun than me. I'm too serious. And you're always making people laugh. You're always hiking, biking or swimming. It keeps you connected and very social. I envy that part, the athletic part. My way is dialogue. I guess it has to be. *My Dinner with Andre* type conversations. I'd rather be in a coffee shop with one or two people."

"But you're funny, too, Babe," she said. "Ron convinces you you're not, but you are. You crack me up. You are an activist. You even marched down Fifth Avenue with the swarms. How did you do that walk, anyway?"

"I got left behind."

"But you're always involved. I walked around worrying about window treatments while you were writing letters to the papers, protesting the war, fighting for everyone's rights and all that stuff."

"Yeah, true. I do that. But I suppose we're alike, too," I said.

I didn't mention it to Nancy but I'd always felt like a shlump when we went out together. Being six feet tall, she towered over me and

always made her grand entrance while her long strides put me half a block behind. Then I'd

Sisters.

Nancy and me.

156

walk in the door and no one noticed because she was already holding court. It made total sense, though, because she felt invisible the whole time we were growing up, while I was the epicenter of destruction. So what started out as an innocent little afternoon break turned into a day that bonded us more deeply as sisters.

We both ducked under the water for a break and to bring our curls back. Returning to the surface, we shook our heads like shaggy dogs.

"You were the star," she said. "You were the pretty one. Daddy loved you."

"Are you kidding? He killed me all the time. He hurt me."

"Yeah, I know, but I still wanted to be you. I copied everything you did, even the bad things like eating too much and getting bad marks because I wanted some of that attention and thought that was the way to get it. I worshipped you. The only time he even noticed me was when I made him laugh. So I learned how to do that and I guess that's just what I do now. I entertain. Indirectly, he gave me a talent. I like that I can do that."

"You were amazing. Do you remember when you got that comic, that little short guy,

to come to your apartment when you lived in New York? You were working on a pilot or something?"

"Oh, yeah, Joey Blanco."

"I was there for some reason, a rare visit. I never laughed so hard. I remember tears rolling down my face and having to pee but not wanting to go because I might miss something. You guys could have made it big together."

"I know. He was hysterical. We had a ball. Too bad that never happened," she said. "You know what? I was so ignored. I was too tall and too loud and Daddy ignored me even though I stood out. So I had to stand out even more. Joking around was how I did it."

"You were good at it while I was the trigger for his rage so I had to hide and keep out of his way."

We both paused and drank in the silence. Everything around us was quiet except for the sound of water and a sudden wind.

"When you went off to Boston, I felt so abandoned," Nancy continued, tearing up. "You left me with them and he still didn't notice me. He talked about you all the time."

"Nancy, I never gave it a thought. I just

wanted to get out."

"Oh, I know, but I didn't get it at the time. I was fourteen."

"I missed you, too. You were my baby sister. I loved you so much."

"I know. When he died, I became Mom's husband, her caretaker, because she was a basket case. I was only sixteen then. Can you believe it?"

"I can't imagine what that was like. You are still wonderful to her. And now you are her star and I am her prodigal daughter. Now I'm starting over in this place I ran from."

We fell into each other's arms, dripping wet and holding onto each other for what seemed like the longest time since we were little girls. It felt so good to find each other's souls again—as sisters and as grown women.

Words.

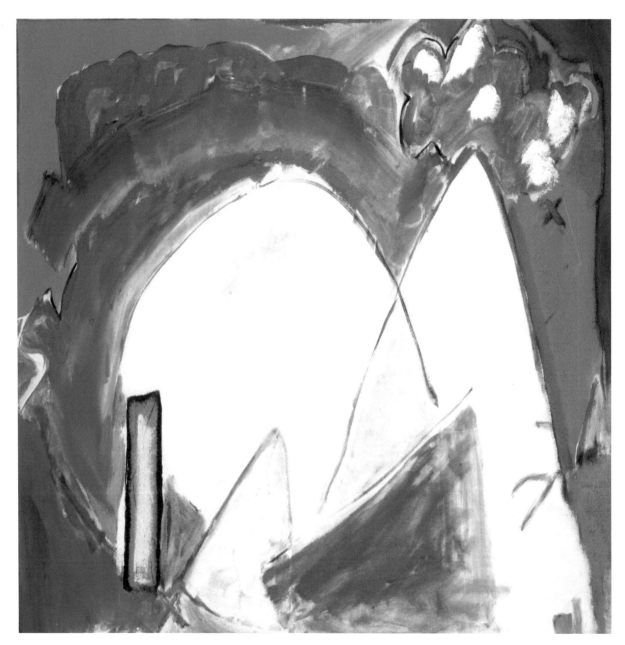

Things Fall Apart

Pilgrimage to the East: Things Fall Apart

The Grandmaster, Waterfalls and Rice Paddies, Kama Kura, The End of Trickery

I was hanging out on the porch, watching the kids ride around the neighborhood on their bikes, when the emptiness attacked me. Would I get that artist-in-residence grant from the state? If I didn't, then what would I do? Hungry for something, anything, I meandered down the street to a jewel of a bookstore, a cozy little place that also sold exotic cheeses and things and featured mainly books of interest to women. There I noticed a flyer announcing a tai chi class at a Kung Fu school taught by a Grandmaster. Kung Fu seemed to be the ultimate in physicality and violence but knowing that tai chi is a slow, peaceful meditation, as well as a means of self-defense, I decided to check it out. Maybe I could do this.

I walked the block back to the house, got in the car and drove to the Kung Fu school and rang the bell. No answer.

I found a spot atop a picnic table in Elizabeth

161

Park, just a block away from the martial arts school. The sky was blue and cloudless. The leaves were glistening red and gold in the sun. I sat on the table and pondered my near future. With this discipline of tai chi, I might just be able to build up the strength I was seeking, physically and mentally. My excitement grew as I made the commitment in my mind to do this. I was thirty-eight at that time, and still hadn't gotten a diagnosis for my mysterious condition, whatever it was. The idea of practicing tai chi gave me a ray of hope.

The martial arts school didn't have its hours posted on the door, so I decided to wait for a little while to see if anyone would show up. I continued to wonder about the next steps to take in my life. What was I supposed to be doing? What was I doing back in Hartford, where I had long ago escaped from years of misery? It seemed like every time I had come back to visit, I would regress. My voice would go up an octave. I would become a child again and now here I was once more, yet everything was different. I had my own family and I was the parent. Slowly, as I pondered my life on this crisp New England October day, I felt

something move within. A wave of joy entered me, bringing with it a glimpse of this new freedom that I wasn't yet sure how to use but here it was, open and waiting for me to grasp.

I walked around, kicking golden leaves until it seemed time to return to the Grandmaster's school, which was located in a large Victorian home. I rang the bell; still no answer. By now, I had become obsessed. I knew I had to find this teacher and learn tai chi. I needed to start some sort of exercise or I would dry up and blow away with the leaves beneath my feet.

After another hour of staring at trees from my perch, I tried once more and an unlikely figure came to the door. I was surprised. He looked like a Sumo wrestler: short, older and Buddha-bellied, with unexpected curly black hair and deep black eyes. He invited me into his office and after announcing that he and his students had just been teaching at the nearby university, he dug right in and proceeded to tell me everything about myself, things I didn't want to hear. At this first encounter, he already had me pegged. I wasn't aware of how acutely unhinged I had become with this move, but he could see it plain and his certainty and accuracy unleashed in me a flood of not only tears but embarrassing sobs that burst forth despite my desperate attempts to control myself. I didn't even know this guy, for God's sake, but he spotted emptiness, loneliness and confusion right off the bat.

And then he blurted out, "Finally you're here. I've waited my whole life to see you again."

What?

A normal person would have walked out the door right then especially after the craziness with Harlan. But I believed him, because he was so unexpectedly gentle and from the minute I saw him at the door, I felt a thrill of recognition rush through my body. His eyes were warm and compassionate. I needed to latch onto something and was compelled to follow this thread and see where it would take me.

After the big drama of his perceptive words to me, he abruptly stated, "Tai chi starts at seven tonight" and left the room.

I fed the family a simple meal and fled out the door at 6:45.

When I rang the bell at seven, I was surprised to find no one there but a bored, young woman who was waiting there to teach only me. The Grandmaster who had "waited his whole life to find me" was nowhere to be seen. No Grandmaster, no students, no one else in sight. Had he created a private class just for me? I was disappointed to be there alone with this very young and very put upon woman but I followed her moves as best I could. Though I was disappointed to not even see the Grandmaster, I was determined to finish this exploration and returned to the school where he taught a diverse group of students, all ages, colors, shapes and sizes, from macho and nerds.

It turned out that the Grandmaster was a bit of an exhibitionist. He created shows for schools, colleges and Chinese restaurants. It seemed to be a cheap way to showcase something as serious and reverent as martial arts. The exhibitions showcased his best black belts doing carnival-inspired feats like walking on hot coals or broken glass, and breaking concrete blocks over each other's heads. The showstopper was his own strike that split stacks of ice with his bare hand in an even more dramatic exhibition of mind over matter.

But the Grandmaster also taught us meditation. I practiced Tai Chi and meditation and often I would hear the kung fu practitioners in the other room shouting fiercely with every punch and kick. It seemed so violent. But because some of the same gentle tai chi students were also kung fu students, I was convinced to try kung fu. Then after learning some basic kicks and punches, I was allowed to try some of the beautiful Shaolin animal forms a la Bruce Lee. Of course, it was a huge challenge for me and I only learned a few basic moves but I was delighted to be among these athletes and the Grandmaster who pampered me because I was so limited and they all respected my efforts.

While Harlan and the Grandmaster both taught about manipulating energy, Harlan seemed to be about power alone and the Grandmaster seemed to be about skill, power, peace and balance. I had always sought a way to be able to protect myself and my children from any threat or emergency and also to find a form of exercise that my body could actually handle. I'd already had my share of sexual assault, enough for a hundred lifetimes, so I was anxious to learn both inner and outer protections to transcend my victimhood and become strong and fearless. I owed it to my kids, if not myself. So between the meditations and the physical challenges, I embraced the concept of spiritual warrior and took the bad with the good and the wise with the absurd.

I felt honored and confident in the Grandmaster's presence. He took me into his confidence for some reason and I sat by his side as he consulted with students when they came to him. He sought my advice on what tournaments to enter and shows to do, how to make kung fu as popular in the states as karate and how to deal with other issues that would come up. I was younger than him but older than most students and I took great pride in being the yin to his yang as he so often claimed. The energy balance between us held us together like glue with deep telepathic knowing and my ego puffed up like a wet sponge—typical, I was later to learn, about cultish relationships. Many women savor the power they derive from their exalted position with the guru. I was no different and how had this fit with my feminism?

At that time, the Women's Movement was gaining influence and also experiencing a schism. Sadly, there remained the disparity of stay-at-home moms who felt unrecognized for their full-time work at home while women working outside the home were getting all the accolades but those workers felt torn by being away from their children. To their stay-at-home sisters, though, they tended to give the impression that they felt superior and maybe many did. That caused an unfortunate schism between the two groups, which made me even more frustrated, having known both sides of the coin.

The Civil Rights Movement, which had inspired the Women's Movement in the first place, had been gaining momentum and continued to inspire what appeared to have begun as a white elitist movement, but I didn't think that was actually true. There were so many factions and tugs of war about what the essence of the movement was. There were those who were specifically and deliberately inclusive of all ethnicities and sexual orientations and those who were deliberately not—fearing, I suppose, that a movement of inclusiveness would never be accepted by the mainstream and would not grow. It was complicated.

Ms. Magazine made a major effort to expose abuses and show support for all women. That magazine opened my eyes ever wider to the still rampant racism that permeated society and the hideous treatment of women throughout the world. Somewhere in there, I bought Angela Davis' *An Autobiography* and during her book signing, she generously wrote, "For Marjorie, sister in solidarity." I was humbled by her inclusiveness and shocked by her writing. It was actually bodily painful to read. The black experience is something those of us who are white can't even imagine if we are even brave enough to try.

I loved the martial arts. Although I was a "token" practitioner—meaning, they encouraged me to practice even with my limitations and seemed to have some innate resonance with them. And to my delight, I did receive the artist in residence from the Connecticut Commission on the Arts. I was given the opportunity to teach at a progressive middle/high school not far from Bloomfield. I went wild gathering materials that I could never have afforded before and the school had a huge frame loom built for me. I taught a variety of art classes and created two other electives for the curriculum: *The Creative Process* and a course called *Sexuality for Women.* I wanted to educate girls about the manipulative methods of demeaning women through all aspects of advertising and how women's bodies were used to sell everything from beer to bras. I wanted to address gender issues to empower the girls no matter what their sexual orientation might be. All of that was challenging and rewarding because it was pretty taboo to talk about gender issues in those days and it was clear to me that there were several students who were struggling with that. Using material coming out of the Women's Movement, I created a course that was empowering to all the girls and our conversations were informative and nurturing. The grant ended after what seemed a very rapid year then they decided to hire me. I use that term loosely as my only compensation was free tuition for Adam and Jennifer. But I loved teaching and mentoring and was grateful for the education that my children would receive.

At some point, I managed to get permission to have the Grandmaster teach a class. Because I was so enamored by his frequent references to Mahayana Buddhism and was convinced that he knew a lot about it, I thought he had a lot to offer the students, both physically and spiritually— and, of course, his demonstrations were dramatically entertaining. Everything was going well on that beautiful spring day of his visit until, to my horror, he picked the shiest, most awkward boy in the school for a demonstration.

"Hey, fatso," he called. "Come over here."

Oh, my God. It was Bobby. In that moment of shock and display, all respect for my teacher came crashing down. I gathered his things and angrily ushered him out the door. This was a side of him I had not seen before. I told him off and rushed back in to comfort Bobby, who had been mortified by the blow. From then on, I continued with my martial arts classes but emotionally distanced myself from him.

The thing is he had planned a trip to Taiwan and Japan with some of his better students. Adam and I had been encouraged to go. I was ambiguous, mainly because I was no longer as connected in the way that I had been but to me it was a spectacular travel opportunity that I thought might never come my way again. Adam, now fourteen, was also taking Kung Fu lessons and wanted to go on this trip so badly that he was willing to spend all the money he had been saving from his Bar Mitzvah the year prior. I was still anxious about any physical challenges I might have to endure and now I knew the craziness of this teacher so I had my doubts, but my love for adventure won out. My love of Eastern teachings, Chinese landscapes and calligraphy, Zen brush paintings, and my desire to see the temples and shrines of the East, plus the knowledge that we would be in the company of trustworthy, intelligent friends, helped make my decision to go.

During the first two weeks in Taiwan, I climbed up the stairs to the top of several multi-storied Buddhas, visited a pottery where dragon and floral vases are painted, and wandered through the National Palace Museum of ancient bronzes, landscape paintings, portraits of monks, and the beautiful Kwan Yin, which all shone gloriously off the walls and pedestals throughout the museum.

With my friend, Margot, a young and beautiful black belt, I visited temples crowded with adults and children silently placing little paper prayers at the entrances. I loved the monasteries that sat abandoned in overgrown grace. One steamy afternoon, I was lost in déjà vu by a wood frame building with a dirt courtyard, stone benches, turquoise tiles sliding off the roof and a lizard that poked its head out then scampered away.

There was something wonderful but also a little spooky about this place until I found an arching wooden bridge behind the structure.

Leaning over the railing of its apex, I stood mesmerized by the water lilies and watery reflections below. It felt as if I'd been there before. It was all violet and green like a Monet painting, which may be why it felt so familiar. A blast from the bus driver's horn disrupted my private moment, as he motioned for me to hurry up. I didn't want to leave this place but the others were already seated and waiting for me with unhidden annoyance.

The Grandmaster would be competing with full-blooded Chinese practitioners and I knew this made him feel insecure because he thought of himself as a mixed breed from Hawaii. Not knowing the culture very well, I had no idea if this was realistic or not and was not in a position to judge. But his insecurity was creating very bizarre behavior; he was making demands on us that we had not expected. He made students stay up until all hours of the night practicing unfamiliar forms and techniques, causing not only sleep deprivation but high levels of stress, which was nerve-rackingly contagious.

As an example, one night he made Adam try over and over again to balance atop six tall, empty beer bottles, an impossible feat for my gangly teenage boy or anyone else for that matter. So now on the bus as we toured the island of Taiwan, our teacher sat alone in silence, where as before his students had vied for the seat beside him where he would hold forth his wisdom. And so we traveled the narrow, winding, jungle-lush roads up and down mountains in fear and disbelief.

The second and probably main reason for his stress was that he had collected money from fourteen of us and bought the airline tickets at a group rate. But unbeknownst to any of us, he had deceptively purchased only one-way tickets out of Tokyo where we would be going next. Did he have magic up his sleeve? Was this another ice-smashing phenomenon? No wonder he was able to give Adam and me big discounts but how was he planning to get us all home? That was his fear and soon it would be ours. He continued making unreasonable demands on us and having so much to prove to the Chinese, everyone's sanity was at stake.

I suppose in order to remind us that he was still a master, he would stand on a temple stoop and in less than a second appear down the street buying a drink from a vendor. Then he would disappear and pop up in another incongruous place. How could he do that? That was the magic that kept us all intrigued. On nights when he would drill the practitioners in villages and cities where we had been invited to compete, I would extricate myself and happily venture out in the tropical air to explore the streets, which were always alive with families hanging out on their stoops in an attempt to cool off from the thick heat of their low-roofed homes and tiny apartments.

One day, I found myself sitting on a bench in a park in the mountains. Narrow waterfalls danced above me, acres and acres of rice paddies rippled in the breeze below and a crumbling hotel struggled to stand on its own two feet— that's where the Grandmaster's inner circle was meeting, in that hotel. I had not been invited because I had dropped out of the inner circle on the day of the Bobby fiasco.

I later learned that it was more about meeting with those he had hoped might be able bail him out with their credit cards and get us all home. Meanwhile, Adam and the others were practicing animal forms behind the hotel while I sat by myself surrounded by tropical birds and their penetrating, multi-octave songs, watching them hop from branch to branch against a cloudless sky and the green terraces of the rice paddies below.

Tiny people in tiny straw hats were busy working in the fields below. This was a foreign land and I was a foreigner in my own skin once again and I was as far from home, here in Taiwan, as Taiwan is far away from Bloomfield. It's the other side of the earth. I studied the ground, watching a family of little brown ants do their work. After moping on the bench for some time I was alerted by a distinct feeling of warmth gathering around me. It felt like a warm wave of sweetness washing over me. My heart began to soften and swell, and I physically felt a smile creep over my face, just like that Easter Sunday on the Charles River. I looked up. Way down the path was a small figure with a broom in his hands, slowly sweeping his way in my direction. As he came closer, my heart quickened and I felt that there was something out of the ordinary about him. I don't know if it was possible but I felt that warmth and love emanating from him and it got stronger as he got closer. I knew (even though we had no common language and he was just a path sweeper) that perhaps he would be the answer, that he would somehow shed some light on my situation. Perhaps he would infuse me with the wisdom I needed right now.

My heart slowed down as he came closer. I was overtaken by calm and humility, and knew that I would not be able to look at him when he got there. There was something holy happening. My eyes simply closed to better take in the moment. As he swept his way up to where I sat, I did not lift my head to look, I was that humbled. But I seemed to absorb the sweetness that came with his presence. Only as he went past me did I dare look up, expecting to see his back, but he had disappeared completely. He was nowhere, not down the path and not climbing down over the rice patties. There were no buildings or objects blocking my view and he was not on the horizon. For a minute, I was disappointed at myself for not engaging him in in some way but somehow I knew that contact had been made without language. Still, where could he have gone? I did not understand what had just happened but my whole mood had lifted, my strength had returned and I sensed there was more mystery to come into my life.

Finally, thank God, it was time to leave

Taiwan. The whole two weeks had been fraught with tension, all except for my strolls through the streets, the fabulous meals we were treated to and this last encounter with the sidewalk sweeper who disappeared.

Our flight to Tokyo was quick and easy and we settled into a comfortable hotel, a far cry from where we had been staying in militarized Taipei. This was 1976, so Taiwan was in flux but nevertheless intriguing and colorful in all its contrasts of ancient and modern; modes of transportation with entire families on bicycles carrying their wares to market, competing for the roads with buses, tiny trucks and cars; the mountain people and urban dwellers; the water buffalos in rural landscapes and the waterfalls dropping from great, green heights. All of that was fascinating even though it was experienced through a lens of uncertainty.

When we arrived in Tokyo, the Olympics in Canada were in full swing, and most of our group stayed in their rooms watching television. As long as I was in this dreamed-about country, I wasn't about to lie around watching television, so I ventured out into the pouring rain, down the escalator where I stood among crowds trying to decode the subway system, and happily found my way to the Ginza and the Kabuki Za.

From my seat in the audience I watched women glide in wearing elegant silken kimonos while others filed in clutching their lunches in Bento boxes, exquisitely enameled and decorated. I was enamored by the gold-woven stage curtain and the people seated all around me, chatting and laughing and picking at their lunches. I walked down the aisle to inspect the golden curtain close up. The Japanese culture is one of immense order and beauty. For me, the performance was not just on the stage; it was in the rows and rows of people in the audience and the glorious interior of the theater.

After the performance the rain was still coming down in torrents so I ducked into a little shop that had windows stacked with colorfully patterned square cloths. The fabrics were variations of classic Japanese blue and white flowers and fans and reds and yellows, as well. I chose one to cover my hair from the rain, tied it under my chin, and bowed to the salesgirls who had bowed to me as I walked out the door. Less than a block away, I decided to turn back to buy more of these gorgeous squares. I found the shop girls giggling behind their delicate hands as I came back through the door and suspected they were laughing at me.

"What?" I motioned to them, not knowing what was so humorous.

They showed me that the colorful squares were for wrapping their possessions, much the way we use purses, and not for wearing on our heads. Once I understood this, I fell into laughter with them. Being a textile junkie, I spent an hour choosing a dozen to bring home as gifts.

One night after the rain had cleared, a group of us decided to go exploring. Once outside, I took off by myself to anonymously discover what was ordinary about the Japanese culture. Adam was safely under the watchful eye of Daniel, our senior instructor, and had buddied up with another teenage boy

It was fun to be out alone in a far away land where no one knew my name or spoke my language. I felt strong and independent and actually relaxed. The path sweeper seems to have had a lasting effect on me. I turned a corner and strolled down the street just looking around and taking it all in. Suddenly Wallace, our group's star practitioner, came up behind me and bodily turned me around. I had been heading into a dangerous part of town. I was surprised yet relieved to learn that the Grandmaster had put a guardian on me. I was grateful for being under Kung Fu protection but embarrassed for being so naïve (perhaps another example of a disconnected antenna).

On another day during our trip, Adam and his buddy discovered a park with a shrine atop a mountain of stairs.

"You will love it, Mom. Just come," he insisted.

The old stone, extremely steep stairs had no railings and seemed overly daunting, but Adam took my arm. Once up there, I was transfixed by the natural beauty in the middle of this city. It was a place of stillness, with overarching trees and meditation benches carefully placed under them. It was lush and green and silent, except for a faint melody moving through the air. I followed the sound coming from a little shrine tucked off in a grove of pine. Lined up on the stoop of a small wooden building was a row of flip-flops and sandals. This too, was a sacred place.

I wandered around in these enchanted woods enjoying the birdsong, the faint sound of the chant, the goldfish ponds and the sunlight pouring down through the trees. Overlooking an ivy-covered wall, I came upon a local woman who was about my age and who spoke English. After some small talk about my interest in meditation and the beauty of Zen, she invited me to go with her to Kama Kura, where the original Zen temples had been attracting seekers and tourists for ages. I jumped at the chance and very early the next morning, Emi and I headed out on the bullet train. The window gave us a fleeting glimpse of Mount Fuji. It was thrilling but at that speed no more real then a picture postcard. Unbeknownst to me, Emi had decided to get off one stop before ours so she could show me the village. That meant walking. But a light rain had just stopped and the sun was bright and everything along the way glistened: the gardens, the trees, the homes themselves. We walked at an easy pace, stopping at a little antique shop along the way. It was amazing to realize how modern our "antiques" are compared to these from so ancient a culture.

The temples were magnificent to walk through and the way they used wood and stone was so, well, Zen. I was surprised to see so many swords on display in one temple but I began to better understand the connection between the monks and martial arts.

On another day, Margot and I took a ferry to Yokahama and visited a silk museum. We got there at almost closing time and the guard allowed me to sit at one of the antique looms. I was immediately transported to another time and longed to finish the cloth that had been started in fuchsia and gold threads.

I was so happy to have had that experience with Emi in Kama Kura and then with Margot in Yokohama, proud of myself for making the best of a difficult situation, trying not to think about the ticket dilemma, waiting and trusting there would be a solution while thoroughly enjoying the sashimi, Oriental gardens and museums.

We were beginning our second week in Japan. Now the Grandmaster had locked himself in his room and only Debbie, his young lover and assistant, was allowed to come and go. Our teacher seemed to be having some sort of nervous breakdown, which created more unrest in the group and several factions and alliances that come from paranoia had begun to form. Some people began sleeping together to ease the stress and to find comfort. It had become both bizarre and frightening.

I walked down the hall, took a deep breath and knocked on the Grandmaster's door. Debbie answered and emphatically told me no one could enter. I insisted on going in and pushed her aside. He was lying on the bed, eyes closed and breathing in a way I had never seen a human breathe before—huge, thunderous breaths, his stomach, a mountain of flesh rising and falling in great rolling waves. I thought he was dying.

"Come in, Mahji," he said, slowly opening his coal black eyes. This was not the same man. He looked ready to cry but I had no sympathy.

"Adam and I have to go home," I said with the same eye contact and depth of voice that he had taught in his lessons.

"I thought you were enjoying yourself," he said.

"I'm making do," I said. "We need to get on a plane tomorrow."

The next day at the crack of dawn, Debbie knocked on the door and told me to get ready, that Adam and I were leaving. We threw our stuff together, raced downstairs and someone I didn't know drove the three of us— the Grandmaster, Adam and me—to the airport. The Grandmaster was all disheveled and reeked of alcohol. There was a brisk conversation at the ticket counter while he did his "tricks" and we were immediately ushered into first class without a ticket or even having to go through customs. Only after the plane had taken off were we able to exhale. I will never know how he managed to pull that off. The others were left back in the hotel with no way of knowing how or when they would get home. I felt horrible about leaving Margot, but what could I do? I had to take care of my boy and myself.

After my crashing delusion of getting strong through kung fu and playing the role of Grasshopper to the Grandmaster (like in that popular seventies TV show), my desire to get physical and spiritual seemed to be putting me two steps forward and one step back. The goal of creating a monastery that the Grandmaster had so often talked about with me ended up being just another fantasy, leaving a vacancy in my entire body and a yearning for something I struggled to name.

Despite all of my self-absorption, especially upon my return from this trip, I have to say that above all else, seeing my girls after a month away was a wide eye opener. My kids were what I cherished most in my life.

My treasures.

They were the grounding aspect through these phases of my life, with their glowing potential as human beings, their beauty, their sensitivities, their talents and their humor. I was vigilant about their well being and watched them like a hawk. Liz and Jenn, being only a year apart, were best friends. I sometimes felt like the outsider in terms of their confidences because they had each other. It wasn't like a mother-daughter relationship where the two did everything together, daughter hanging onto mom's arm, mom scrubbing daughter's head, polishing each other's nails. They had each other for that. I loved watching them together, arms around each other or in a huddle. They were so different from each other and perhaps that's what kept them from competing.

They were my girls and they are so beautiful. I would walk into a place with my girls, one on each side, and I was proud to be their mom. Adam being the eldest, and having an outrageous sense of humor, was fun to be with, too. He could have been a stand-up comic. We had good conversations, too, and I felt that we were close but he was growing into manhood. Although it was a joy to watch, he slowly began to pull away and make choices I was not happy with. He was becoming a teenager and starting to explore his independence. That was the way of things.

That March, we visited Ron's parents in Florida. It was during the thick of my longing for something I couldn't name. I snuck away by myself for a slow stroll along the beach. What was I so desperately looking for? Wasn't my family enough? My art? Along the way, I picked up shells and bits of sea glass. I laughed and cried from the beauty and from a loneliness so deep that my heart hung beneath my ribs like a wet rag. I thought this laughing and crying was a sure sign I was losing my mind. I simply had no choice but to let it go. Tears and wind stung my face and it felt good.

What I needed, I decided, was a Zen mother. Not a Zen master but a Zen mother, someone who was raising children, someone who knew how much the heart could stretch, someone who could love so deeply it hurt. I needed someone who understood the excruciating search for the Divine. I needed Mother Mary, a good Jewish mother who could lead me by the hand.

I yearned to know how to have God in my life and raise my children at the same time. Time was running out. They were teens already. I had read metaphysical books written mostly by men, not mothers, and I'd had mystical experiences, some of which I wanted to repeat. I'd had teachers in Harlan and the Grandmaster who showed me who I did not want to become; now I needed an authentic teacher who I could admire, someone with integrity and a true role model of that which I aspired to be, a wise and loving mom and a spiritual warrior at the same time. I was still in the process of *becoming* and I wanted that for my family and for myself. I was determined to honor the contract that my soul had made before I was born. My love for my children was more than I could have ever imagined or barely even contained and now that they were growing up so fast I wanted to gather the skills to walk them into a bountiful, joyful adult life. I didn't want a guru and I didn't want strange phenomena. I wanted something pure. This was my prayer as I tearfully collected treasures off the damp, sandy floor.

Emergence

Seeking a Zen Mother: Finding a Way

Laughing and Weeping, Teens: What are They? A Book from Dreams

I've heard it said many times that when the student is ready, the teacher appears. Still, to my amazement, soon after I became clear about my desire for a true teacher, what I sought came knocking on my door.

I was carrying two bags of groceries onto the porch when a VW Beetle slowed down and a young woman with a generous smile poked her head out of the window. Our eyes locked as she opened the door and stepped out of her car.

"I think I know you," she smiled.

"Don't think so," I said, struggling with groceries and my key but acting polite.

"Do you have a minute?" she asked. Being a slight bit curious to see what this stranger had to sell me, I let her go on.

"I don't usually go this way home," she said, "but something told me to drive up Kenyon Street. I knew there must be a reason why, so I followed my nudge. When I saw you on the porch I intuitively knew I had to stop."

It seemed a bit strange when she began a conversation and out of curiosity I let her continue as we walked up the porch steps into my home. She was an art student at the university and there was something different about her. She seemed giddy with happiness. After chatting for a while, all of that exuberance, that perkiness, in contrast to my ambivalent mood, made me want to throw a shoe at her. What did she have to be so happy about? What was her secret? What sort of act was this? She couldn't be for real.

This young woman told me her name was Susan and proceeded to tell me about an event that was coming to town, a seminar of some kind. I knew it. I knew it.

"Not religious," she explained, "but spiritual, something I was sure you'd be interested in or I never would have had the impulse to stop you like that. Things seem to happen that way, with synchronicity."

Synchronicity? I didn't know what she was talking about and by now I was bored.

"No, no, not interested," I said unpacking the groceries. "I'm done with this kind of stuff."

"Okay," she said, still smiling. "Just so you know, if you have any questions, here's my number."

I had no questions and was glad when she left. Her over-the-top chirpiness had gotten to me and without a second thought I threw her number in the trash.

Several days later, I noticed a full-page ad in the newspaper for the event this woman had told me about. *How pretentious for a spiritual path, I thought, to advertise like that.* But the day of the event came and despite my cynicism I found myself in the shower. I threw on some respectable clothes, burst out of the house with unexplainable fervor and drove myself to the coliseum. The annual World Wide Seminar of The Path was taking place.

Wanting to be anonymous, I took the elevator to the last row on the highest level of the coliseum where only a few of the 7,000 attendees were scattered around. I had no idea why I was even sitting there and I certainly didn't want to bump into anyone I knew.

As the evening program went on, I began to relax. I was becoming filled with the gentleness and sweetness from the words and the music. The indescribable vibe that filled the space had, to my amazement, also filled my heart. Rivers of tears poured down my face as I sat transfixed, unaware of anyone else. The discussion of reincarnation, the eternal life of the soul and the concept of karma was what I had wanted to know about for years. It all struck a nerve that nourished my whole body.

One speaker told the story of her personal journey, which was a rough and winding road deepening in to the very core of herself. She was a charismatic woman who spoke about her process of having to let go of her personal power, how she used to do fantastic things, similar to what Harlan and The Grandmaster did—not for selfish reasons or for personal power but rather with the belief that she was helping. She worried all the time about the ills of the world as she generously put her well-intentioned powers to work. She spoke about her process of having to let go of that personal power, how she had been able to manipulate people and things with her mind but never once thought of her skills as manipulation.

As she spoke, I couldn't help but relate my own experiences. I had felt so good about helping that oil truck up the hill on that blizzardy day when the guys dug the elderly woman's car out of the ditch. That was a positive thing to do but now I wondered what would have happened if I hadn't helped the truck up the hill. Maybe the driver needed to stay in Covington that night. Maybe he would have avoided an accident up the road or maybe he would have met the love of his life if he had stayed back in town until morning. But leaving the woman in the ditch may have ended in tragedy, so wasn't that the right thing to do?

This speaker described so elegantly and clearly that this kind of subtle distinction ultimately takes practice. It's about listening to an inner guidance that comes through us rather than acting out of our ego's preferences. *But how do you know?* I wondered.

Her story and the description of her transformation had a huge impact on me. I became aware of how people do this all the time, consciously and unconsciously, because we do worry and we do care and we do think of ourselves as "good" people. She worried all the time about the ills of the world and felt gifted and obligated to put her well-intentioned powers to work. She felt blessed to be able to do these things but on this path, she what she called "The

Law of Discernment." If we pray for someone to recover from a disease, for instance, we may be interfering with their soul's plan for themselves and who are we to say what needs to happen? So I was learning that praying for God's will to be done is a cleaner way than praying for a person to have the result we think is best for them. We just cannot judge what is supposed to happen for someone else.

So here was a new way—a different way and that required forgetting the skills I had learned about personal power with such enthusiasm. That meant letting go of fear, not worrying about fixing things for others or even for myself. It simply meant to" let go and let God" and relax fully into that state of being. The phrase "Thy will be done" suddenly made perfect sense to me. It not about doing nothing but rather, listening with the heart from a nonattached perspective.

This was a challenge for me because it felt like I was removing the inner armature I had built over the years that was holding me together and I feared I would collapse back into a weakened state without it. Yet after that seminar, one thing was clear: I had to make a shift into this new way of being. This change

turned out to be seminal to my progress.

After that event, I continued to read The Path's literature and went to a few meetings to further test the waters. Though my mind did not yet know it, fate had brought me to my destiny—for the time being, anyway—because self-enlightenment is a never-ending process. Once again, I was open to all possibilities but now I had a new skill set to learn.

Before deciding whether to join The Path as a member, I talked with Ron and my kids about my discoveries and new insights. They know too well that when I become interested in something, I become obsessed. "Here she goes again," was their general reaction to my exuberance for this latest one. That was to be expected but nevertheless, they each, in their own time, made the decision to join me on this journey, and for that I am glad.

As it turns out, The Path was full of answers to many of my questions and had somehow seemed to satisfy my longings. It opened the way to a clearer sense of my purpose, untainted by the shadowy ominousness of Harlan and the charismatic, mocked-up love of the Grandmaster. I felt like I had found a home and in that home was pure love, plain and true. This seemed like what I'd been looking for all along.

In the days that followed, I asked for help in letting go of my "tricks" and somehow a clearing came in with a whoosh, like a tidal wave rushing through me. It washed all that away and made space for spirit to come through instead of my own well-intentioned efforts. I had released it or it had released me, and in the process, I became empty and fragile. It was a new kind of emptiness and it was good because with it came a gentle stream of love, blowing in like a warm wind and filling the space in my soul.

At once I knew I would no longer need self-defense, that I would be "told" when I was in danger. I would be guided to move to where I needed to be. The antenna that I had repressed as a defense mechanism in childhood would be returned to its rightful place but only if I kept my connection with the Divine alive through constant receptivity. It had been there before the abuse and now I was reclaiming it. This awareness would become my way of life. I vowed to be receptive through stillness, chanting, singing, prayer and deep breathing whenever I wanted and wherever I happened

to be. All of my nightmares and dreads simply vanished. No more images of babies crawling in the road at night or inescapable fires or perpetrators lurking in shadows, as I'd had most of my life. All of the horrors that had haunted me beneath my consciousness had vanished. I became high on love, ease and my new sense of security.

I knew whatever was down the road, my children and I would be okay. I knew I was here to serve God and in turn that would serve humanity; but how that would be, I wasn't yet sure. To talk about it sounds so self-righteous but in truth it was extremely humbling. I knew there were millions of others doing the same thing in their own ways all across the planet. Now I was among them; and it was not some religious thing, which made it even better. It was a human thing to be personally connected with the Divine.

My response to things that happened shifted. If I go lost, I knew it was for a reason. If I was late, it saved me from some mishap or it put me in a position to help someone else. If I called a friend, it was at exactly the right time. There was always a reason. I was being used in ways I could not predict or design and I loved that. I seemed to just have to follow those inner directions and not have to make the usual decisions whether to say yes or no, whether to go here or there. I had to be flexible and it made life simpler.

The Path was based in male hierarchy, but this time I knew how to work with that. This time I could assert myself as a woman in my own way, as a mom and as an activist with a whole new perspective. In my meditations, I was reaching glorious heights. I felt I was beginning to shine with the same bliss as the woman in the Volkswagen that pissed me off so badly. But now I got it. Now I understood. It was exhilarating. With the same curiosity but without the crazy risks I was coming into a deeper faith.

By now it was about 1978 and we had moved out of the rental on Kenyon Street and into a lovely old farmhouse that had once been part of a dairy farm before the suburbs grew up around it. Ron had been happy in the city but I wanted our kids off the streets and back onto beautiful land. I wanted that for myself, too. The realtor had shown me the farmhouse in August, when everything was in full bloom. Sweet smelling phlox and day lilies bordered two buildings, a row of tall pines lined the drive, a gigantic mountain laurel graced the doorway and three stately maple trees were scattered down through the yard that would bring me joy in every New England season. It was a setting worthy of the Fauves.

We needed money and I had wanted to learn the techniques of power weaving so I was thrilled to get a job in a large silk factory where they had once even raised their own silk worms. But even with ear guards on it was so loud in there with all those huge looms chugging back and forth. I took a good long look then ran out the door. Instead I took a job correcting by hand the mistakes that the power looms had made.

I joined the union and that winter, I stood on a platform from nine to five in a rambling brick factory building with acres of worn wooden floors and sunlight pouring into the many enormous windows. I actually enjoyed the work. But it was a typical factory culture with cliques and factions, everyone from that same little town, not my town. The only people who could take breaks back then were the smokers, and everyone was a smoker so I had breaks, too. Consequently, I would take my half-hour lunch in the parking lot in the refuge of my car with a sandwich and a book. When

I'd get home, dishes were still piled in the sink, the remains of snacks and school accouterments littered the table, music beat heavily from three teenage rooms and everyone was starving. I was exhausted and Ron in the shop day and night was averse to getting involved.

I tried often to set up family meetings to democratically find a way work out a plan to get chores done while meeting everyone's needs. Ron belittled my every attempt.

"I don't sit down for meetings," he'd say and, of course, the children followed. I didn't blame them. I understood that they had school and work and friends, but there needed to be house rules and I was the one to make them. I was the one who worried when there was something to worry about. Maybe Ron worried, too, but he'd rather not let on.

"It'll work out," he'd say.

"We have to help it work out," I'd say but he wanted to be the good guy.

"Don't make me the bitch." I'd plead.

"Then leave them alone," was his answer.

One winter's night, the phone rang and a customer of Ron's wanted to know if we knew anyone who would like to stay in his lake house for a few weeks. He was going away and didn't want the pipes to freeze. I jumped at the chance for a retreat and dashed off to live by myself on the lake, equidistant from work at the factory and home in Bloomfield. At sunrise I'd jump into the hot tub on the deck, stretch into wakefulness slowly as I listened to the ice crack across the lake, and watch the light flow into a new day. At night, it was a different story. The house was basically an open space with no interior walls, and no shades or curtains. Any snowmobiler racing by could see into the house and I felt seriously vulnerable. I'd sit in the faint light of a kerosene lamp, reflect on all that was going on in my life and write in my journal. I had so much emotion built up inside of me about things that were working out and things that weren't the words rushed out of me like water over rocks.

This practice of The Path and the silence of the lake house slowly returned me to an experience of expansion and connection with myself and a gushing sense of gratitude for everything. This formless, soundless rush would enter me unexpectedly, filling me with indescribable love for my kids, my husband, my house and yard, for my body and my work. For some reason, it came natural for me to call this rushing "God."

"Please, God, I want to write about all of this," I'd say. Then these became letters to the Divine and they ignited a fire within me. I wanted to tell the world what I had found but more importantly, I wanted to hold this sensation in myself, tightly in myself.

After a week at the lake, I realized how much I missed my family and invited them out. I decided that Saturday I would shop and Sunday I would cook. They'd drive the fifty miles to play on the ice, skate and slide, and hang out over hot cocoa. At dusk, we'd sit down to a beautiful feast in front of the fire. Then everyone, satisfied, would pile in the car to go home while I remained.

I was still worried about the kids during these years, some days more than others. Drugs were rampant, booze was available and sex was atmospheric. So one day, I asked God, "Where does my job end and yours begin? What am I supposed to do?"

On The Path we had been told that Spirit will often appear as a blue star or a blue globe of light. If you see it in meditation, it is a comforting thing. I came home from the lake house and went into their rooms to check on them as I always did after they went to sleep. I opened the door to Adam's room and there it was, a blue globe of light bouncing around the bed like a glowing beach ball. I couldn't believe my eyes and the feeling of presence in the room. I was so humbled that I backed out of there in awe and silently closed the door behind me. I peeked into Jenn's room and the same thing happened. I peeked into Liz's room and there, too, was the blue globe of light. My question had been answered. They were being watched over, all three. I don't know how that works. It was a comforting mystery to me, rather delicious but there it was, a welcome mystery and my worries drifted away. I was in partnership with God.

Jennifer, our middle child, was the wild one, a free spirit, as they say. She was always active and independent and there was very little communication between Jenny and myself. Children from other families were running away from home to Haight Ashbury in San Francisco long after the hippie movement. Some thought that San Francisco was a haven, a dreamtopia for restless young kids, seekers or those who needed to escape from their homes. Yet it was a utopia in rumor only. Kids were getting lost, swallowed up by the city, on their own and inundated with unanticipated challenges as parents were abandoned in helpless terror.

Jenn had been doing well in school. She also had a small paying job and two volunteer jobs. She was a doer. And, of course, she had a vibrant social life, spending time with friends from different cliques. I don't know how she did it all. She could communicate with everyone, but not us, and so I was challenged. If I got too tough with her, I feared she'd run away. She was that independent. With all of her busyness, she was only at home to sleep and sit on her bed listening to music. Despite the reassurance of the blue globe of light, I occasionally kept her out of school to take her to breakfast, one on one, to encourage some real communication. She assured me that by the time she got home from school most days, she was exhausted and had nothing to say to any of us. She loved us but had nothing to say. She was fourteen. What was I to do?

A few days after I saw the blue light, I took her aside. "Jenn, I cannot be sitting on your shoulder watching every little thing you do. You are making decisions that will affect your entire life. From this moment on, I am handing you responsibility for yourself. Every action you take and every decision you make is your responsibility, so do it from a state of consciousness." My kids understood that kind of talk. "Do not slide into what other kids are doing just because they're doing it. Take your time, stop and think it through or just let it come to you. You are smart and if you let your immediate instinct lead, you will know what to do. I am always here for you. You can always come to me with anything. I love you."

I literally put out my hand and ritually handed her responsibility for herself. I felt a sense of relief because I could actually feel it transfer. Jenn took this seriously and seemed relieved. Her behavior changed almost immediately. She found time to talk to me with no need to be distant. She made her own rules and followed them. She began making excellent decisions and seemed to have little to rebel against. She knew she was trusted and wanted to keep that trust.

Years later, she told me that giving her that kind of responsibility was the best thing I could have done. The idea to let her own her actions came from somewhere other than the limited reasoning and logic of my mind. Could it have had something to do with that blue globe of light that reassured me the night I asked God, "When does your job end and mine begin?"

Just around that time I had to make a point with Adam, too. I had to put my foot down regarding his behavior, but he had been ignoring me. He stood at the kitchen window looking out at the rain as I babbled on pedantically in my usual manner. But silence. That's all I got from him. Then I asked God for help. All of a sudden I was crystal clear, the right words pouring out of me, startling me with their relevance. When I was done speaking, Adam turned to face me, looked me in the eyes and said, "Why didn't you say it like that before?" and then things were fine.

My higher guidance had kicked in and the wisdom flowed out. It wasn't my wisdom. It was more like the universal intelligence I had opened to, Spirit, the Loving All. Or maybe this was the voice of the Zen mother that I had been searching for. Who cares what name is used? I know it is all the same Divinity.

I discovered that this newfound connection to a higher intelligence was what I needed in order to give my kids what they needed. Mainly that was the understanding and access to their own higher intelligence. Each of them differed in the amount of freedom and responsibility they could handle and the amount of receptivity they had to these ideas. I was able to appreciate how different they were from each other and what they each needed in relationship to me and how I could better serve them now as their mom.

Soon after I returned home from the lake, I had a dream. I was asked in the dream if I wanted to write a book called *The New Woman Warriors Handbook.* I said, "Yes."

In the morning, I told Ron that I was going to write a book with this title, since I figured that announcing it solidified my commitment to writing it. Since I wasn't a writer, I was just as surprised as he that I had set this goal for myself. Yet I had made the connection while at the lake that in my altered state in retreat I had asked to *write for God.* What in the world had I meant by that? I just knew it had been joyful and fulfilling and that I wanted to keep doing it, writing my thoughts from this new perspective. I never expected an "invitation" like this could come in a dream especially with the title already there. I was thrilled to comply.

The next night, not having a clue as to what I should write about, I sat down at the typewriter and waited for something to come into my head. And something came. The words poured out of me just as they had in my journal. They came when I was chauffeuring the kids and when I was standing at the loom, in the middle of the night and even when I was down with a migraine (an occasional occurrence I later discovered was caused by birth control pills). No matter what I was doing at the time, I knew that it was my job to get the words down. When I was done exactly nine months later, I sent a copy of the manuscript to the powers-that-be at The Path, just to be sure that I was not misrepresenting anything about the program.

You, the reader, may be wondering about all of this business of The Path so let me explain. The Path is a fictitious name for the actual teaching I have been talking about because I have felt the need to protect the people and the teachings from my personal opinions about my experiences there. It is a sacred path, a love path at its core, and the masters I've spoken of both living and ascended are those I had loved enough to keep their pictures on our mantle. They were as inspiring to me as a view of the mountains or the glisten of ocean under the moon or of a V of geese screeching across the sky. Their faces in photos and drawings for me emanated strength and loving kindness.

All of the literature up until that point had been written by the founder so this was an extreme surprise and honor when the publisher said that they wanted to publish my book, a book that was full of personal insights, experiences, successes and failures. *The New Woman Warrior's Handbook: Not for Women Only* came out later that year, in 1982. I soon began receiving letters from all over the world from students of The Path and the general public. The biggest thrill for me was the day I walked into Dalton's Bookstore in New York and there it was, my book on the shelf.

The publication of my work changed my status with The Path. It gave me opportunities I had never before had and provided opportunities to speak in front of audiences large and small, to teach, to have my ideas taken seriously, and to lead seminar workshops for people from around the world. It gave me a sense of certainty about my experiences, interpretations and beliefs, thereby making it easy to talk freely. This made me a tiny celebrity within The Path, which was both awesome and awkward. All of a sudden, everyone was talking to me. I loved it and I didn't. It was overwhelming but being recognized for something that I had done was gratifying.

While this was going on there was much joy. We had all lightened up, found a kind of settling in to a real home in our house, town and within ourselves. The family had become strong and our house had become a kind of sanctuary for friends of ours and friends of the kids, a vastly different kind of social life from our years in Maine. The young people would come over to hang out and were comfortable participating in our intense conversations, rehearsing their music and attending numerous parties that Ron and I chaperoned most often in the beauty of the backyard. There we hosted potluck picnics, talent shows and crazy dancing under the moon. We also traveled all over the country to seminars and savored the sights, museums and restaurants in various cities and on California beaches. Sometimes on road trips, some of the school friends would be allowed to come with us. We'd all squeeze into the van and go. Despite a little discomfort, we were riding the spiritual train.

We each volunteered in our own ways at these seminars. I did my thing, Ron ushered, Jenn taught classes to teens and served on panels, Liz worked with the preteens directing and writing little plays, and Adam basically listened. Probably like most religions do, we enjoyed the camaraderie of like-minded people, although most of us never thought of The Path as a religion. It was more a way of life made up of people from all religions and cultures and having been taught that all religions eventually lead there, it made us feel relieved that we had found "the true path." We were relieved to believe we were ahead of the game but we had an overblown sense of righteousness and didn't yet know it.

So who were those ancient men and one woman gazing out of their frames into our lives from the mantle? They were simply our teachers appearing in dreams, carrying messages, ideas, love and protection much like what some would consider to be a guardian angels, the presence of Jesus or the imaginary friend some have as children. Very real. One of these masters who visited me often in my dreams, whose presence I could feel and even sometimes have silent conversations with, was one who brought me poetry and calmness. This master was Chinese and as it turned out he was, yes, mysteriously the very same man I had seen in Taiwan, the one who had calmed me down, the one I thought had vanished not into the rice paddies but into the ethers. Was he the path sweeper? How could that be? All of these new experiences were a welcome mystery and a surprising adventure.

Still I always suspected that whatever way we are comfortable perceiving the Divine, It/She/He will come to us in that form. Whether there is scientific proof or not is irrelevant. It is the love energy that appears, sometimes in these familiar human forms.

My mantra had become *anything is possible* and my search had always been to know the deeper truth of that love energy that streams in to my heart, to my whole body and I longed to know what is real. What is the difference between what is accepted as real and what is not because there is so much reality that cannot be seen, heard or measured.

From the beginning of my involvement with The Path, I had wondered what it would be like to talk to the Living Master, one on one. This man was our spiritual leader, one of a long line of masters walking the planet right now. He was the considered "The Way Shower", a teacher that would lead us into our own "mastership." For me, that meant I would eventually have the ability to continually operate not from my ordinary self and ego but from my higher self or soul the part of me that is eternal and closer to God.

So the idea of standing before The Master was both humbling, exciting and terrifying. If I ever had that opportunity, I knew I would get all flustered and tangle my words imperceptibly.

Then one day, having finished my own presentation, I was stepping off the stage as he was about to go on. He stopped me with a question about my book. There was no time to get flustered. I looked into his eyes and my shoulders dropped and my breath came easy. Being in his presence was lovely. It was elevating. I became more of myself, not less. We were in perfect harmony as we stood there while everything else fell away. I found myself asking him a question I had been mulling over in my head for months, something about the value of publishing books on all the religions and philosophies (not just ours) and as he listened he showed genuine enthusiasm. How did I dare make a suggestion like that to him? But that moment in his presence showed me what it is to be totally, genuinely and deeply myself. It felt great. He was not someone who was superior but someone who brought out the best in me, drawing out my own qualities.

He said, "I too have been thinking about that but it is not yet time."

I had been enjoying the ripple up in status, but at the same time didn't approve of it because it placed me in a new position in a long stretch of hierarchy, and that hierarchy was in large part one of the reasons I would leave The Path after eighteen years. I was aware that there were those without any status who were far wiser than myself. I was beginning to get an uncomfortable feeling. Just the idea of the attention that some seemed to get and most didn't and by way of what? I wasn't sure. Initiations? Seniority? Hours of volunteerism? Amount of donations? I didn't know but there were definitely many stars closing in on celebrity level and many more aspirers and suddenly here I was sliding into the arena of the "stars." For a while, I embraced the attention, the opportunities and the invitations that came with it. I would be able to serve in bigger and better ways. That was the good part. But the hierarchy in the organization, as I suppose exists in any organization, was beginning to make no sense

to me whatsoever and there was also a certain phoniness I began to sense. There was simply too much bliss. Everyone when we got together was perfect. Everyone was overjoyed. No one showed the sorrow that life inevitably brings to everyone sometimes.

Spiritual paths can open up the doors to growth, love and wisdom. It reminded me of that first day when the young woman in the Volkswagen came to my house spilling bliss to the point that I wanted to throw a shoe at her. The thinking was that all they had to do was chant their mantra and everything would be fine, all life's problems would dissolve. But that isn't how it works. To be in integrity, there also have to be some blues followed by an investigation of what is causing it. There must be some self-inquiry, as well. There must be an investigation into the darker side, the wounded side, the hidden side, the illusory side that is in everyone's life. There has to be a balance to become whole. (I used to hear people talking about healing ad nauseam. What the hell does everyone have to heal, I wondered.) Little did I know yet about all the silent suffering and the shoving down of pain and neither was I in touch with my own. All I was aware of was a longing I could not name.

The question then became, "What is truly motivating us? What is motivating our ideas, beliefs, decisions and actions? What made me sink into a dark whole when someone I respected didn't praise me for a job well done? Why did I care?" I started to see that all of us would eventually have to own the unpleasantness within ourselves or we would be walking around living a half-life and I didn't see that happening on this path. I had a lot to ponder.

No matter how careful, caring and conscientious Ron and I were, how well we thought we were doing with our kids, we were still imperfect parents. Who isn't? I hadn't wanted to repeat what my parents did to me by dismantling my young self, inhibiting my growth by their behaviors and their words so my reaction was to swing the pendulum to the other side and try to make my kids feel good about themselves. I wanted more than anything for my children to have a deep sense of who they were as individuals, to discover what their gifts were, to discover their innate wisdom and their blossoming potential. I wanted them to have a healthy sense of self and understand the uniqueness of every individual in the whole world. I encouraged and rewarded them but I probably should have leaned on them harder, demanded more of them academically instead of praising them to the hilt. I overcompensated. Liz once chastised me after a Christmas concert in which she played the flute with her school orchestra: "Mom, I hate when you beam at me like that. It's embarrassing."

The hardest thing for me to learn much later was that the whole time we were on The Path, Liz hated it. She wished that we were being Jewish like her friends. She wished that we were not in some weird spiritual group that no one had ever heard of with pictures of weird people on the mantle. She was embarrassed. We did not know that or the consequences that would eventually have. It drove her as far away from my beliefs as she could get. So, no matter how hard we tried, our babies were bound to grow up with pinches, bites and booboos that would eventually become their own task to heal. We were doing our best from who we were at the time. Parents are not given a handbook and even if they were who would be the author? We all have our own philosophies even when we are not yet wise ourselves. We so wizen up with age and in retrospect can see the beauty and the errors of the past. But that is life and life is good. It's what each of us does with what we were given that counts.

No matter what, at some point in their precious lives, happiness is their own responsibility. Whatever healing needs to happen, whatever gifts need expressing, whatever flaws need fixing, whatever love needs dispensing, all will become their own small contribution to our collective human evolution.

Ron and I stood in the middle of the driveway watching the little blue VW back away from us. Our daughter was headed for California. Ron was dumbfounded. "Where did the time go? She was just a little girl," he gasped. I was proud and confident that Jenn was ready, ready for school and ready for the world.

Revealing the Concealed

"I was once a sleeping ocean and in a dream became jealous of a pond."
–Rabia

The Year of Almost Drowning: Diving for the Pearl

Leaving The Path, The Shock of Cancer, Diving In, Becoming Frances

I had always known that my physical limitations were not psychosomatic, as I had been repeatedly told by healthcare professionals over the decades. Just in case they were right by a slim chance, I would periodically push the outer limits of my body with dangerous challenges. One summer day while visiting Ron's family at the beach, we took our little sailboat out, just the two of us. When we got out to what seemed a reasonable distance, I jumped off the boat to challenge myself to swim back. I knew how to swim but endurance was the issue.

As soon as I was in the water, I found myself in a riptide. Ron was already facing out to sea with his back to me, while the wind carried away my cries for him to turn back and get me. There I was, kicking and pulling and getting nowhere. I stopped yelling for him in order to conserve my strength and right myself out of the vertical position I kept slipping into. With one great breath,

I lifted my belly up onto the surface and into a dead man's float, giving myself the opportunity to rest, something I had learned at Brownie camp. But I soon noticed that I was drifting out to sea and began to panic. As I panicked, I went under. Bobbing back up, I could see the distant sailboat, as well as tiny figures sunning themselves back on the beach—Ron's relatives, chatting away, totally oblivious to what was happening to me.

Under I went again and again. Then I heard myself sputtering out loud, "Oh, my God, this is how people drown." I righted myself again and noticed a line of buoys strung diagonally in toward shore. I headed for them, alternating between breast stroke and floating, breast stroke and dead man's float, and while I alternately stroked and floated, I prayed. Sometimes, I kicked while my arms rested and sometimes I pulled with my arms while my legs rested. Much of the time, my face remained in the water. It went like this until I finally reached the buoys. But to my horror, when I got there, I saw that the rope was not taut but dragging down in giant loops and would not hold me up.

I spotted two boys further out in a rowboat. "Boys! Boys! Can you come over here?" I didn't yell for help, which obviously would have been more effective.

They yelled back, "We saw you swimming."

They laughed and didn't come towards me. At that moment, I thought that I might not survive. I turned toward the beach and float-kicked my way from one buoy to the next. Hanging onto something was better than hanging onto nothing. When I finally reached the shore, I was like one of those cartoons of a person barely touching land, feet in the water, face in the sand, while the relatives further down the beach continued their chatter. Apparently it wasn't yet time for me to leave the planet. Whose voice was that that came out of my mouth in that moment of panic reminding me that this is how people drown? I do believe that was divine intervention coming to me in my own voice.

By the time of my near-drowning situation, I had long given up trying to get a diagnosis for my mystery ailment. Every time one of those docs told me it was in my head, I wanted to punch him in the face because he couldn't bring himself to say, "I don't know."

Then one day in my mid-fifties, I was carrying a box of books into the library to give a talk about the teachings of The Path. The box got heavier and heavier as I made my way to the building from the car, as my arms got weaker and weaker and finally gave out. I dropped the books all over the sidewalk. After my tantrum and a string of swear words at God (for here I was doing something "spiritual"), my question was, "How come now this has to happen?"

That night I dreamed of another life. It was me in Mexico in the 12th Century. I was young and leggy and brown skinned. I thought I was doing something good but it was harmful. My present life was the time for me to balance out that karma. For every action there is an equal reaction and here was the reaction. Now I knew why. But in my dream I was also told what I had to do was start looking for a doctor again. It was mind blowing. I woke up on a sopping wet pillow. I had been crying in my sleep. I had been crying in gratitude. The person I had unintentionally harmed in Mexico in that former life was a person who was again in my life right now. I was grateful for the opportunity to have a second chance.

I went to the University of Connecticut Health Center, where they put me through a series of very unpleasant tests, including a biopsy taken from my left thigh. Ultimately, that led to a diagnosis of the rarest form of muscular dystrophy. Finally, a diagnosis!

Only forty people in the world were known to have this metabolic disorder in which the body cannot use carbs for energy and has a low-exercise tolerance that causes muscle pain and actual immobility. In infants and childhood, it can be fatal. I've had it all my life but here I am still and that feels good.

At the health center, seventeen doctors came to view the slides of my biopsy. I was allowed to attend this meeting with all of the physicians. They told me at the time not to expect a cure because with it being so rare, there was little demand for a cure and therefore no money in it. I accepted that and went about my life with the same anxieties about stairs, hills and where to park the car but I was satisfied to have a reason for this misery.

On the first warm, sunny day of summer, I was ready to begin something new. I found myself thinking about making a small circle with stones, a private meditation place as special as those I'd seen in that shrine in Tokyo. I had been looking for a spiritual discipline outside of an organization or religion, just a way to meditate and deepen my connection with the earth. I had dissociated for years, leaving my body because of my childhood traumas and the disability and later, the emphasis on soul travel, a skill taught on The Path, which involved leaving the body for higher spiritual realms then returning with knowledge gained. This was not what I needed. What I needed was to get grounded. What I needed was to get out of my head and enter fully and solidly into my body so I could experience what it was to plant my feet, my whole self, on holy ground.

I wandered out on this perfect day to survey the woods beyond the muddy stream that cut through the far end of our yard. I struggled to get over to the other side, pulling myself up the bank, slipping and sliding and grabbing onto low hanging branches and small trees. I sat down where I landed and sang a little song, asking my heart for guidance.

I was drawn to a place with the high point being a moss-covered mound, soft and sweet beneath a maple tree, just budding red. I gathered sticks and branches that had been lying on the ground and dragged them over to form a circle. It took me awhile to do this work but the sun felt good and the circle was already turning into sacred space. I sat and chanted and sang and prayed under the dappled sun and found myself just loving everything. A chorus of birds joined in with their different tones and rhythms. The circle had grown larger then I had anticipated, about twenty feet in diameter and not on level ground but this was what was given.

I rested awhile and when I was ready, I climbed over the stream and back to my life but was soon drawn out there again, this time with a sack of flat rocks and things from my collections. I managed to get across again and took my place. I laid out the objects down all around me. The biggest rocks ended up marking the four directions on the outside of the circle. I don't know how long I sat with the hot sun pouring down through the trees onto my face. It was a sweet thing until I got up to leave and walked around the outside of the circle. Tiny thorny branches grabbed and pulled at my hair. I wound them around a nearby branch to keep them high enough and out of the way, but still they found me and clung and scratched. Now they formed a kind of course weaving above my head.

Across the middle of the circle, barely visible was a moss-covered log rotting softly into the ground almost as if it had just been placed there, and then a sudden flash of white. It looked like a roll of birch bark. I thought maybe I'd take it back to the house and keep a little piece of sanctuary on my desk, but when I got up close I saw it was not what I had assumed it was but rather a perfect little skull complete with little fangs and teeth. My first thought was that it was Jake, my favorite "panther" cat, one of a number of our beloved cats we had buried out back. But on closer scrutiny I found the head to be more like a kitten than a grown cat or any wild animal I could think of. It was no doubt a kitten we once loved and it was a sacred thing to come upon the realization that it had been there unseen the whole time I had been making my circle. It jolted me into the facts of death. Then birth. Then death again and how many lives our souls actually inhabit. *Who was this kitten now?* I wondered.

But why was it there, atop this log instead of within the earth? It gave me bodily chills that it had probably once played amongst these very rocks and trees and that it had once been loved by us and grieved over with its loss. Now here it was again dug up by some other animal, so perfect in its structure and a reminder to me to appreciate the present moment, as well as the ultimate beauty of impermanence.

By this time, Adam was a young man of twenty something, well on his own. He'd met Louise on a train traveling from Hartford to New York where he was studying at The New School of Social Research and The School of Visual Arts. Louise was a legislative assistant for a New York City council member and had been filling out an application to Columbia Graduate School of Journalism. Only after the train had stopped and they rose to leave did they begin to talk. Adam had been reading Long Days Journey into Night and was balancing some boards on his shoulder. Louise was intrigued.

"What are those for?" she asked.

"For a sculpture I'm building," he said and that was the beginning for them. Months went by and he and Louise were soon committed enough to move together to New Mexico where Adam had received an Artist in Residence grant from the Art Center in Roswell.

Liz had also gone to art school at SUNY Purchase, New York, where she met Ben. They had been married right after graduation and were the first to have a baby. When I had gotten the news that she was in labor, I quickly called Ron, who was out on an installation job and couldn't be reached. Then Ben called again and told me she was now the mom of a beautiful baby boy. Ben was out of breath with excitement. I called my mom, who was not home. Adam and Jenn were unreachable and my sister Nancy didn't answer her phone. Frustrated and ecstatic, I raced to the store for flowers. To whom could I tell my news? Who would rejoice with me? As I walked into Shop Rite, who did I see but my old friend Sandy from the *Happy Huddle,* my very first friend from the sandbox when we were three. Though we lived in neighboring towns, we hadn't spoken in many years, having drifted apart by life.

"Sand!" I yelled, as if we were still best friends. "We have a baby. I'm a Grandmother!"

I spun her round and round as we laughed like little kids, like we used to laugh those many years ago, as if no time had elapsed.

Ron and I sped to New York that night to meet our first grandchild. He slept sweetly in the arms of our radiant Liz. When I got to hold Jacob myself it was, of course, pure bliss and that would be the start of our eventual ten grandbabies.

Jenn, who was now studying to be a chiropractor, wanted all of us to get together for Christmas but this time in New Mexico. Our visits had been sparse throughout her years in California. The visit promised to be a great reunion with Adam and Louise hosting us in their little house of love and art-making.

So that December, Ron and I took one of our rare vacations and flew out to Albuquerque, rented a car and drove south to Roswell to spend Christmas with our kids. It was like the honeymoon we'd never had.

The landscape was vast and beautiful, and driving along in our automobile, we discovered story radio, the first time we had ever heard Garrison Keillor, with his slow nasal voice accompanied by extraordinary musicians. We bathed in profound loveliness, the intimacy, the laughter, the singing along and the strange sky, the Capitan Mountains, the eagles, the mule deer, the big horn sheep and just the two of us floating through all that enchantment away from everything familiar, on and on endlessly it seemed through three building desert town after three building desert town until there it was at the horizon, a twinkling of lights. We were coming into civilization and closer to the reunion with our grown-up children, which made our hearts race with anticipation. They would all be waiting for us and we couldn't wait to see them again.

"Too bad Liz couldn't come," I said, longing to see all the kiddos together and our new baby boy.

"Yeah, well it's their first Christmas as a little family," Ron said.

"Hannuka," I corrected him.

"Yeah, right, Hannuka," he said, remembering that Liz was now long gone from The Path and had become a culturally committed Jewish mom.

With big hugs and greedy kisses, we had arrived. It was great to see our children so happy. We marveled at the way they had grown into adults with intelligence and independence and enthusiasm for what they were making of their particular lives and how they had been learning from the world and people other than ourselves.

We savored every moment. New Mexico was a foreign land to us Northeasterners, and exploring the landscape and the culture was an adventure. Some mystery enabled me to walk the earth as never before. The land itself seemed to help me place one foot in front of the other and I treasured the mysterious beauty. I loved the beauty, slowness and depth of the people, which I tucked away into the back of my mind for future exploration.

Back in 1977 when we stepped onto The Path, it had been dramatically transformative for us. It had become our home and the people had become family. But now after almost eighteen years, I felt that I must leave that family and Ron felt the same. I had lost my passion for seminars, was bored with hotels, and sick of getting up at outrageous hours to volunteer. I'd had my fill of being taught to let go, to just chant my word and all my emotions would fade away. I was sick of a culture that didn't honor the wildness inherent in all of us. Most importantly, I needed to break through another barrier within. I needed to find a way to bring that light into some hidden darkness I harbored deep down that had not yet been uncovered. I had to get away from that blissful culture and address the doubts that I had been avoiding. It was time to descend into the deeper truth of myself and on this path it was sacrosanct to remain positive without a negative thought able to surface. So now I needed people with passion and courage enough to stand at the edge of darkness and dive down through the light into the shadowy realms within. Scary as that was, I knew it was my present calling. It was time to say goodbye with the utmost gratitude for all it did for us.

For My Sisters and Brothers on The Path

When I came to The Path
I had been searching, stumbling toward it
For many years.

It became, for me,
A cocoon to keep me safe
While I unfolded inside its walls.

A container, a covering,
Like a magic sweater
That kept my body warm
My mind cool, a shimmering film of light
While I inhaled the love

And rapture and crumbled
The remains of ancient fears.

Strands of brightness woven of the minutes
Of the days, the years
Dreams of glistening fibers
Woven to a perfect fit
The right temperature for day or night

Each moment it grew more cozy,
Fit my form,
I fit softly, snug
Inside its silken threads.

This sweater kept me dry through every storm
Protected me from fires
And kept me true in times of testing
*
Only now there's something wearing thin
In certain places
There are holes
It's lost its shape,
No longer contains the body of myself

Wrists dangle out, get chilled
There's scratching round my breasts

And 'round my throat
Its tightness
Keeping me from song.

With trepidation but determination
I tear it off

And search now for a garment of a fluid yarn
One loose enough to leave me room to grow.
So I can travel the unknown
Without restriction
Into daunting /fearsome places I'll dare to roam.

"As important as it is to believe, it is even more important not to believe. Pure belief is too thick. There is no room for movement and no motive for reflection. When belief is rigid, it is infinitely more dangerous than unbelief. And belief becomes thick and rigid so frequently that it is often difficult for a thoughtful person to want to believe or admit to being a believer."
–Thomas Moore

So it was time to finally heal my childhood. I interviewed five therapists before I found the right one. Unlike the other five, I would not be able to pull the wool over this one's eyes to escape the pain that lay before me.

Dottie said, "Just because I was once a nun, don't let that fool you. I'll be neither too kind nor too harsh. We will work together to stay balanced and keep you going at your own pace. Okay?"

"Yes, that sounds good," I said. "You know, when I was looking for a therapist I avoided calling you because your description said something about being spiritual. I do not want any New Age talk and I don't want to get away with anything. AND I want to get through this as soon as possible. So please don't spare my feelings. I need you to call me on my stuff."

"Don't you worry about that, "she laughed and she was right. She saw through my masks and pushed me through the stories I'd been telling myself by asking the tough questions.

Together, we did deep work over the course of two years. I was diligent with my sessions and as part of the plan, she required me to attend one of the sexual assault crisis services groups that met at the local "Y." So there I sat, in a supposedly safe place to talk out our stories and get support. There were six of us and two facilitators packed into a small windowless room with stuffed animals piled in the corner. I did not want to be there. The stuffed animals and these scary looking women who seemed like they were hanging onto life by a thread only emphasized the fact that I was different—that I was okay and that I didn't really need support from them, that my abuse was nothing compared to theirs. I was a happy person and functioning fine, thank you very much.

At my next session with Dottie, I walked in confidently, sat down on her couch and delivered my prepared speech: "I really relate more to the facilitators than I do the clients. I think I was able to be supportive of the women, but I don't want to go back."

"You either dive in or you find another group," she told me. "You are not a facilitator in this group. You are here to heal, and you need to make that dive."

"You don't make it easy, do you?" I said with a smirk.

"Is that what you think this is?" she laughed.

Reluctantly, I went back rather than look for another group. I fortified myself for the following week by telling myself that I would be able to take my turn with much less pain than these other women because my experience was not as bad as theirs. My father didn't beat me up or throw me down or any of the other horrible things that made them victims, but just by association I feared that I would become one of them. I was relatively normal, pretty functional and these stories were so horrendous that I was scared, I was triggered. I wanted to hold it together but it was not to be. As I sat at the edge, afraid to push off, trying to summon my courage like the others had done, some gate opened in my head and my body followed, seeming to become fluid, and I sank down into a deep, dark pit. This was the descent I had asked for so I could finally rid myself of the effects of that trauma. I was falling.

It was deep, lonely and endless in there. I don't remember words, only sobs that seemed to come all the way up from my toes and out my skull. I was unaware of anyone. They were there, though, and seemed to be holding me inside the space of a container so that when I was ready I could come back, rise into my body, my chair, and back into the circle.

Something had given way. I was emptying into dark water and when I finally rose to the top and took a breath, it was as if I'd come up from the deep ocean having decided not to drown. I emerged into an atmosphere of the most loving energy I had ever encountered. Up until that day, I had held it together. I had not cut myself, or become an addict, or been promiscuous. I had just become an imposter passing as a normal person. Now it was like I was naked, holding nothing. What I experienced from these women was real compassion, palpable and beautiful energy that greeted me with victory. The form of compassion that I thought I'd learned on my spiritual journey was nothing compared to what these women gave me in their silence: no words, no hugs, just simple, beautiful presence. They could do it because they knew.

After weeks of engagement in that group, Dottie sanctioned my desire to become a facilitator. I did have some reticence because obviously I was not a therapist and these were deep wounds we were dealing with there, but I thought I could do it with the training provided by the organization and with Dottie there for me as a backup. They paired me with a young woman who had taken the training with me. Most of these people were younger and my partner volunteer froze by my side as we listened to the stories of

several women who had multiple personalities and many excruciating stories to tell. This, I was unfamiliar with. We had not been trained for this. One story was so devastating I could hardly bear hearing it. The room itself seemed to be stretching, tightening around us. I didn't know what to do. I wanted to be professional but all I really wanted to do was run.

I went to my next session with Dottie. "I can't do this. I am not a professional and all I want to do is cry."

"You are not expected to be a professional," she said, "and the best thing you can do is cry if that's what you're feeling. You are there to listen to the story, to empathize, to be a witness, that's all."

So I went back. As the woman told more of her story I did cry and that night all the others softened. The energy in the room shifted because of my new honesty, which made them feel safe. I had learned how to be real in the situation. I had learned how to cry with them.

After several months in this support group, it was time for me to tell my mom what I was going through. I had some lingering resentment toward her and had been keeping a modicum of distance from her all these years. She had a right to know why and she had some questions to answer for me. This was a big decision because if she refused to believe me, I understood that it might throw me back in time and trigger memories I had been repressing. But it was time. I had to do it. She came over for lunch and when we were done I told her about Daddy.

"That's impossible, I don't believe it," she said with anger and that disapproving look I knew so well.

She stood her ground and I stood mine. "Get out of my house." I screamed.

I must have sat on the couch for an hour staring at the wall. We'd just had an honest-to-God fight. I said what I felt for the first time in my life and I felt sorry and confused.

Then she called.

"I'm remembering things," were her exact words. She was crying. "I was always so happy when he was with you," she said, "that you were getting along. I never knew. I just never knew. I'm so sorry," she cried. "I should have known. Now I remember…."

That's all I needed to hear.

She came back and we held each other

tight and then tighter. Once again, I was shown evidence of the beauty of impermanence.

Mom and me just out of Nancy's hot tub.

I continued to help run support groups, man the hotline, and work with a women's psychotherapy group before I decided to create my own "Writing to Heal Workshops" out of my home. The writing was very therapeutic for the women and after a few months, I added art-making to the workshops.

I did that until I encountered one woman who was so full of rage that I was frightened of her. She was much bigger than me and was a firefighter, very tough. Here she was in my living room, unleashing torrents of rage. I kept telling her firmly to put it all on paper, everything on paper, and once she got going she poured it all out. But she had been so close to violence that I didn't want to put myself in that position again. It was too risky without deeper training. Meanwhile, I was still doing my own work with Dottie and because of her skills, humor and honesty, I soon reached another level of inner freedom.

Some Women

Some women
Walk through walls at night.

Some lie awake
Afraid to toss or turn
All frozen into silence.

Some women hold
Pillows against their eyes, against the dark
Against their ears and mouths
And all the portals
Where childhood memories are stored.

Some hold their pillows tight against the night
And fear to let them go when it turns light.

Some women wear tailored suits
Spike heels, walk briskly
Bravely into day
Making names for themselves
And at night handle razor blades
To make the blood flow
Proving their is life beneath the skin

Some can't be with others or by themselves
Some step only on the brightest stones
Daring not to peek into the dark
Wells that are the archives of themselves.

Some women tremble with each sound they hear
Tripping over obstacles of grief or fear.

Some women reflect the red and orange of the night
They walk through caves of fire and burn bright
Some of these are the same women, one leading another into solace,

The Beauty of Impermanence

Some are magical alchemists,
Turning leaden memories to gold.

Some of us are the same women.
We eat our dreams like medicine
Or fresh sweet melons
Depending on the night, depending on the
mood
And when the panic's past, the sorrow
We keep our lives moving along
Praying it is only our best
We are expected to do.

We reside here in holy love for one another,
Knowing what we have in common with each
other.

We have swallowed, alternately, periodically,
Bits of broken glass
But we have also tasted the sweet juices
Of sun ripe mangos as
We dine at the table of time.

We are the women,
Rooted in the earth the way we are
Touching with our fingertips, the heavens,

Caressing with our palms, the sky
Smoothing sweet salve over our skin
Reaching each other with our song
Longing to know where we belong
For we are the warriors,

The healers, the poets
And together out of compassion and love
We are the feminine face of God.

During this new stage of my life in which I was finishing menopause, I was beginning to reinvent myself. I decided that I had outgrown the name Marjorie. For me, it carried the heaviness of childhood, of my teachers calling on me when I didn't know the answer, of my parents' inexplicable anger. I had done enough healing work and menopause had brought with it a time to take inventory, to set new goals and actually shed my old skin and leap into a new identity. It was time to change my name.

Frances had been sitting in first place on my birth certificate all along, ignored by my parents and unknown to me until I was in my twenties when I had to apply for a liquor license to work in a New Jersey restaurant. To do that, I had to send for my birth certificate, which I had never before seen. There in black print was "Frances Marjorie Slonim."

That decided it. Instead of Marjorie Slonim, my maiden name, I would now be Frances Curtis (my married name). I always had an affinity for Saint Francis of Assisi, the animal lover, and Saint Francis deSales, the mystical writer and founder of the women's order of the Visitation of Holy Mary. I was born in St. Frances Hospital and Saint Francis deSales died on my birthday December 28 (in the year 1622). So it felt utterly natural to reinstate my true first name, and I fell into it as comfortably as falling into bed.

But now I had to ask myself, *What do I want at this point in my life? What now?*

Economic insecurity was always there and the scars that remained from Ron's affairs in Roosevelt and in Maine still held a latent sting, compounded by the way he gazed at young women wherever we happened to be. I knew that despite all of that, though, I was becoming free. Now that I had done significant healing work, that taste of freedom was rising again onto a new level. Still, I knew there was always more to come. I guess it's true that we are all works in progress. The inquiry would need to continue. There was always something new as something old dropped away.

Ron was supportive through all of my changes, including changing my name. It is always hard on the spouse when one partner is working on their self-development because it brings up hidden issues for the other. But he was good in so many other ways. His enthusiasm had been an impetus for continuing to make my WiseWoman dolls and any creative endeavors I was involved in. This was really what had brought us together in the first place. The dolls had a simple raffia base but were elaborately decorated with found and purchased objects, including silver, other metals and semi-precious stones. They were covered in cotton and drawn with paint, ink and oil stick. Some had real hair, others were made from a variety of materials. I had been selling them to women along with their names and stories as power objects and in some cases would mentor women in making their own as part of their own healing process.

Nancy, who taught writing and was a commentator for NPR, had received an Artist in Residence grant from the Isabella Stewart Gardner Museum in Boston. She was there to give talks to fifth graders and later the patrons of the museum. I had a meeting in the city during that time so I stayed with her for the night. I always kept a few dolls with me so I could show them around. The curator of the gift shop liked them and took some. They stood tall and powerful among the books and *objets d'art* on display and I was happy to leave them there for the right person to find.

It was an amazing feeling sleeping upstairs in one of the guestrooms in that elegant and historic building. After hours, we crept downstairs like two little kids sneaking in to see Santa Claus at Christmas. One of the guards let us in and gave us a tour of his precious domain. One sculpture was more beautiful than the next. All along the perimeter of the main hall were masses of orange nasturtiums dropping down against a white background, a veritable vertical garden.

"White coral bells upon a slender stalk," Nancy began to sing, and I joined her.

We slid onto the piano bench, puzzling it out on the keys, singing the song that still rang through us from our childhoods, harmonizing like we used to, our sister-voices echoing throughout the great hall. It was a stimulating visit.

It just so happened that as I was exhibiting my dolls in a Hartford gallery later that year, Ron was showing his furniture in Farmington. Both openings were on a Friday night. We were excited and proud of each other's work. In fact, Ron had built a shelving display for my dolls, which showed them at their ultimate best. Kathleen, Ron's apprentice, was still in the shop as we got dressed to go. The plan was to all go to my opening first, as it was on the way, then drive up to Ron's show.

"You go ahead," he said. "I'm not ready so we'll follow and be there in a few minutes." They showed up at my opening together, made their brief appearances then suddenly and conspiratorially dashed off, leaving me humiliated, suspicious and alone.

When I got to his opening, Ron was working the room and hardly said a word to me as he shared the spotlight with Kathleen and flirted with another young artist there, which I could see was infuriating Kathleen while I hung by myself in the background observing.

Afterwards, the three of us stopped to eat on the way home, with the two of them in her car and me driving ours. They claimed they had to discuss a potential sale and a pending commission. When the hostess seated us, Ron slid in beside Kathleen and our conversation consisted of the two of them opposing me on every subject we broached. That night was the first time I had seen this, and as I sat there practically gagging on my food, I tried to look cool because I wanted to process what was happening right before my eyes without making any sudden assumptions. It all seemed so unreal.

When we got back to the house, I went upstairs to take a bath to reflect on what just happened. As the bath was running, I looked out the window and that's when I saw the kiss. I don't know how to describe rage except that it is given the color red for a good reason; it makes the blood boil.

When I read *Sisterhood is Powerful* years prior, it had been such a revelation to discover how many of my vague dissatisfactions were right there in that anthology. It crystalized for me that the personal is indeed political. I had worked to be strong in other ways. I had pushed for equal rights for all women, for independence and freedom from the status quo but now I was beginning to face the fact that I was not an independent woman and I could end up on the street because of money (or the lack thereof), the lifestyle I had chosen, and how my disability had all worked together to show me how vulnerable I really was.

I had to swallow the suffering and keep the faith that I'd come out on the other side, and I had to remember that everything has its reasons. But first, I just had to boldly look at the truth while trying not to see myself as a failure. As Lucile Clifton says in her poem, "The Light that Came to Lucille Clifton":

"You might as well answer the door, my child, the truth is furiously knocking."

Years ago, a wise astrologer told me that there is a crossroad in life. Somewhere in our fifties, we choose from the deepest part of ourselves whether to live or die. We choose to live fully or roll away down the other road. The first choice gives us a second wind, an enthusiasm for the changes, a plunging into life from a new and mature perspective. The other is the one set before us continually, the expectations that life is downhill from here, that opportunities have shriveled, health is on the decline, wrinkles are ugly and gray hair is dull. One has gone about as far as one is going to go, and if you haven't made it by now, forget about it.

"So which one will you take?" That's the perpetual question.

With my foray into deeper healing, I'd made the decision to live because some part of me knew that there was a lot more in store for me. Without thinking about it, I had already chosen the road to live . . . or so I thought. For me, continuing on with drive and vitality was a no brainer. I saw myself

as only half-baked and half lived. I wasn't done. I had paid too many dues and there were bound to be some rewards down the line. To slow down now would be defeat and a cop out on myself.

Yet despite all of these truths I had been encountering, there was something deeper hiding in the cracks, something that I had yet to discover.

The talk of the town was that this Raphael, a Nicaraguan shaman was coming to town. A psychotherapy group had invited him to visit from New Mexico where he now lived and practiced. There was much excitement. All of the healers, therapists and New Agers had come to hear him speak and sign up for private sessions with him. The place was packed. He gave a delightful talk, powerful and sweet. His words and his transmission captivated us all, and more people than he could handle wanted time with him, enough to have to bring him back at a later date.

Even though I had left The Path, I was still saturated with its teachings and had gone to hear the shaman's talk out of curiosity. In my arrogant certainty, I was "above all this" but still, I was intrigued. After the presentation, I jumped in line with the rest of the crowd. I was there to thank him for his purity and innocence. He was very refreshing. I had no interest in a session but I wanted to show my respects. When it was my turn to step before him and thank him for his talk, he said simply, "I want to see you."

"Oh," I said, surprised and somewhat flattered, "I'm not here for an appointment. I just wanted to thank you for your talk."

Again he said, "I want to see you."

"Oh, no," I said again. "I don't have the money and I am fine. I'm fine, really."

"Come and see me at one tomorrow," he insisted with an urgency that I couldn't refuse. "No money needed."

That was worrisome because I had been waiting for the results of a biopsy taken the day before that wouldn't be back for several more days. I had been through breast cancer scares before and it had always turned out to be nothing so I hadn't been concerned until I walked away wondering why he had singled me out. When something comes at me three times like that, I pay attention.

I brought the required supplies and a gift, as was the custom. I brought him one of my favorite dolls. He was delighted. He told me that his grandmother and mother were both curanderas and my doll reminded him of his grandmother.

"Would you mind if I gave it to her?" he asked. I felt honored. Then I was asked to lie down on a blanket. I didn't know what to expect. He then began to drum and rattle and chant in another language while circling slowly around me. I felt ridiculous, like a cliché in a grade B movie and soon began to bolt. Then suddenly something shifted, as if I had been slammed back down by an invisible hand. I knew this was no joke and my little voice told me to be still; there was nothing to fear and nothing to laugh about. Without any further conversation, Raphael went straight to the breast in question and hovered there for what seemed a long time.

Something was happening deep inside of my body and I heard the words inside my head, "You better start listening to your wishes. Listen carefully, not the wishes you think you want but the desire beneath that." I heard the words, and became still. Then it was done.

When the diagnosis for breast cancer came a few days later, I was shocked but not as shocked as I might have been without the shaman's concern. Who isn't shocked when they receive such a diagnosis? No one in my family had ever had cancer. They were heart condition people. So where did this come from?

As fate would have it, years prior I had been driving home from somewhere distant and, for some reason, was listening to a tape by the writer and pacifist Deena Metzger. It was about her experience with breast cancer. I remember she said that she must unconsciously be at war with herself and this was alarming to her because she was such a dedicated peace activist, and wondered how could she be attacking her own body.

"Because," she said, "that's what cancer is."

I don't remember who loaned me that tape or why but I had been intrigued by her inquiry into that question and her deep honesty with her answers. So, now, years later, when it happened to me, something in me remembered Deena's wisdom.

The day of the diagnosis, the doctor urgently walked me into a conference room, where waiting for me was an oncologist, radiologist, social worker and two others whose functions I don't remember. They were my new team, there to help me devise a plan for my treatment. I was by myself and overwhelmed and told them I needed two weeks to think about my next step. Because my tumor was small they didn't argue too much.

"Two weeks only," the doctor cautioned. First I had to go home and cry. Then I would have to think about how I would even get the treatment without insurance. And then I would have to learn about all my options before I let anyone touch me.

I bought and borrowed a bunch of books on the subject and began to read. I found all sorts of contradictory recommendations. I called my own doctor and some alternative practitioners I knew and consulted with each of them, creating a team of advisors.

Adam said something to me that would stick forever: "Mom, you have the inner and outer resources. If anyone can beat this, you can."

The certitude of Adam's words made me believe him. And then I remembered, years prior, reading Audre Lourdes' *Cancer Journals*, and I set about to journal fiercely, too, listening intently to what might be a hidden desire, letting the words come through a stream of consciousness and I went into prayer simply asking for guidance and the ability to hear deeply.

During two weeks of intense journaling, meditating and praying, what came up for me was depressingly clear. I knew that I could not depend on Ron to grow old with me with that restlessness and roving eye of his. He would never take care of me but originally wasn't this part of why I was attracted to him in the first place, forcing me to become strong? Had I set all this in motion?

I recalled one night just a few months before we were sitting at some art event and this young woman came running over to Ron and kissed him on the lips, passing by me as if I didn't exist. He was all lit up over this "girl" as they acted like they had some secret going on that she didn't care if I knew about. He ate it up and whenever we'd go anywhere there'd always be another one, some "skinny girl" with tiny breasts, a major contrast to me, so I had good reason to feel insecure with these young ones always fluttering around him. In all possibility he could one day walk out for greener pastures and I could become one of those street women pushing a shopping cart down some sidewalk, piled high with all my possessions. That possibility led me to believe that I could not survive on my own—which was bad enough, but worse was the conviction I held that I would r*ather be dead than be a burden on my children.*

That script, I discovered, was hiding deep in my psyche until now when the meditating, prayer and journaling brought it to the surface. I could now see clearly that I was nurturing a death wish and my body was complying. *Holy Moly.* The words that covered my journal pages showed me what lived beneath my awareness. I had always felt a little lazy because I hadn't meditated regularly or stuck to any one spiritual practice. I would have given myself a "D" in discipline. Much later I realized, though, that writing was my true way of meditating. The revered old yogis and masters had their ways of doing it and their disciples followed, down through the generations. I tried many of these methods but my mind would go rampant trying to sit in lotus position or other suggested ways of quieting. But one day it dawned on me that these were all techniques handed down by men, holy men, beautiful men but it simply was not my way as a woman.

After feeling inadequate long enough and finally delving into inquiry around this, I began to see that women are different from men even when it comes to meditation. Many of us have naturally invented our own ways of connecting with the Divine without ever naming them. I began to realize that my deepest connections happened when I made up love songs to God in the tub or in the car, when I sang my heart out with whatever was in there at the time. That was meditation, too. I began to realize the writing in my journals and writing my poems were a form of meditation also. Writing had always been there for me, not only as a practice but also as a form of serving whatever cause moved me.

So it doesn't matter to me now as long as it brings me connection, love, and reverence for the Divine and as a result the sense of the Divine's reverence for me.

Through the writing, I learned how amazing is the extent to which the unconscious can take control. At the top of the mind, we think we want something, but underneath is where reality actually rises into manifestation. I thought I was loving the life I was living but despite the image we cherished of ourselves, we were not living the freewheeling, joyful life that everyone seemed to admire about the two of us. It is such

a paradox. I guess what I had been doing all that time—moving around, changing jobs, making art, going without a bra, wearing my hair out to there, looking cool and laid back to the rest of the world—was, in reality, living in denial. In many ways, it was real but there was so much more to uncover. I had to acknowledge that I was living in dread, in shadow, in fear of something that did not ever need to happen. I was waiting for some heavy shoe to drop without articulating that to myself. I was a living contradiction. I was a pathological optimist, numb to my innermost feelings.

As soon as I realized that, I knew what I had to do about my cancer treatment. I convinced the hospital to put me on a payment plan. The financial guy was great. He suggested that I not choose my treatment according to the cost and encouraged me to schedule whatever I needed. Radiation alone would have cost $27,000 for ten minutes for six weeks, to say nothing of the chemo, the Tamoxifin and the lymph node extraction, but he insisted I do what I needed to do. Despite the cancer team's best efforts, I decided, after all my reading and all my consultations outside of the hospital, that I would have the surgery, nurture my body with the best possible foods and supplements and, most importantly, revise my thinking, and that would be the end of it. No chemo, no radiation, no Tamoxifin, and no messing with lymph nodes. I would have the surgery, period, and I would never, ever have cancer again because I would no longer carry that hideous death wish around in my head and in my body.

But I did a few other things, too. During that time I had met a young Indian woman at a pow wow. She and her husband had a booth displaying their beautiful ceremonial leather regalia. They also had medicine bags on display. I was so taken by the power and beauty of those little bags I ordered one for my baby granddaughter, Jessica. Sara, the maker, wanted specific information about the baby before she proceeded to make the little bag using her intuition to bring in Jess' essence. All these years later, now at nineteen Jessica still considers the bag a treasure. But more than the bag, there was a reason Sara had come into my life. She was good at other things, too. She knew about the medicinal properties of herbs and had begun to create programs for young Native women to learn about them. Among her

herbal wisdom she knew about a blend of herbs that were said to help cure cancer and she boldly recommended them to me. I had my doubts but at the same time I had faith in the natural ways of indigenous people so I bought some tea and a little handmade booklet that showed how exactly to make it which ended up being no simple affair. Ron and I spent hours brewing this tea then pouring it into sterilized brown beer bottles and sealed them up. I drank and drank of it for weeks.

The tea story turned out to be about a nurse who worked in a cancer ward and had a patient she was very fond of. The traditional medical model was not working for her and the patient was failing. The nurse, who was Native American, knew of a "folk" remedy called essiac tea. As the patient departed from the hospital to go home to die, the nurse whispered to her about this tea. The story goes that as a last resort the patient took the tea and miraculously recovered. Later her healing story was validated by many other healing stories regarding this tea, so I had my hopes for the same.

Another thing I did as part of my hopeful recovery was contact a doctor up in Canada who had supposedly created a formula that worked

219

wonders for getting rid of cancer. He had been a doctor in France during World War Two but had lost his documents, including his license to practice. Still, under the radar he had developed a so-called cure. Since I knew and trusted my source for this guy, who was a doctor, I went ahead and for forty dollars ordered the formula and also made an appointment to go to Canada to see him. He was booked far in advance so I settled for an appointment months away. The medicine arrived and Ron had to give me injections into the groin that lasted for twenty minutes each. Of course, it was not something I looked forward to each day and neither did Ron. For me it was quite painful. For him it was a drag to come upstairs, take time out from his work in the shop with his precious helper, Kathleen. I would have to beg him each day to bring up ice and wait while I numbed the site before he stuck me with the needle. He was annoyed that I bothered him for the ice. It took too long. I thought he was hoping I would die so he could be with his apprentice forever. But I would not die. Ten days before my appointment with the doctor in Canada I reminded him about the trip.

"Oh, I can't go now," he said. "I have too much work to do." (Code for "I want to stay here with Kathleen.") "You can drive up by yourself, can't you?"

No, of course I couldn't but the serum I had been taking may have been enough. Between the journaling that revealed my death wish discovery, the shaman, the injections and the tea and—oh, I almost forgot, at the last minute it dawned on me that I needed to make my own Wise Woman Healing Doll—I have no idea what cured me of cancer. Maybe it was all of these things but I strongly feel it was mostly because of the discovery I made in my journal and how I was able to reverse that desire to die rather then be a burden on my children. I deeply wanted to live.

I would never recommend any or all of these methods to anyone else. Everyone has to find their own way because every situation is unique, and every body is unique but this certainly felt like the right way for me. It was all a leap of faith and maybe a little inner guidance. I was choosing life on a more conscious level this time, all the way down to my bones. I had discovered what I consider the real cause of this disease into my body because I know that the mind, emotions and body are not separate from each other, that all the parts communicate with each other all of the time.

Within that month, after all my research and combinations of healing methods, I had the surgery, and that day twenty years ago marked the end of cancer for me. Healing had occurred and I will always be grateful to all who had a part in it. Sara had become a friend and, by the way, she bought one of my dolls to add to her collection of Indian artifacts. I was honored.

At times, people had asked about the dolls, the wild ones and the calm ones, the fierce and the beautiful, the textiles from all over the world, the beads, the hair, the amulets. People asked if each doll represented a certain culture, tribe, clan or country. Are they African or Indian or Gypsy? Did you co-opt them from different cultures not your own? I say no. They are me. All the things I've ever seen and loved from whatever culture, I've internalized. It's all become a part of me, and the dolls were an expression of my own voice. I think in some ways we all live inside each other. Everything we see and hear is inside of us and we always nurture what we love. From that, I believe, art emerges.

Storm

Truth or Consequences:
If Only I Had Known

New Mexico, Mom, 9/11, Adjusting the Trajectory, Entering Seminary

It was time once again for me to get away by myself. This Kathleen thing was too much to bear. I knew it wasn't love; it was infatuation, an illusion, a vanity and I wanted to save my marriage. There was much to think about. I would fly into Albuquerque and decide where to go once I got settled in my rental car. I shoved my bags in the back seat then triple checked my maps. Everything that anyone had ever talked about was north: Santa Fe, Taos, Chaco Canyon, but I heard that Silver City was cheaper and attracting artists at that time so I took the road less traveled. I drove south.

I had come to the Southwest to find a way for Ron and me, or if worse came to worse, just for me. In any case, something major had to change. I snuggled in for the miles ahead with my down pillow scrunched in behind my back and reaching up over the armrest, a perfect comfort zone. I donned my shades. The road was wide open, straight, and dazzling from the sun.

My wild, diverse journeying companions were also strewn in the back seat: Rumi through Coleman Barks, The Stones, Aretha, Thelonious, Tosca, Krishna Das, and Elaine Boosler. But it turned out the car had no CD player, and only fundamentalist preachers and songs of lost love blasted the airwaves up and down the dial. I didn't need either but as soon as I was safely on 25 South, I started singing, "Amazing grace, how sweet the sound" at the top of my lungs.

I planned to stop in Socorro for lunch then head down to a town named Truth or Consequences, where I had made reservations at a hostel right on the Rio Grande. On the map, Socorro looked like a good-sized little town and I had heard that Judy Chicago, an icon of feminist art, maker of *The Dinner Party,* lived there. Wouldn't it be great to bump into her?

I felt good. I was alone, a little bit scared, and a hundred times more excited. Everything was where it needed to be—my water, my gum, my Trip-tick, my jacket, my phone numbers and directions to each destination. I was cruisin'.

Soon I approached signs to Socorro. The main drag was one long strip with streetlights—

motels, a laundromat, hamburger joints, car wash, low buildings—no hills, no curves, but in the distance, mountains—beautiful, beautiful, mountains. My stomach was making noises so I chose a little mom-and-pop place. There was a lone cowboy type at the counter and all the tables and booths were empty. It was an odd hour to be eating so I figured that was why the place was empty. I took my seat at the counter for a little conversation, a little local color. The server greeted me with a "howdy ma'am" and took my order. Through a window to the kitchen I watched a young boy put my salad together. He didn't stop sneezing the whole time.

Outside the sky was clouding over fast. I gazed out the window at the town and watched the transition from light to dark. The guy behind the counter delivered my salad with a nod.

"Travelin' far?" he asked.

"Not very," I replied.

"Good," he said. "This is unusual weather for these parts."

With a quick ripple of anxiety, I looked out again then down at my salad. The tomatoes were sickly pink, and the cucumbers and onions were wilted, but the lettuce and green pepper rings seemed crisp. All I could think of was that sneezing kid and the ominous weather. I didn't want to be a snooty tourist by not eating, but the weather gave me an excuse.

Thunder was rumbling in and I needed to get to Truth or Consequences before dark. I jumped up and paid my six dollars and fifty-two cents, my first expenditure out of my tiny budget, and I didn't even eat one bite.

Damn! I had checked for weather with Triple A and the New Mexico Tourist Bureau. They both said there'd be fine weather this month. Even my little travel book told me so. Now the sky was deepening into blackness while lightening careened across the mountains, right in front of me, long, jagged and highly charged. Not that close, but I was headed in its direction.

I turned on the radio again but now even the preacher wasn't getting through. At this point, I would have loved his company for there was no one on the road but one truck ahead of me. I decided to stick close. In fact, I thought, maybe I'd get off at the next exit. Truth or Consequences could wait.

Back in Socorro, it felt safe, familiar, sheltering. I cruised the street again, stopping for the night at the first motel I found that had an AAA Motor Club discount.

It had cleared by morning so I started out for Truth or Consequences. After an uneventful trip, I checked in to the hostel and the owner lead me to an aging camper, which I would be sharing with two other women, a curtain drawn between our sleeping quarters.

After settling into this stark little space, I wandered out to survey my surroundings. Situated five feet from the Rio Grande were three one-person hot tubs overflowing with running water from the hot springs. These ancient springs were naturally between ninety-eight to one-hundred-fifteen degrees Fahrenheit, with traces of more than three dozen minerals, though I didn't know any of that when I made my reservation. I was just looking for a place to lay my head and catch some Southwest color. All three tubs were occupied by young blonde women smoking and speaking a northern European language that I could not identify. I waited my turn and excitedly climbed in. All worries evaporated with the liquid heat. I was thrilled in my anonymity and the proximity to this Rio Grande I'd seen in all those Westerns throughout my life.

All during the windy night, the camper rocked and shook and stunk of stale cigarettes. I rose early in the morning, grabbed a coffee and buttered roll, and hit the Turquoise Trail in my Geo rental, heading toward Silver City. I had no idea that I was about to approach a wilderness area with endless hairpin curves. The signs told me to keep my speed at ten miles an hour. I picked my way along the narrow road, excruciatingly aware that to my right, steep cliffs rose into a cloudless sky, and to my left a drop-off, way down, onto the tips of evergreens and tangled branches where no one would ever find me if I happened to miss a curve. I muttered myself along, aware of the smile on my face from the exhilaration of this fine line I was traveling alone.

Out of the corner of my eye, I saw movement. Passing me on the right was a herd of something. I dared not take my eyes off the constant curves of the road for a better look but they were four-legged, with horns, rapidly trotting along the narrow edge alongside my car. According to a sign I saw, I was somewhere in the Guila Wilderness.

I held my breath from the gorgeousness of the earth I was moving over and my slow movement into the unknown. It all felt electric. Then I saw the first signs of civilization—a few trailers and a few cars parked up on a hill—and I exhaled.

I had made reservations in an historic lodge in Bear Mountain that turned out to be nothing like the photos from its glory days. Our communal dinner all seemed to be out of a can, everything was bland and the bevvy of guests along with myself were shocked.

The widow who owned the place laid out some very strict rules as if we were seventh graders. But the good thing was I had been seated at a table with a charming couple from Chicago who invited me to explore the cliff dwellings with them.

It was a delightful outing even though I wasn't able to climb the ancient, fragile stairs for a better look. Even so, the sun-spattered trail was alive and lush with botanicals of all kinds and I sat on a rock studying the miniscule bits of life surrounding me while the couple from Chicago explored the ruins above. When we returned to the lodge, I showed them my dolls, which I had with me because friends back home had said they would go over big out there. These Chicago folks invited me to their second home in Santa Fe where they wanted to introduce the dolls to a friend who had a gallery.

Also, Raphael, the shaman who had helped me in Hartford, offered to meet me in Albuquerque on my way back north and take me on a journey into his sacred mountains where we would meet his grandmother. He was third generation *curandero* (as I've mentioned) and I so looked forward to the privilege of meeting his mother and grandmother.

An arts festival was in full swing in Silver City with lots of music, crafts and southwestern food. I spoke with a few artists to find out more about the area and its potential for Ron and me.

But wait a minute. Isn't this what I did before? Didn't I drag us out of the quagmire of Roosevelt to Maine because of his affair? And did that change any behavior? No. So why would I think a new place this time would do any good? We take our problems with us wherever we go so I pondered and daydreamed and pondered some more until I decided to make no decisions, to just look and see and imagine what might be. But the image of that kiss kept haunting me. Maybe I should move here by myself like I moved from Boston to New York. Step into a new world alone. I've done it before but it certainly wasn't my first choice.

I called Ron to see what he was feeling and despite myself maybe sell him on the idea of moving. "Do you remember how beautiful New Mexico was, how much we loved it, that Christmas with the kids?" I asked him.

"Yeah, it was nice," he said.

"I met some artists who said they were part of a vibrant community and the art culture is growing fast down here. Tourists are starting to come south and it's affordable," I stammered. "I walked into a real estate office just for kicks. The agent showed me this sprawling Mexican-style ranch. You would love it, Ron. It has…"

"I'm going with Kathleen," he blurted out. "We're together now."

What? I couldn't believe it. I pleaded my case until my face was red and dripping with grief. I was a pitiful sight as my body rapidly collapsed into a severe case of bronchitis over the next few days. I drove right back to Albuquerque and caught the next plane home, forgoing Santa Fe, the gallery and my journey with the shaman.

When I stepped off the plane, we talked for hours about love versus lust and reality versus fantasy. After all, he was how much older than

this "girl"? In the end, there was nothing for me
to do except back off.

If Only I Had Known

If only I had known there was a difference
Between theory and practice,
That the political
Doesn't always have to be the personal,
I would have said "no."

But when the very, very, young woman
With the turquoise eyes
Came for her interview
And convinced Ron
She was just what he needed in an apprentice,
When she told him how she had researched
The files of the Arts Commission
And decided he was the best,

And when she insisted
That despite her small size
She was strong enough to do the job
Because she had once been a gymnast,

He was convinced.
And I should have said "no."
Not because of her qualifications
And her cuteness
But because I know Ron.

Still I didn't say no,
Because, to tell you the truth,
I had fought for over twenty years
For gender equity.
I had railed against tradition
That said women couldn't be
Firefighters, soldiers, doctors,
Politicians, garbage collectors, and cops.
So how could I, of all people, say "no"
To this would-be woodworker?
And how could I say "no"
When I have my own two strong daughters
And would fight like hell
To open any doors for them?
So how could I have said "no"
Just because she was cute.

If only I had known
That you shouldn't always put your money
Where your mouth is.

If only I had known that thirty-seven years
Isn't necessarily for keeps.

But I did know, of course. Soon after, as I was making plans to leave the house and the town, Ron changed his mind.

"I *will* break up with her," he said. "I'll do it right away."

Then I got a call from her, the woman who had been eating her brown bag lunches with us and bringing me fabric and beads for my dolls and talking to me as though we were best friends. Now she had something she wanted to say. We met in a neutral place and over a cup of coffee and she began to apologize. I thought she was graciously stepping out of the picture, but instead she said she was sorry she had taken Ron away and she felt oh, so badly.

"That's not the case," I told her, "because we have resolved it and Ron is going nowhere with you." *Are we still in junior high?* I thought.

"That's impossible," she retorted. "He said that we would be together."

"Well, let's go ask him," I suggested.

We drove our separate cars down to the gallery where he was working. I thought he would die when he saw us together. When we asked him about his plan, he said something about his commitment to marriage and the mortified Kathleen ran out of the building as fast as her gymnast legs could carry her.

But that wasn't the end of it. He still managed to convince her that he was leaving me, and from his sneaking around, I saw that he was still undecided. He, too, poor thing, was in pain with conflict enough to make this piece, which he called ACHE.

From a conflicted heart.

229

The Beauty of Impermanence

I began looking at our history:

Trading Places

Miles of flat land, blonde grass
Red buttes, antelope herds,
Bald eagle silhouetted against sun
New Mexico

Now, since we've come back
To this doldrum town
The snow has thawed
Only to freeze again
This stubborn suburb in Connecticut,
It's warplanes, submarines, and sirens screaming
back and forth.

Zig-zags from the undersoles
Of our boots press in
Match the ribbings and skiddings of our tires
Still there is no money
And the local news is rotten.

I used to want to leave this place
And move back to Maine

where snow stays clean.

packed hard against the road
Where the plow came through.
Stacking up walls on either side
To make a dazzling tunnel.

That winter hush
From the whole galaxy,
Embraced our place on the hill.

We'd return from somewhere late night,
The children looking to the stars
From their wrappings of blankets,
It might have been six below

Now we hear the house is up for sale again.
It stops me in my tracks

But no, that cannot be
It's New Mexico that calls,
That tangerine sky
That land, *El Capitan Mountains,*

all that space between one thing
And another—

Yet it is with reverence
For the place in Maine that I conjure
Cold forests, black bears moving through early
morning mist
And the afternoon discoveries of pre-digested
blackberries
In clumps among the apple trees,

We were in our thirties then,
So how we got to here and now
I'll never know,

Me, I'll be leaving soon, thirsty for the sun,
I'll trade the slender white-tailed deer,
The tamaracks, the few remaining elms
And all my favorite maple trees

For the big-eared deer that winked at me on
Christmas Day
From her hillock on the Turquoise Trail.

I'll trade all my treasured beasts of this

Northeast
For just one of those red and yellow license
plates
They give you when you move
To New Mexico

And I will cry going and coming
So many things are beautiful.

But in the end, New Mexico was unrealistic, as it was too far from family and friends.

So I drove to one of my favorite little towns in Massachusetts about an hour away and took a room in a bed and breakfast just for the night. I needed to develop a strategy for myself. After a night of rampant scenarios in my racing brain and an abundance of tears, I jumped out of bed, grabbed the classifieds while avoiding eye contact with the overly exuberant proprietor of the B&B and directly secured an apartment down the road, right next door to a quaint little library. How perfect would it be if I could land a job there? After all, I had excellent library experience in New York City. No question. I would have to quit my job as an employment counselor. That, too, is ironic, isn't it? Me, an employment counselor.

The hour-long drive into the Berkshires would become a harrowing experience in the winter so I would put my hopes on the library.

I was creating visions of life as a monk in this tiny but adequate place. I would bring nothing with me but my computer and all I would do is stay holed up there and write. Of course, there was the matter of the job but I would do whatever it took. I had a good feeling about the library and if not I'd take a job in McDonald's or Shop-Rite or anything that would free me from my old life.

When the critical moment came, a week later when Ron thought I'd never have the courage to leave, I began to pack up my essentials. It was then he had another change of heart. Now it was his turn to cry, apologize, beg and promise, and that is what he did.

I was ready to leave despite all this sorrow on both our parts and then again it seemed so much easier to stay. The library was fully staffed, as much as their budget allowed and I had not yet found anything else. Much as I was accepting the fantasy of my life as a recluse in that tiny apartment, staying put was, by far, the easier path. A copout? Maybe. Maybe not.

But this would require new and radical conditions. I had to have my own space. Trust had to be earned back. I was not about to sleep with a husband who had been intimate with someone else. Not only the physical thing was repulsive to me but the fact that she was more than thirty-five years younger than him and his student. It stunk. Time had to intervene before we could be together again, if ever, and the prospect of being a recluse in my own home had some appeal.

Meanwhile, I was happy to take over the bedroom. I bought white down bedding and soft, fluffy pillows, set up my office, and lived in that room with a new kind of ease. Ron was assigned the guest room.

For a while we lived like strangers under one roof. Then we started eating together. And then over time, little by little, trust began to build and life began to almost normalize. We both had our work and our passions. Ron was now a serious martial artist, I had my nine-to-five or -six or -seven job and my metaphysical explorations but we found time for the little things. Laughter came back as we emerged into a new way of being together. I convinced myself that we were repairing this union that had begun in that makeshift wedding thirty-six years ago.

Meanwhile, on another front, because of growing health limitations, Mom was ready for assisted living where her parents had once finished their own earthly journeys and where many of her acquaintances had taken up residence. She had been in her treasured apartment for many years until she had outlived her three best friends and couldn't bear to be in that building any longer. So she moved out of Hartford to Martha's Vineyard where Nancy had been living for years by then. And now it was time, but it wasn't easy to get into the Hebrew Home, as there was a long waiting list, so I spontaneously invited her to live with us while she waited.

Days turned into weeks, weeks turned into months. Even though we had come together that afternoon on my living room couch talking about the abuse and all the realizations that were the effect of it, despite myself, I was still hanging onto some resentment toward her. After all, she didn't take any chances to nurture me or provide any warmth for either of us girls growing up. She was too frightened to do so. But the day she moved in, all of that vanished. It was as if we had always been close, loving each other unconditionally and it was a great feeling. Nothing had been forgiven because no one was to blame. It was as if a wall had dissolved.

I was able to take a leave of absence from my job. I brought her juice, eggs and English muffins, her coffee (black), and the paper each morning in our sun-drenched porch that she loved. Ron was good to her, too. Up until then they had always brought out the worst in each other. I think she must have known his inclinations to wander so it was always tense when she was with us. But now it was good.

What Our Eyes Miss

Out the sunporch window
First I see the goldfinch,
Their feathers getting yellower each day
It's been a long winter,
Almost April
And still three feet of snow

Between the still bare branches
A purple finch perches,
Eyes darting back and forth.
I take my mother's hand,

Pull her up to watch the flutter
Going on between feeders

When splash,
A frantic scramble on the snow,
Like ink spilled on paper
Or birds ensnared in sudden tantrums.
I cannot make it out.

Then whoosh,
Gone,
Quick as that,
The grackle,
Tiny now,
Tucked up against the belly of the hawk,
Against a firmament of gray

Predator took prey
Right before our eyes,
Leaving us dumbfounded,
Leaving us four black feathers on the snow.

"Why don't you stay forever?" I asked Mom.
"We'll cancel your reservation at the home."
"But who will find me when I die?" she asked.
"I will," I said. "Who better to find you?"

And so we agreed.

One day, I was puttering around downstairs making breakfast while Mom was upstairs getting ready for the day when I heard her yell from the bedroom.

"There's been a horrible accident. A plane just crashed into one of the Twin Towers."
We sat in front of the TV with our coffee, covering our mouths in horror. We watched as over and over again the towers burned, the smoke, people running, screaming and jumping. We watched with the rest of the world in agonizing disbelief.

A few days later, I was online when I discovered a workshop that was being presented at Fordham University in New York. It was being given by an international organization that deals with trauma all over the world. I was compelled to go so I called my friend, Carmella, and the next day we made the trip. We weren't allowed to drive into the city so we parked nearby and hopped a train. The streets were eerily empty.

Participants lined the halls waiting for the facilitators to come and unlock the room. Next to me, leaning against the wall, was one of the most striking young women I had ever seen. She had black curly hair and the blackest, brightest eyes. She began a conversation and right away we seemed to make a connection with the kind of small talk one would expect under such circumstances.

The room was packed with trauma experts, clergy of all kinds, social workers, teachers, psychiatrists and a variety of healers. One teacher described how she rushed to the window with all the children as they watched the smoke and chaos. She held back tears as she described watching the buildings where these children's parents worked and how she tried to respond to questions for which there were no answers.

A woman walked in. Her hair was a mess and her clothes were disheveled. *How is she going to be able to help anyone,* thought my fat ego. As it turned out, she had just spent two days and three nights helping out on the sidewalks of Ground Zero. She was ruffled in shock like the rest of the city, and a rush of heat crept over me to think I had made a judgment about her or anyone else.

During the workshop, I felt a horrible pounding in my chest and a fire rising up inside of me. This, I knew, was my queue to speak up and say what I was thinking. These people were all professionals and I didn't want to open my mouth in this packed room, but the pounding got worse and I had no choice but to speak. The words spilled out of me without me even knowing what they were. When I was on The Path, I could speak before thousands because I felt certain about everything, but that day, I would have given anything to just be still and listen. I can't remember what I said but a thunderous silence blanketed the room and the dialogue turned in a new direction. It was impossible to understand the full scope of what had happened at Ground Zero, but this community of shared voices helped me to feel that there might be a way forward for us all.

When the workshop was over, the striking young woman and the one with the ruffled hair invited me to join them at Starbucks. Carmella agreed and we ended up sipping lattes and talking for hours. Everyone was grieving. Everyone was turned inside out from this tragedy but there was a commitment on the part of all to find ways to come together and heal.

As I learned that day over lattes, these two women were recent graduates of The New Seminary in New York. After a marathon of shared storytelling, they insisted the seminary would be a great place for me to go, that I would be a perfect fit and that I could make a contribution. The idea of me going back to school at that stage of my life seemed crazy. Still, when I got home, I did two things. I bought an American flag. The right wing had co-opted the red, white and blue, taken it for their own, preached that they were the only patriots and the only believers in God. That was not true. My patriotism was ignited and I made that statement by flying the flag on our front porch. Secondly, I Googled The New Seminary, was impressed by the faculty, printed out an application, and without a second thought sent it in.

I had been inspired. Destiny had called, finding myself at that workshop then connecting with those women so deeply. What's really funny is that I never saw them again and I don't even remember their names, but the Divine was at work and my life on that day began a shift that would change me forever.

That same week, the nursing home called. They had a room ready for Mom and, much to my surprise, she jumped on it.

"I'm useless here," she said. "I need to be with my peers. I can help out there. I can have friends my age and you can go back to work. You will have plenty to do now with school."

With endless hugs we packed her up and brought her to her new home, only a mile away, where at ninety she thrived as a volunteer and found her passion in the art classes and with her new roommate, red-headed Libby, who clicked around in heels and earrings and bright red lipstick, playing the piano and singing in her vaudevillian voice at all the nursing home events. She was four years older than Mom and had outlived two other roommates. She and Mom became immediate sisters who held each other's hands, smoothed each other's foreheads, looked into each other's eyes like lovers and shared each other's secrets.

Although I maintained my privacy in my own room at home, Ron and I had been sharing our mornings, afternoons and evenings lovingly. Somehow, good behavior and joy had crept back into our lives. In 2003, we celebrated our forty-third anniversary by reviewing the scenarios we had squeezed into those years—all the changes, joys and sorrows we had shared, especially our love and joy for our children and grandchildren.

This poem celebrates the miracle that we

were still together and that we did have a lot to celebrate, the moments that acted as the glue that held us together, such as it was.

Me, Then You, the Black Belt

I mourn, then welcome the not knowing
I knew so much once, was certain as rain
And then it turned,
Dissolved like grains
Of sugar in black tea

Nothing left to claim, hang on to.
As far as beliefs go
Everything seems true.
"Sorrow is inseparable from joy."

You can hear a tune by Bessie,
A riff by Lester
And you shiver to the bone.
Then that's gone.

They say being uncertain
Is a sign of wisdom
At noon I question nothing
At midnight, everything.

Cardinals dart about,
Red and reddish brown
Against the snow, against the dark
Frozen rhododendron leaves.
They know exactly what they do.

Today in the morning, in the kitchen
I grind beans, squeeze grapefruit, mill about.
Across the room we grin at each other
You come close, shoot out a front kick,
Duck my punch and we start out the week.
I think maybe that's what counts with God,
Beginning the week . . . grinning.

Forty-three years . . . my God, I remembered going to Ron's parents' fiftieth anniversary and they seemed so old. Living with someone that long seemed impossible. Now there were seventeen in our family—three kids, ten grandkids and us—and we both felt that after all that living, we were at the beginning again. We were and are evolving, and with this new millennium, the world is evolving.

We soon learned that al-Qaeda, a Muslim extremist group, had been the perpetrators of the 9/11 tragedies and it brought to mind Blaise Pascal who said, "Men never do evil so completely and cheerfully as when they do it from religious conviction." This was applicable to so many incidents but nothing in recent years like this.

Over the following two years of study at seminary, we learned that this was not Islam. This had been an attack by people who, it seemed, had co-opted the religion and used it for their own aberrant means. We also learned about—and, for me, the biggest surprise was—what religious scholars had written about Judaism, bringing me a new understanding and a new respect and connection with my own roots. I was pleasantly surprised to learn that the early Jews believed in divine intervention, not a common belief in the world. This meant to me that anything could happen at any time for any reason and yet we always have free will. How does that come together, I wondered. I also learned about the impact Jews had on the world with their early insistence on justice and the potential for social change. Up until that time, life was simply accepted as it was without the possibility of transformation. Apparently, the concept of

justice and social change had not yet entered the collective consciousness before the Hebrew prophets brought it forth.

In this still early part of the 21st Century, when things seem to have gone wild in the U.S. and all over the world, it makes me long for divine intervention. Will humanity be able to get it together before it's too late? Will Israel follow the teachings of the prophets and embrace justice for all? Can they find a just way to peace?

To me at this moment in 2016, so much is broken, not only in the Middle East but all around the world. Our government is broken. Threats are coming from within and without the United States and the earth herself is struggling for survival. So much is heartbreaking. I continue to look for answers, in my own head and in the hearts of the people I meet, in books and magazines and online. There is so much to learn, so much to do, so much to change that it becomes overwhelming. But this is what I do know: That possibility with a capital "P" floats around us, in between us, above and below us. It floats around waiting to be grasped and brought down into reality through minds that are open and still. That's what keeps me hopeful. When I was on The Path, it was taught that everything was in order and as co-workers with God, we needn't be activists. All we had to be was love. My question has always been, "but is that enough? " John Lennon said it is.

I discovered that there is a word in Judaism called "tikkun." It means: "it is each person's job to help repair a broken world." But on The Path, we learned that nothing is broken, that everything is in balance whether it appears that way or not and that is quite a different story. Even though I didn't know about tikkun, I have always held that urge, that desire within me for as long as I can remember to do something for change. For anyone with the inclination to heal the world—whether we are on any path, Jewish, Hindu, Christian, Muslim, Buddhist, Agnostic, Atheist, or any other faith teaching—our guidance, which comes in many forms, is to do something. But there are several definitions of activism.

Being an activist, to me, involves using whatever gifts we have been given or that we have cultivated in order to better our world. We become co-workers with The Universe through the development and use of our creative abilities, which are unique to each of us. For some, the guidance to become an activist may involve only meditation and a conscious effort to radiate love through kindness and attention. For others, it is marching and carrying signs, signing petitions and sending money or doing something very difficult for change within our own selves, something in our lives that needs to change first, something we do not want to face. All of these things are forms of action and the way I see it, everything is not yet in order. Far from it, I have always believed that as conscious humans we are a vital part of creating that order. We are the instruments of change in our colorfully unique ways.

Only our awareness, our thoughts and actions and our ability to discern what is being asked of us can help initiate those changes for justice and well being for all. Yet this discernment is a very tricky thing, a very fine line because one's believed needs and cherished opinions can get in the way. Ego, craziness and self-righteousness can get us way off track. But when we let go of our personal stake in the results it is authentic and if we follow that guidance, intuition or whatever we choose to call it can lead us to love, which seems to be an evolutionary driver.

All we need is love is a beautiful concept and I

239

love John Lennon for saying it but is love enough when it comes to my marriage, I wondered. Through flash images and words that would pop into my head no matter where I was or what I was doing, I could feel that I was not fulfilling my contract for this lifetime as long as I stayed with Ron. I kept pushing those flashes away because it was a terrifying thought to consider a life without Ron, especially at the seasoned age of sixty-seven. I loved him. I always have and as rocky as things sometimes were, I seemed to belong in this life with him despite our ups and downs.

But there had been a whispering in my ear for several years now that I did not want to hear and the fear nagging at me to leave but the thought of being on my own and away from all that I loved was too frightening. Where would I even go? What would I even do?

The thing is, if I was sincere in my commitment to my "life's purpose", what I came here for in the first place, what I vaguely remembered from far away, and I sensed something was tugging at me, how could I keep turning away?

One day after meditating with Dorothy as we often did, I blurted out, "Oh my God, Dorothy, with all this surrender we're doing, what if we're required to leave our husbands?"

We both cringed at the thought and quickly changed the subject.

Tree of Life in Winter

Tree of Life in Winter:
A Frigid Wind

Standing Naked, A New Gestation, What Will Be Born?

Weeks later after that fearful question I had asked Dorothy, this happened: I was still working in the field of employment for young people with disabilities and I needed to check on one of my favorite clients. Ron's Tae Kwon Do class would be starting in two hours. He seemed to be deep in concentration at his computer. I kissed him goodbye and ran out the door, jumped in the car and was on my way. Suddenly, I remembered that I had a gift for my neighbor's baby in the back seat. I spun into their yard and out of the corner of my eye, I saw Ron rush out of the house and without noticing me he backed the car rapidly down the driveway and took a right turn toward his school. Something was wrong with this picture, so I called him on my mobile phone to see where he was going in such a rush.

"To pick up some beer," he lied. It was the opposite direction from the beer store.
My heart sank. I knew. I just suddenly knew that

he was meeting that woman, his student from Tae Kwon Do, who had conveniently hired him for some carpentry work where he was spending his days. Now I was beyond suspicion and livid once again, beyond anytime before.

I raced off to check on my client then drove to the school to get proof. I was like a crazy person. It was dark by then and I parked with my lights out, adrenaline rushing, waiting in hiding for them to come out of class. After everyone had filed out and driven away, the two of them intimately strolled out together and got in her truck, Ron at the wheel. I raced to the end of the driveway where I could block their way. Shocked by my confrontation, they began spitting out lies as fast as a ticking clock. I had caught them. I said some choice words then sped away to parts unknown. I just drove. Obviously it wasn't the first time we had skidded into this wall.

I was still driving, blinded with tears, when he called my phone.

"Hey, Hon, c'mon. Everything is okay. Honest. Nothing is going on with her. Just come home."

"You pathetic liar. And what did you promise this one? I'm so sick of it. I'm on my way home but don't expect to pacify me with your sweet talk. I don't want to see your face."

I walked in the door seething. "Why can't you keep that thing in your pants?" I screamed as I threw his miserable beer in his face, stormed off to my room, and sunk immediately into despair.

It was then that things began to unravel fast and my life came tumbling down into tiny, furious pieces, once again. If this weren't so excruciating it would be monotonous.

Each time he was confronted with me leaving or throwing him out, he had gotten on his knees and begged and cried. Then after a last ditch attempt at therapy, I would make certain stipulations while he made certain promises and I would end up staying. It had been easier to try to rebuild trust than face the reality of going it alone.

I thought he was done with all this. It had taken eight years to mend what had been ripped apart with that little Kathleen. I was still sleeping alone and comfortable with that. He had not approached me even once so I thought that meant I was pretty much retired "down there" and that maybe he was, too. I was hoping that we were finding common ground. We seemed to be having fun together and I looked forward to the sweetness, laughter and inspiration that had been part of our past; it felt to me like that had been returning and it felt great. He had seemed happy, fun and at ease and I had no idea it was because he was getting satisfied with yet another student.

"It's okay," he said. "I'll be back. I'm off to Nova Scotia for a week and then I'll be back. We'll work it out then. I promise."

"Are you crazy?" I asked. "You think you're going with her and then come back to be with me? You think I'm going to wait for you? No way."

"I do have to take her to Nova Scotia. We've been planning this kayaking trip for months," he said. "Don't go crazy. It'll be fine."

And off they went in her yellow truck, two kayaks tightly strapped on top.

The worst of it was that in three days from their return, we were scheduled to go to the Maine Coast for our first family reunion with all our kids and grandkids. I was set to give a baby blessing ceremony for Baby Hannah, my youngest grandchild at the time, and now that was ruined. How could I go through with any of it with so much anger and hatred? But how could I not go and ruin the reunion by my absence?

Do I tell my kids it's over between their dad and me or do I just for these two weeks pretend that everything is okay?

I felt so uprooted that I could have fallen over in the first summer breeze. For now, thinking about Maine would have to wait. And, God, what about money? We were one of the few couples I knew who had not planned for a future. The present was hard enough. Who could think of the future when the present took up every cent and every ounce of energy? I guess simple hope and faith had been our guideposts but without a clear vision to focus on, we hung on year after year assuming that eventually we would get to the point where we could do what we called our "real work", which was painting and for me, also, working with women on spiritual exploration.

Tillie Olsen, author of *Silences,* says it so well: "I know that I haven't powers enough to divide myself into one who earns and one who creates." I had worked at so many jobs. One of them ironically was getting jobs for others. It started with the disabled. I spent both discouraging and inspiring time teaching people with all kinds of disabilities how to interview, write resumes, find jobs and supervise their actual work. The state gave me two weeks with every group and I did that for three years. Then I found myself on the other side of the fence working for a big corporation where I had the satisfying responsibilities of recruiting and hiring people, a whole different perspective. Some of it was on college campuses recruiting graduating seniors and many others were older women returning to a workforce that had radically changed.

A new social movement had come about in the 1970s following the Civil Rights Movement. Women either needed to get back to work to help with family finances, or they were single moms or simply single women of all ages. There were suddenly a lot of divorces as a result of women now finding the power to improve their lives, many bored to death with being at home in the routine and isolation of a homemaking lifestyle, others just in bad marriages or perceived bad marriages. Women wanted to get out there. They all needed money and for those who hadn't worked because of their years raising families, they answered my ads and came to us. I was able to hire those who qualified and presented themselves professionally but so many didn't.

It was these women I found myself counseling instead of simply sending them home rejected. It was empowering for them to get some much-needed advice, and empowering for me to be doing something fulfilling that seemed helpful. Then the recession came and there was no longer a need for my position so they let me go. Now unemployed, I joined many men and women who were competing for the few jobs that were out there. I had loved mentoring people so I asked my friend, Pete, a retired banker, to partner with me to open our own business. He could do the finances and I could focus on people.

Downtown was no longer a bustling business center, which made it affordable for us. People had fled to the suburbs and malls were the places to go, although there was still much commerce with a civic center right down the street. We found a delightful place with a great view of the city and windows that opened wide to let the breezes in, unlike the high rises that surrounded us. And so we launched Directions Unlimited, a place to teach job-seeking skills as I had done before. The women who came to us had been out of the business world for so long they needed a lot of help to know the new rules, even when it came to "dressing for success"—a big concept back then. So much had changed. Many men who had lost their jobs found us, as well. I loved our stream of clients but because we had so little capital to start with and our clients were always stretched as well, there was only so much we could do; eventually, that little dream of ours failed. So there I was again, back to the drawing board. I began to develop healing and empowerment workshops, taught sporadically as a guest in schools, colleges and the museum, and ran spiritual exploration groups out of the house. Ron's work wasn't steady either.

During that vast span of time, Ron had refined his woodworking skills in the serenity of his little shop. His furniture had been featured in many national magazines and even named one of the top ten designs in 1987 by *TIME Magazine*, and while both of us managed to exhibit in galleries and museums, it never got us off the ground enough to consider saving for the future. Yet we were often so close that those rare moments continually nurtured our hope.

247

Now I was starting my ninth year working as an employment specialist for the state. I was pretty good at training and placing young folks with disabilities into the workplace but it was both inspiring and discouraging. My clients were people like any other people. There were lovable folks and obnoxious ones and everything in between. It was often an uphill battle to keep some clients employed but the victories were joyful and worth the frustrations. Still, I kept my eyes open for something more creative but I resigned myself to the idea that no job is completely fulfilling so there I stayed making enough to keep me afloat.

On top of it all, the end of my marriage had begun and I was drowning in fear and anger. Money . . . now was my biggest worry. I wanted to be rid of him but how would I survive? I'd heard talk from many sources that the coming millennium would bring financial devastation, that the institutions would soon be crashing and burning as a result of corporate greed. Maybe that would equalize us all. But more realistically, maybe we could sell the house and split the proceeds. I didn't know what to think and then I decided that it was best not to think. It only

brought me round in circles so without thinking I started to pray.

I have learned that God does answer my prayers in one way or another, and I also learned that prayers are not always what we think they are. Sometimes they are the energetic longings and yearnings and hidden desires (key word: hidden) as much as the clear petitions of our wants and needs. Everything stirring in the depths of body and mind is a kind of prayer because it is alive with energy, and energy eventually leans into manifestation.

The poet Jericho Brown once wrote, "Today, I believe that anything one visualizes consistently becomes reality. Isn't that what prayer is?" Simone Weil, the French Christian Mystic said brilliantly: "Absolutely unmixed attention is prayer." In so many ways and when it is this authentic, my experience tells me that we are heard. How and by what or whom I can't be certain. To many of us, the word "God" is sacred and to others it is a concept that conjures pain and cynicism. But as long as we can just be open to the possibility that there is something greater than ourselves that is working in our lives, that seems to be what counts. We can call It anything we like. Being a *Star Wars* fan, I could just as easily call God "the Force" and that would do.

It seems that we pray all the time, perhaps without knowing that this is what we are doing. Our prayers silently rise from the deep vessels of ourselves, whether it's a nagging wonderment, a song in the bathtub, a dance under the stars, a narrative with the self, or maybe even an unrecognized longing from the bottom of our hearts, I trust that these expressions are heard by the Divine as prayer and that they are answered in ways that we may not expect or even notice because the answer may come much later. We don't always make the connection, or we may get what we truly need but not what our ego wants. There are individuals who proclaim that we have to be in a certain position or a certain type of building to reach God flying around above us. I know from experience that that is a grave limitation for so many of us.

At the lake house that winter when I journaled my letters to God, I sometimes stuck the most haunting questions into an envelope, tucked them away in a drawer and forgot about them. At a later time, I'd come across the envelope, open it up and realize that, in one way or another, my questions had been answered and my problems had been solved without me ever having made the connection that a *prayer* had been answered. The universe has its ways. Where do all these deep desires come from? Could it be that this larger It, All That Is, Great Spirit, The Creator, or God is what nudges us toward the fulfillment of our life's purpose, which we may have long ago forgotten?

Rabbi Marcia Prager says in her book, *The Path of Blessing,* "Taken together, the opening six words to all brachot (blessings) are an invocation or an overture, announcing our intention to channel blessing and raise up sparks of holiness. We begin in the silence that precedes any sound or movement. Jewish tradition asks that we not say a brachot until we have quieted the mind and focused our intention on the blessing's purpose: 'One should not toss a brokot (blessing) from one's mouth'."

When we do such an invocation from this silence, we experience an inner shift redirecting our soul toward All That Is, and that shift is a beautiful feeling in the body. Every cell seems to breathe. I don't know what comes first—thought or emotion—or a bodily sensation but I know it doesn't depend on any religion. It can happen to anyone anywhere at any time because it is about internal universal connectedness, and however that happens for any of us is personal.

Maybe this is what Anne Sexton described as "rowing toward God", or as Paramahansa Yogananda once expressed: "Words saturated with sincerity, conviction, faith and intuition are like highly explosive bombs, which, when set off, shatter the rocks of difficulties and create the change desired." To me, that is prayer, and the result—whether we notice it or not—is always some sort of expansion or instruction that occurs, carried along by love.

So as I sat in the sanctuary of my room with a candle lit and the angelic sound of the harp, thinking about Tillie Olsen and what she said about not having the powers enough to divide herself into one who earns and one who creates. I began to accept that fact. I also knew Ron didn't love this woman at all. He was just having fun but I was finally ready for finality. Now I needed a lawyer. I was done no matter how he might have cried and pleaded when he got back, and I knew that's just what he would do. I knew I was strong enough this time to resist his crying act and in knowing that I began to feel clean and somehow strong as I rose triumphantly out of anger.

My epiphany was this: I realized that this was what I had surrendered to. My prayer had always been for me to fulfill my purpose here on earth. Who knew what road that would take, what pain that would involve; and since I did not have the courage to leave the marriage on my own, and it was what my soul insisted on, divine intervention would enter and create a way for my marriage to leave me. As much as a part of me felt sorry for myself, I also felt a pronounced freedom, even a kind of joy, knowing that I was on my way to growing into myself. As much as I was terrified, I was equally exhilarated to start anew. My prayers for my destiny had been answered. Being with a man I loved, but who always seemed to have one foot out the door was not the way I wanted to live anymore. But then as the lesser self would have it, I started agonizing over why I had not left earlier. Waiting until I was this age to be out on a limb made me feel ashamed, probably the most unbearable of all emotions. And the psychologists would agree: It was weak of me to have stayed that long.

In the silence of that room, I tried to face

the naked truth and found that I had simply been enjoying the richness of what we did have and hiding from myself what we didn't. We had spent so many days and nights holding hands, snuggling on the couch, laughing at the cats, mourning our losses, rejoicing in our triumphs, expecting success, marveling at the finches dropping seeds at the feeder, discussing music and arguing over articles in *The New York Times,* lingering over meals, and engaging with our kids, our greatest treasures—marveling at who they had become and congratulating ourselves on the fact that we did it, we had gotten though parenting together, having created a clan of seventeen, including ourselves, and we were joyfully proud of that. We shared life. We brought to each other our individual flaws and attributes, our vague but common dreams. Some would say that there is no love if one partner cheats. Maybe one thing has nothing to do with the other. It is complicated and I tend to think that maybe, just maybe, the experts are not always right. These things are not *always* black and white, right or wrong, weak or strong.

Once I had begun to learn about reincarnation, right after the rendezvous with my dead father way back in my college days, I have strongly felt that we were all in this together. It's possible that Ron and I were together because of unfinished business from previous lives. We had to clean up our relationship and complete it, and that was the original attraction. We were together to teach each other things and we came apart when we were ready for the next chapter.

Underneath all of the emotions, I felt gratitude that the other shoe had dropped and a new phase was finally opening up for me, a chapter I had so deeply surrendered to and that I probably could not have followed through with without the betrayal and the anger that preceded it. The whole thing was about timing and now was the time to leave. In the end, I would say that I felt as Beatrice Wood described: "When the bowl that was my heart was broken, laughter fell out."

I walked out across the yard and lied down on an emerald patch of moss that June had brought. There was the sacred spot that my body knew, the far end of our backyard where I often listened to birdsong or watched September leaves spiral down. Now, in this field with the babbling stream and maple trees, which would soon grow a canopy of shade for the coming heat of summer, the same beloved trees that etched their grace against the white of winter, I was finding peace.

This yard had been host to picnics and parties and Liz's magnificent bridal shower, the tables set with splashes of forsythia and bunches of violets in May. This nature space had also been host to sunbathers and teenage talent shows, band practices, yard sales and candlelit dinners. Flower blossoms bordered the house and shop with irises, coreopsis, cosmos, pink and white and magenta phlox, Shasta daisies, crystal lobelia, foxglove, lamb's ears, geraniums, delphinium and oriental poppies. Orange day lilies crowded against the shop and nasturtium climbed to its roof. Everything was in various stages of bloom. When no one was home and the summer days were hot, I would lie naked and soak in the sound of buzzing bees and the scent of pine. I could have been forever in a state of adoration beneath the shelter of those trees, but it was now time to move on.

Just Trees

Slender branches write in esoteric script
Against the sky, entwined as one,
Recording silences and storms

They stretch up out of solid trunks
Along the rock strewn banks
And do their work remembering,
Reaching deep to musky loam,

Their rambling roots make love
And grow together through the weather

While beneath our heavy lids and leathered feet
We do not see.
We make assumptions they're just trees.

So this all began right before we were to drive to Maine for our first-ever, two-week family vacation and to celebrate Hannah's baby blessing. For us it was, of course, a devastating, dense, conversation-less trip, all the miles and all the hours it took to reach our destination. As it turned out, all of the children knew about this scandalous betrayal and here it gets unforgivable:

The Christmas Eve before Ron, Adam and Ben had ducked out to a local bar leaving us women cooking and baking, hearts aflame with holiday cheer and chatter while in the bar Ron stupidly bragged about the affair. Adam seemed not to have heard anything in the cacophony of the tight-packed place, which put Ben in the awkward position of carrying an unwanted secret that he'd held tight until now, this first day of the reunion. From then on, no one knew how to behave around me because they didn't know if I even knew. Ron was turning seventy that fall and with everyone together, the kids had planned a party for him but that was not to be. They did not want to celebrate their father just now.

I officiated Hannah's Baby Blessing as planned, a beautiful event that welcomed our latest into the family with open arms and open hearts despite the underlying weirdness, and we carried on from there, a fake smile stretching across my face. After two weeks of utter awkwardness, we all drove back to our respective homes.

Finally home, I firmly kicked Ron out of the house and watched him on his cell phone in the driveway making arrangements with the "other woman." Once he was gone, the house became fresh and open and airy. It was as if it had been swept through. I couldn't eat or sleep but I felt clean and strong—sad and lost but clean and strong. I seemed to expand into the emptiness of the house, filling the rooms with dance and song and easy breathing. So many emotions at once, a cacophony of transformation. I wandered into the yard again as if for the first time in thirty-four years, with all the maples and pines singing out just for me. I began to fill the space with song, more song, circling the trees as I sang. A grieving, mournful sound mixed with some glee spilled out of me onto the lawn and into the receptive earth.

But life required that he return to the shop each morning for his day's work. It was agonizing seeing each other and painfully disruptive when he had to use the facilities in the house. In the meantime, I did secure a lawyer. Ron really never thought I would go through with it because I hadn't in the past. He was sure I couldn't live without him but because of my trust in my Divine purpose, I knew that I could.

The next order of business was to figure out where to live. Adam and Jenn had both invited me into their homes to be with my blossoming grandchildren. Grateful as I was, I knew I needed my own space and couldn't fit into the intensity of family life just yet.

So the first order of business became figuring out my finances. I discovered something called a reverse mortgage. In my sense of justice, I demanded that we file for one so that I would have enough money to start a new life. I no longer wanted to be in that house or that town or the state of Connecticut. He could have the house, its contents, his precious shop and live with whomever he wanted without having to pay the rest of the mortgage but he could never sell it. That's the way that system works. It seemed plenty fair to me.

I would be okay. Being in no position to know anything except that life had some bigger plan for me that I was not yet privy to, I surrendered to the universe and waited. I instinctually knew that the sacredness that had brought me this far wouldn't let me down now.

Still, knowing that everything was unfolding as it should did not take away the grief or the sense of dissolution of my identity, which was half of the legendary Ron and Marge, a couple that was not only loved but for some unknown reason admired by others, so it remained

challenging seeing him pull in the driveway those mornings. We'd look at each other with sadness, confusion and despite ourselves, a bit of longing. Everything was breaking apart in slow motion. I don't know how June turned into September, but I suddenly needed some definitive closure besides the pleasure of having served the divorce papers. That was satisfying but it was just a paper and I needed some inner finality, something to break the emotional hold. Timing is everything.

"Let's go somewhere to do a closing ritual," I said to Ron one day as he was pulling out of the driveway to go back to his new home. I wanted to finalize this for myself and for us as a couple. I wanted the severance to be marked by a physical action, an emotional and spiritual action. I wanted a rite of passage. He had always hated that kind of thing but he reluctantly agreed to do it.

The day of the ritual, I led us up to an ancient Indian ceremonial site in the woods in a little town that Dorothy had introduced me to. The leaves graced us with their gorgeous dance, slowly, slowly drifting to the ground. The sun shone through the brilliant autumn trees. We stood inside a circle of rocks and I made a little prayer-like speech in which I blessed both of us, what we had together, and what we were about to have apart, the journey that we were each embarking on now. We hugged for a long moment, the first physical contact since June, the length of our bodies together in old familiarity. He was wearing his Levi jean jacket, which I knew the touch of so well. We wept and wrapped snugly in each other's arms, knowing this was the last time.

"Are you sure you want to split?" he asked in a final ditch effort.

"It's done," I said, and we walked back to the car.

We had decided before we went into the woods for the ritual to "celebrate" what we both wanted, or thought we wanted, by having one last elegant meal together at a fancy restaurant I had always wanted to try. The food was lovely but we found ourselves sitting there looking down through our tears into our plates of untouched delicacies. We walked back to the car in silence. My heart was so broken that I thought it must be bleeding.

Again, in another last ditch effort, Ron said softly, "We don't have to do this, you know."

"It's done," I repeated.

Both of us, devastated to the core, drove back to Bloomfield. I studied my red puffy face in the side mirror. A voice came back to me clearly. *Wait,* it said. *Look at yourself right now and remember this misery because you will look back on this someday and laugh. You will be fine. You will be happy. You will have a future you cannot yet imagine.* My own face was speaking to me, actually giving me this message through my reflection in the mirror. It was real. And though I half believed it, it did nothing to stop the pain.

So now it was high time to move, but where to? My musings over California to make a go of it with Jenn's family was a possibility but like I said, not a great solution and with all of the kids and heavy schedules, all the comings and goings and constant interaction I would not be able to think.

And then the phone rang. It was my friend, Lila. Lila had wanted to move from Connecticut to a warmer climate with her doctor husband, Bruce and their sixteen horses. They had been exploring Virginia and tried to get Ron and me and some other friends to consider it, with its gorgeous mountains and perfect weather. I wanted to go in the past, but Ron hadn't been able to even think about moving. Lila needed to get out of the New England winters, as she spent so much time out of doors and Bruce was ready for a change, too. Once they got down to their new home, though, they realized they needed help. Lila knew about our breakup and wondered if I could come down. The young couple that had come to work with the horses suddenly reversed their decision and now there was an opening for me. Divine intervention or what?

Within the week I had one bag packed and was on a Southwest Airlines flight to D.C. Lila picked me up at Reagan Airport and we went to eat at an Indian restaurant (one of our favorite things to do). We talked, shared food and made plans. Little did I know at that dinner that Lila would be instrumental in changing the course of my life.

My room was on the lower level of the hillside and my dear friend had furnished it with a canopied four-poster bed with fine linens and a desk equipped with everything I would need to continue seminary as a correspondent student. The deal was that I would cook and do whatever needed to be done.

Ron left the woman soon after I left and moved back into our house. It turns out the woman wasn't the point. She was simply a vehicle to get him away from his life as it was. He had been quietly battling dissatisfaction, a kind of weariness that can happen once you reach a certain point in life and wonder if this is all there is and if so it's not enough. So instead of talking about it with me, finding a new and loving solution, he had created another adventure with yet another woman. And after I was gone, he broke another heart and moved back home. Even though we were in different places now, miles apart, he still believed I would never go through with the divorce. He knew that leaving the marriage meant a huge rip in the fabric of my life and he wanted me back.

We were in Massanutten for a year in a house halfway up the mountain. We were all trying to adjust that first year—Bruce to his new practice, Lila to her commute to the horses (who were being boarded on another farm until they could find one of their own), and me, to my new life as a single, unhinged but grateful housemate who nurtured high hopes. Stress was thick by the time everyone came together at the end of the day because of all our adjustments.

Then they found the horse farm they had been looking for in Staunton, a little town a bit south. It was a beautiful expanse with rolling hills, big old guardian trees and broad pastures everywhere. Best of all for me, it had a separate little cabin on the property, a cozy place for me to settle in. Life was looking up. I brought down my favorite things and fixed up a sweet little home for myself with a front porch, where I placed a rocking chair overlooking a pasture where the elegant horses would graze.

It was during the real estate boom and I wanted to invest the money I received from my reverse mortgage. If I could grow that small amount by buying in a run down neighborhood that was gentrifying in this charming little city, I would feel secure.

Those days, I was so grateful to Lila and Bruce but at the same time felt enormous pressure to make amazing meals every night for two diverse eaters. My dinners would be gobbled up within minutes and then there was the mound of dishes. Lila would escape to the computer and Bruce to the television. I'd plop down on the couch and watch for awhile then make the "climb" up the little hill through the pitch-black darkness to my cabin, allowing a moment to study the stars. There is no autonomy when someone is helping the way they were helping me, and I felt indebted and guilty if I didn't do enough.

One night after dinner, we were watching a TV show about fatherless girls and from the description, I seem to be identified as one of them since I am a survivor of child abuse. That show further confirmed for me what I already knew: We "daddy-less" girls try to fill the hole in our hearts by acting out in several ways. Some become promiscuous, looking for closeness. Others cut, eat, drink or drug out to numb the pain of emptiness, and others become obsessed in love.

I was beginning to understand how I had filled my empty space by falling obsessively "in love" with Ron when he was nowhere near ready or interested in a committed relationship. He had just wanted to be a lone ascetic with the freedom to make art and play hard but he was passive and malleable and my heart was hungry. I can see how easy it was to manipulate him into marriage but never into the closeness I yearned for, and that challenge, I'm sure, was part of the attraction.

So, what was it about these other men that I'd had a magnetic attraction to (though not in a romantic sense)? Why did I get involved with the sorcerer type instead of blissful gurus in robes like most of my friends did? First it was Harlan then it was the Grandmaster. It bothered me that I was attracted to such bizarre men and it took a long time before I recognized that something about them was resonant with my dead father and something in me needed to overcome that fierce patriarchal hold still hanging over me. Somewhere in myself I must have thought they were filling in for him, allowing me to finish whatever business was not done by the time of his death. I had to move from victimhood to conqueror. I had to bring myself up and out of that role with my father. There was something I had to win but what I hadn't yet known was that I had stepped into dangerous territory.

I had found these two men, one right after the other, and I would learn what I never wanted to become. What a gamble that had been because that involvement could have killed me. Turns out the universe had scheduled me to learn about danger, good and evil, and the guises they can come in. I needed to learn my own limitations and the difference between the love of power and the power of love. I had to learn discernment. Those two were proxies and maybe Ron was, too. I didn't yet know.

Now I see how much sense it makes that Ron was never really committed, escaping his original entrapment by having an affair every decade even though we had become an institution as a family with no conscious thought of ever breaking apart. We did have love. We did have fun, and we had camaraderie and intellectual stimulation but at the same time, there was that cracked foundation underlying everything. I wonder now, is it our own hand or that invisible hand guiding us toward our eventual potential? What a sacred journey it all becomes and how delicate and subtle are the ways in which we make our choices.

The required year had gone by when I flew back to Connecticut to finalize the divorce. Being apart we had some good dialogue over that year, both of us understanding more about each other after our forty-four years together, but now I was excited to get the divorce actually finalized. He picked me up at the airport, the hug felt good and we went out to dinner. The next day, we drove in silence to the courthouse and joined the long line waiting there. I was feeling free and Ron was being his lighthearted self. We were doing this thing together as if nothing unusual was going on. The judge didn't get to us that morning so those of us remaining were sent out to lunch. We went to what had been one of our favorite restaurants near the park and had salmon mousse and arugula salads.

When it was our turn, the judge asked each of us if we wanted alimony. We both said no. She asked me a second time. I said no. There was nothing either of us had to give to each other.

Ron told me much later how difficult that time and the actual divorce had been for him. He just couldn't believe how it had ever come to this but he hid his feelings well. He told me with sincere sadness that he realized he had been afraid of losing himself if he ever expressed the love he really felt for me. That was very sad but I suspect he is not the only man who holds back for that reason.

That next week, on June 10, 2004, I would be ordained as an Interfaith Minister by the New Seminary in New York City. That meant I had a week to spend with my mom and catch up with girlfriends. Ron offered to drive me to New York, which was a great thing because he knew how hard it would be for me to drag myself around the city. On the way, we picked up Liz, who gave me a corsage of assorted white flowers from all three kids and helped me dress into my clerical robe backstage at the Cathedral of Saint John the Divine. I thought of the two women I had met at the workshop in New York right after 9/11 and how our conversation at Starbucks had convinced me to take this path, how absolutely right it felt at the time. And indeed it was right and in that moment I was so grateful to them.

The ceremony lasted about an hour and a half. We came in two by two, lit our candles and took our place in the choir. We were each colorfully dressed according to our own taste and imagined function as clerics then we were ordained by our faculty representing the different religions. After the ceremony, Ron and a few of our dear friends went out to dinner and celebrated my life and new beginnings. The comfort and ease of Ron and me together among these friends seemed natural.

While I was wrapping everything up in Bloomfield, I got a call from Lila. She had found a sweet little house for sale that was already rented to students from Mary Baldwin College across the street. I took the next plane home to check it out and buy it before it was swept up. The house sat in a small yard where the trolley teetered past. A majestic walnut tree shaded the backyard. A brick pathway lead up to the front porch and although it had once been a single family home, it was now divided into two flats already rented by tenants, which would take care of the mortgage and allow me to live in the cabin on the farm.

So there I was, free. By choosing life and listening to destiny calling through those two women I met after 9/11, I had gone through a radical change and found my way here to a new adventure and perhaps my unique purpose. I had become an interfaith minister and was inspired to marry people and perform commitment ceremonies for all combinations of faiths, ethnicities and genders—and to celebrate through writing and painting what I was beginning to see as a unique moment not only in my life but in the history of our species.

Ron's actions were in line with our dharma. His affair was a fact in the story but it was not the truth of the story. Over time, I relaxed into grace and ease as I came to understand that there was no forgiveness needed because there was no blame incurred.

On Having Come Through It

After the divorce, the calamity,
All that,
Comes the pause, comes breath, comes fire,

Poised in the scent of dreams
Tuned to the sound
Of poplar trees flowering
Or the bell-like sound of rain

I prepare for the glint of fresh waters,
For the hint of knowing something new
For first strokes
Clear light
An expectation of surprises

I hum to myself
To the world
To the beginning.

260

Stillness in the Field

"Grace is the palpable presence of Divine Love."
—Miranda MacPherson

Coming Into Grace

Coming Into Grace Slowly

Shopping for a Nightie, Behind the Tree, Leaving the Farm, Bye Mom

Meanwhile, back in California, Jenn and Brian had purchased and fixed up a house, made some money on it, and my enthusiasm had them wondering if they could do the same on the East Coast. Jenn had moved out west to attend college and to our dismay had never moved back. Brian had always lived in California and Jenn thought he would never come east. Their chiropractic practice was successful, their four kids were thriving and life was great for them in Santa Rosa.

But the opportunity for investment and my enthusiasm about Staunton made Brian want to investigate. He fell in love with the Blue Ridge Mountains and for the first time considered moving away from his native land. Jenn was thrilled and to our total delight and everyone's amazement after nineteen years, Jenn was moving "home"—well, back to the East Coast anyway, and that was a huge thing. She would now be near her single mom, give the kids their grandmother, invest in property, and finally be closer to the rest of the family. They bought a house in Staunton and one in the tiny town of Batesville where they settled in between the farm and the growing city of Charlottesville. I couldn't be more thrilled.

Nine grandbabies and me
(Easton Raine had not yet been born).

However, circumstances on the farm involving all their changes were driving Lila and Bruce apart. I loved them both and I seemed to be acting as a liaison that was keeping them together longer than they might have—at least, that's what I was told. But it didn't last. It was a difficult time as all breakups are and none of us knew, once again, what kind of future we wanted to create for ourselves. For the two of them, this had actually been a long time coming, which I hadn't known. So what were we now to do, we wondered, as the uncertain days came and went?

During all this speculation, Lila convinced me to go online to see who was out there in the world so that I could feel optimistic about "someday" meeting someone. I thought she was overly optimistic. I was too old for dating and didn't know much about the Internet anyway. But being so much younger than me, she was closer to that reality. So for the fun of it, we signed me up on Match.com. Without thinking, I impulsively wrote a list of requirements for my own clarification. This was the list off the top of my head for what I wanted in a partner.

1. I want a partner with integrity, honesty, self-expression and whom I can laugh a lot with.
2. I want a partner to touch and love and get exasperated with when the world seems difficult.
3. I want a partner to drive through the mountains with, one who will stop and marvel at the view, a hawk, an oak, a praying mantis.

4. I want a partner so if I break down in the mountains he will know how to fix the car, get us out, and be happy to build a fire.

5. I want a partner to discuss situations with, make decisions with and cook for.

6. I want a partner to talk to me about what he is thinking and feeling and be consoled or inspired by what I have to say.

7. I want a partner to laugh with, giggle with, fool around with, watch TV with and read in bed with.

8. I want a partner who will look deeply, lovingly and searchingly into my eyes, one who will stroke my crazy hair.

9. I want a partner I can caress, cry with, take care of, be taken care of by.

10. I want a partner who will listen to me and hear me.

11. I want a partner who respects himself for what he has done in his life and what he is doing now.

12. I want a partner with whom I like walking down the street with, walking across a parking lot with, walking on a forest trail with (but not too rambunctiously).

13. I want a partner who enjoys my kids and becomes part of the family and whose family I can embrace, as well.

14. I want a partner who I can trust when he goes away, or sit around with on a rainy day whether we are doing things together or not but just knowing he is there.

15. I want a partner I can have fun with, take a break from, make love to, be made love to in what ever way that works for us both.

16. I want a partner who loves kitties.

I wrote my true age in an overly extensive profile, simply because I love words, then sat back to enjoyed watching the photos come in. Lila and I giggled through my diminishing grief as we looked at guys, big and small, cute and not, some very, very old and most looking for women twenty years younger then themselves. What did I expect?

And then one caught my eye.

I liked his face and his written profile. I answered back and that was the beginning of something new. After a series of emails, we began talking on the phone. That meant we were no longer anonymous but had achieved a level of trust with real names and real numbers. The Divine had been intervening since my big surrender, so why not now?

Mark and I spent all of our nights on the phone, our voices traveling between Pennsylvania and Virginia with great enthusiasm and optimistic intimacy. I trusted him early and I was right to do so. We had everything in common. We were both into the arts and music, both humorlessly dedicated to our spiritual search, both politically aligned. We shared books and tapes and CDs and discussed our respective day's events, as well as our emotional challenges. This went on for months. We were solid and grateful and talking about the possibilities of building a future together. There were no games here. Everything was candid. Two-hour nightly conversations of deepest sharing and serenading brought us closer and closer. Yes, he sang me almost to sleep every night with his smooth, deep, sexy voice and in that state my dreams came in light and lovely.

It was time to meet in person.

We studied MapQuest and had finally figured out a middle ground in Hagerstown, Maryland. I got off at the exit before mine to primp and pee so I would be all set when I arrived at the appointed mall parking lot. He was shorter than he looked in his picture but that was okay. His car was older and smaller than mine so he packed his guitar into the backseat of my Corolla, locked the car, and off we shyly went looking for a place to eat and get acquainted, real person to real person, somewhat surprised by our mutual shyness after all our intimate phone conversations.

We strolled into the food court of the strip mall, which, of course, had a poor selection of offerings, varying from mall Chinese to mall Italian to mall hamburgers. I ended up with a soggy plate of spaghetti and a wilted lettuce-and-cucumber salad. He got a plate of lo mein with those insidious packets of soy and duck sauce and, to my amazement, we found ourselves struggling with conversation. It was certainly not romantic.

Our meal only took up 30 minutes so we drove around until we found a sweet little park. What else were we supposed to do?

It was surprising how awkward I felt, especially when he started singing to me on the bench of the picnic table, leaves blowing gently in the breeze with a temperature hovering around seventy-five. What setting could be better? But it was weird. And it remained shockingly awkward as if we didn't know each other at all, so I kept it short with the sorry excuse to make it home before dark. I tried to figure it out. I pulled everything apart. I analyzed, I swore, and I mumbled to myself all the way to Adam's house, not too far down the interstate, where they had settled. I was excited about seeing my babies again and it took the edge off my disappointing encounter with Mark.

Still, for some reason, we picked up our nightly ritual where we had left off, regretting that we didn't take good advantage of our time together, laughing about the strangeness. On the phone, we were back in the comfort zone and immediately began planning another trip. This time, Mark would drive to Virginia and brave an entire weekend, and we would commit to not being shy with each other. We had so much going for us that it was absurd to not follow through with another attempt at love. I would be the hostess and I could determine the tone.

Okay, so now, just in case, I needed something on hand that would be fabulous to wear, something that could make a man's hand glide gladly over the ground of my body. I was hungry for intimacy, especially since I had this amazing connection with him, even though our

first meeting was a disaster. I felt close to him from all our deep and sassy conversations. Desire had begun to trickle back into my body after years of feeling retired "down there."

So where was Victoria's Secret now that I needed it? Most of what hung on the racks around town were "cutsie" little pajama sets. You know the kind—low-slung bottoms with little puppies printed all over and tiny tank tops for college girls with perky breasts. Then there were racks and racks of flannel cover-ups for the God-fearing women in the neighborhood.

I tried Goodwill . . . and the Salvation Army . . . both great for jeans, sweaters, scarves and bags, but I soon discovered that second-hand lingerie did not hold any, well, sex appeal. The likely ones of lace and brevity gave me the creeps when I touch them. Who knows what they had lived through before they ended up in this place?

I knew of no adorable boutiques in the area, but JC Penney's had a pair of tailored blue satiny pajamas. That could be sexy, I supposed, in a Katherine Hepburn sort of way. But I had my doubts, hardly being of the Hepburn species. I bought them anyway, just to be sure I had something. Then I raced over to check out

Belk's Department Store. Lo and behold, there on a rack was a tiny blue nightie with spaghetti straps, low neck, and some fancy work running up the sides. Trouble was my breasts fell just under the place where they should be landing, though not by much and, in the dark, who would notice or even care?

I wasn't sure if I would even get to wear a nightie with this new man, and if I did, would there be need for attire at all or would we simply tear off each other's clothes before he was all the way through the door, like in the movies? Maybe we would be shy again and avoid the whole thing altogether. After all, having slept with the same man for so many years, simply preparing for someone else was excitement enough.

Finally, the big weekend arrived. The eggplant caponata, truffle pate, and cheese plate were ready. The merlot was mellowing on the counter and I'd stashed some Sam Adams Seasonal in the fridge the night before. We had been checking in on our mobile phones as he was getting nearer, and I had been talking him through the farm-strewn roads to the cabin. I turned the music down so I could hear the car coming up the drive. I looked out the window.

There he was already parked.

He stepped out of the car and I studied him meticulously.

After all the wonderful conversations that brought us this close, this was the real thing, a visible, movable body. I walked out onto the porch with a great big smile and open arms. It was so easy.

His kiss was sweet, sensual and lingering. He smelled good, too, and that's a big thing. I felt immediately adored. I knew I was in for a delicious two or three days, or whatever it was going to take to know something about this relationship, to know if we would be able to make it work. At that age, there was no time to fool around. I wanted to know right quick.

He began pulling things out of the car, bag after bag, as if he were staying for a month and then, of course, the guitar. He had stopped by Burger King about an hour before and wasn't hungry, so feeling somewhat crushed by having to leave my carefully prepared meal, I took him for a walk around the farm. The whole farm was set on a steep incline from the road, up the long driveway, past the yellow barn to the main house on the right where Lila and Bruce lived. Then my cabin. We walked around the back first to show him my little sitting area and the garden and sculptures that Adam had made. Behind it was a huge manure pile. We laughed a little at the (lack of) Feng Shui of it all and he took my hand.

Right then, I had an inkling that the sweetness of the porch kiss was not an indication of things to come. We seemed to have depleted whatever chemistry lived in that porch kiss. After shuffling around for a few hours with very little to talk about, and since Mark wasn't tempted by my appetizers, we headed to town for dinner. That, too, was tedious. Turned out that he was a picky eater, dragging his food across the plate in small cut-up pieces and, to top it off, he was obnoxious to our server. You can tell a lot about a person by the way they treat their servers. Mark stared into his plate during most of the meal. Where all of our stimulating discourses went, I had no idea. He decided he wasn't feeling well and seemed to have become suddenly over-focused on what was turning out to be a number of ailments.

Back at the house, he began pulling out tissues for allergies, smelly creams for a backache, and a mammoth vibrator, which he asked me to help him with for the places he couldn't reach. I was not into it but did my best while wondering how the guy I liked so much by email and phone had been replaced by this one in person. Maybe being stuck with me for the next few days in this small place was scary for him and brought up all his issues. I was mad at myself for not being more sympathetic, but, to tell you the truth, I was totally turned off and also feeling stuck. I couldn't bear the overpowering smell of that medicinal cream and the proximity to his body in my small bed. Oh my God, it was so bizarre. What had I been thinking and what was I going to do? I certainly didn't think it would be very gracious of me to send him to my studio on the floor with a sleeping bag or away to the guest room in the main house but we both knew without saying a word that we would not get through this night together. So I slipped away over to Lila's extra room with the soft cotton sheets and down pillows and I know he was just as relieved as me.

When I came back in the morning, he was on his knees looking for a lost hearing aid.

"I know I left them both right here on the table," he said, "and I can't find them anywhere."

For hours we searched. These things cost thousands, but we finally gave up and he went home. If we had been dogs, our tails would have been between our legs.

After Mark left, I went into the kitchen. There she was: My beloved cat, one long, white paw behind the stove batting something around and, yup, she had stolen the thing in the night, right off the table. I sent it off in a little box later that afternoon and returned from the post office to devour the caponata, pate, cheese, crackers and two glasses of Merlot. And that was the end of that.

The next day, I awoke with a heavy heart, not only because of Mark, but the gloss was fading from the situation on the farm. Fragments of my dream still lingered in that in-between place of sleep and wake. In it, I had crawled into bed. Ron was already there and I snuggled in. That hadn't happened in years and I had no desire to ever have it happen again. But I guess I did long for the comfort I once felt, the familiarity, the constancy and, yes, the love I still had for him. My longing, though, was really for the void to be filled and a touch of love on the body. It was the emptiness that hurt more than the loss of him because the loss of Ron was a loss of the idealization of him, the good memories of him, not the reality of him as he related to me.

The laptop that I had gotten free from one of Apple's promotions lay in wait among books, folders and the instruction manuals that I hadn't once glanced at—but were at the ready whenever I might get motivated to activate that side of my brain. My office had projects piled high. Loose papers and manila folders covered the desk and the seats of the leather swivel chair. Folders that had slid out of their piles now covered the floor. I couldn't even open that door for fear they would follow me around until I dealt with them. My dining room table—where I would have preferred to have a vase of Queen Anne's lace or a pot of geraniums—was littered with papers, stuff from school, names of wedding venues, phone numbers and designs for a web site for my imagined business as a new interfaith minister. If I could see that far into the future and design really sacred ceremonies, I thought, maybe those relationships would have a better start than ours had. There were stacks of printouts for properties Lila wanted me to look at and there I was running around with a jungle of keys, dragging myself up stairs and down, showing homes in the boiling heat and freezing cold, always searching for new investments. Still, there were stacks of paid and unpaid bills as Ron and I were still sorting out our financial discrepancies.

Was it any wonder that I just wanted to lie there under the fan, reading, staring at the ceiling and trying to stay cool? Aside from the littered table, the bed was my home. I would write there, sleep there, read there, dream there, pray there, and be as private as I wanted to be. For the past half hour, I had been reading Eduardo Galeano, who was blowing my mind with his quick, gorgeous imagery and profound description of pain. He is a historian, storyteller, poet, scribe and revolutionary. Reading his life and version of Latin America and Spain in the near past gave me pause to reflect on the concept of democracy and our life in the United States, and my own little life there in exile, in a bed, in a cabin that did not belong to me.

Ram Dass once said that there is complication between the helper and the helped. The helper has expectations and the helped takes on a subordinate position and the uncomfortable feeling of indebtedness—although, in fact, the helper is being helped by simply being in that role, doing something good for someone else. Yet in our case, it had become clear to both of us

that we were helping each other. How long could it last? I wondered.

Although I was so grateful that the universe, through Lila and Bruce, had brought me down to these Blue Ridge Mountains and the beauty that surrounded us, I felt it would be some time before I would settle into a life of my own. I had no idea what I wanted that to be but I trusted something would change to lighten things up. I had no choice but to trust. Since their move from Connecticut, things had gone steadily down hill for them. There was talk of separation. I was a friend to them both. Of course, Lila and I were close but also Bruce and I were friends, too. They were both dear to me. Eventually, they were on a clear path to separation. It was decided that Bruce would move out. This was hard for all of us but it seemed the only way.

Lila and I began to consider turning the farm into a women's retreat using both our skills to do therapeutic work and support for women in transition. We were becoming experts in transition as we plowed through our own and we thought with my workshops and weddings, and perhaps even some cooking and Lila's equestrian skills and therapeutic background, we might be able to make something work that would not only help ourselves but help others a lot. And our excitement about inviting special guest facilitators convinced us we could create something really valuable. I would move into the house with her, which would leave the cabin open for others. We thought, also, of other entrepreneurial possibilities and relationships, and wondered if either of us would ever find another male partner to love, but for now we had each other.

At twilight, my favorite time of day, when the veil between worlds is thin, I tossed a slice of leftover pizza into the oven, threw a salad together, raced to the porch and watched the light fade gently into dark. The apple tree laden with apples, distorted and small for lack of care, seemed to feel as sad as I did. I was learning how to be a recipient of many compassions but also learning to follow my feelings and let them turn into melancholy when they needed to.

Was I projecting that onto the poor tree? I don't think so. If trees could talk, it would have told me how hard it was to produce those hundreds of green apples and then have them fall to the ground before their time, only to get stepped on and run over as if nobody even cared. I looked at the beautiful branches, some drooping almost to the ground with the weight of ripeness, and I realized how much I cursed those little things under foot, turning my ankles constantly on the way to the car, the mush turning into fly-attracting magnets. But on occasion, a rash of black butterflies with blue markings, almost iridescent, would flit in, fluttering around the mess and then up into the branches. It was a gift to have such visitations and I pondered all of these things and all of the little things I didn't do while living there that year and a half. I didn't take care of the tree and protect it from bugs. I didn't weed the back garden that was so extraordinary when I came. Frankly, I didn't quite ever settle in. There were still boxes of clothing and supplies crowding the attic and stuffed into the back room waiting to be opened and placed around with some semblance of order. But I rationalized: "You've been healing. You've been grieving. You've been adjusting to aloneness, singleness, homelessness, voluntary exile, and learning to be a recipient of grace."

There was little left at the end of the day for all the things I would like to have done. I convinced myself that it was okay. It just was okay. There would never be a conclusive finishing. I, as a woman, would never be finished. I, as a person, as a soul, would never be finished. I knew that to be true. And it was soothing.

One night, Lila and I were hangin' out and started to talk about the false hope that I'd had with Mark, and simply how you can never know if you're going to have that all elusive "chemistry" with someone unless you spend time with them in person.

"Well, Mark was just one man, one person. So let's see who else is out there," Lila suggested.

I revisited my written "requirement list" to remind myself of my desires, then I pulled up a chair near the computer and logged into my page on the online dating site. Lila and I squeezed in tight to view the screen together, and she began to scroll, laughing about how we were "trolling for guys." Most of the men my age were looking for forty-year-old women. I couldn't help but wonder who these studs thought they were—especially since they didn't really look like great catches themselves. Then there were a few forty-year-old guys who had winked at me, the sign for being interested in further exploration. That gave me pause, as well. Why would they want a woman twice their age?

Buddies.

"Keep scrolling," I said, really getting into it now.

Then: "Wait. Stop." My eye caught another man "winking" at me. I liked his face immediately, not an overly handsome face but a good face, one that telegraphed integrity, strength and wit. I winked back, which I understood to be what I should do if I wanted to express interest.

I thought about what President Lincoln once said when asked by his assistant why he didn't hire a particular applicant for a job: "I didn't like

275

his face," Lincoln responded.

"How could you not hire him based on that?" asked the assistant.

"After the age of forty, every man is responsible for his own face," Lincoln reportedly said.

So, I liked this man's face, and there were only a few words in his profile but also, an important factor was that he was looking for someone his own age—my age.

As with Mark, this man and I lobbed emails back and forth until we both felt safe enough to reveal our identities. Then a phone call.

"I drive through Staunton sometimes," he said, "on the way to visit my daughter."

"Where does she live?" I asked.

"Harrisonburg. With her husband and two kids."

"That's right on the way. Why don't we meet somewhere for a cup of coffee or a glass of wine?" I boldly suggested.

He wasn't very outgoing but what could either of us say in this delicate tentativeness? After Mark, I was wary of revealing too much over the phone and this guy, Maurice, seemed happy to make a plan to meet in person versus talk from a distance.

It was almost Christmas and the ground was covered with snow. We planned to meet for Sunday brunch at The Pullman, a local restaurant where the trains speed right by the window as close as the width of a bicycle path. After trying on several outfits, I decided to leave the house early so I could arrive ahead of our appointed time and get the first sighting when he walked through the door.

"I'm expecting a gentleman," I told the hostess at The Pullman. The place was empty and I was sure she'd have no trouble bringing us together. She ushered me into a booth and when I took my seat, I seemed to sink down in, much too low. I must have looked very dumpy with the table level to my chest so I moved to another booth facing the door. The same thing happened. I kept jumping around to different booths hoping to look stately and tall but they were all the same. Finally, after this game of musical chairs, I settled into a booth and posed as nonchalantly yet elegantly as I could.

It was now time for Maurice to arrive but he hadn't come. *I'm being stood up,* I thought, or maybe, God forbid, he was in an accident. I went into the lobby to take a look and there he was, looking at his watch with a frown on his face and the hostess, totally oblivious. We greeted each other with mutual apologies, took our seats and buried our faces in the menu. We ordered and began to get acquainted. He was nice enough but not exciting. We enjoyed our eggs benedict and some ordinary conversation then got up to leave.

The sun was shining and the snow was packed down in the parking lot and slippery. I was about to thank Maurice for walking me to my car when he said, "I wonder how a hug would feel." It was an appealing invitation. I tossed my bag onto the passenger's seat to make my arms available while being careful to keep my feet from sliding on the frozen snow. His body, even through our winter coats, felt good against mine.

Back at home, Bruce was still in the process of moving his stuff out when I came through the door. Knowing that I was on a kind of blind date, he asked how it went.

"I don't know," I said. "He wasn't that interesting. I don't know if I'll go out with him again."

"Not so fast," said Bruce. "He's could be a Zen master in disguise. Ya' never know."

As is turned out, Bruce wasn't too far off. Maurice had been in the process of getting a horrible cold and wasn't himself that day, and he did turn out to have an understated wisdom that was perfect for my extreme opinions. We began to go out. He seemed to be actually courting me. I thought that it must be a southern thing. We came out of the movie theater one night and had to walk across an uphill parking lot. I was trying to be cool and get all the way to the car without my legs turning to lead, but could not make it.

"I have to stop here," I said.

"Okay," he said nonchalantly. "What's wrong?"

"Umm, well, I have this thing. It's kind of strange," I said, not knowing how to explain it. I didn't want to scare him away by saying I had a muscular dystrophy. I never use the word "disease"—particularly in this kind of circumstance—because, thank God, mine is not progressive and I don't want it to sound too horrible.

"Well," I said, anticipating awkwardness in trying to explain what I, myself still didn't understand. "I run out of steam," I said. "It's like trying to drive a car when it's running out of gas. My muscles are like that, always

277

running out of fuel. So I need to stop every so often and wait till I'm ready to go again. It's weird and no one can tell me what it is. Sorry," I said, feeling embarrassed.

"Oh, sure, okay, I'll get the car," he said, as casually as if I had asked him the time of day. Then maybe to change the subject, he pointed to a nearby building.

"Isn't that beautiful? It's a Jewish church," he said.

"It is beautiful, but it's a synagogue. I know 'cause I'm Jewish." It just came out for no reason. I was letting it all hang out. Take me for who I am, I guess.

"Wow, you're full of surprises," he laughed, and off he strode to get the car.

Okay, I thought, now everything is out: my disability and my Jewishness. I wondered if this was the last time I'd ever see him.

But it wasn't. To my delight, the more we went out the more I enjoyed him. He made me laugh and would always offer to drop me off in front of wherever we were going and pick me up on the way back. No big deal. I had been worried about what his politics would be, being a "southern boy" but there was no need. He thought

things out for himself and usually arrived at the same conclusions as I did. He almost matched the things I had on my list for the perfect partner. But he was a white bread man and I was rye. He was ham and cheese and I was cream cheese and lox. He drove a fancy car and I drove an old one.

Yet the most telling differences were these: He was a well-behaved, proper man. One day soon after we'd begun dating, he took me up on the Blue Ridge Parkway, which is the actual ridge at the mountaintop that winds its way slowly through the forests down to North Carolina. He had packed a bottle of wine, some crackers and cheese and some CDs that I loved. It was quite romantic until I had to pee. Of course, there was no bathroom for miles and miles so I asked him to stop. I wound my way deep into the woods until I found a tree large enough to conceal my action. When I returned, he was amazed that I did such a thing.

"Well, what did you expect me to do?" I asked.

"I don't know," he said. "I've just never seen anyone do that."

Where had he been all of his life? I wondered. It was almost a deal breaker for me to see how sheltered he had actually been and I teased him for being such a prude. My reaction made us both laugh and brought us closer.

I came to learn that Maurice had no interest in spirituality and was not a fan of kitties but all of that mattered less and less as we spent more time together. I loved being with him. I loved being able to laugh so easily, to actually have fun without the ponderances I was accustomed to. We continued to go out and I stopped responding to other men on the Internet site. Still, I couldn't help but wonder if I was making a mistake by putting so many eggs in one basket. So just to be sure that I wasn't rationalizing or acting out of desperation to be with someone, just to be sure his spiritual indifference didn't matter, just to be sure I was being honest with myself, just to be sure it didn't matter that I wasn't feeling passion, only sweetness and ease, I made an appointment with the woman who had been my therapist during the toughest days down here. After telling her everything and hearing my own voice speak the words, I knew that I was on the right track with Maurice. I had felt it from the start but it had seemed so incongruous, a Yankee Jew and a Southern country boy who had never even met a Jew. I was learning that none of that matters when it feels so right and that you don't have to be over the moon to make a good match.

Spirit had been pushing me at him and now with this session I was beginning to trust that, a case of heart versus head.

From then on, Maurice and I spent a lot of time together, celebrating holidays with each other's kids, driving around in his '62 Morgan that he had restored himself, and dining at my favorite restaurants. Love was growing, as was the romantic attraction. Then one night after we had been going out for almost a year, he dropped down on both his knees. I looked into his adorable face and said "yes" to what he called the "M" word.

It was as if, in that moment, some glorious gate opened and the blush of love whooshed through us in a heightened flow that I'd never felt before. Our mutual commitment literally opened us to each other on a newer, deeper level. It was as if we both exhaled in sweet perfect ease for the first time together. We had admitted and we had committed.

Now that I had taken ample time at the cabin on the farm to rediscover myself, I had embraced the new me and was ready to love someone else. Now I could wholeheartedly move into this new life with Maurice. At the same time, I had more to let go of: this cute little town and the gorgeous sight of sleek horses and big, old shade trees framed by every window. There was none of that where I would be going and the little patio development where Maurice lived had only baby trees and no place yet for songbirds. But I knew that loving the person was way more important then loving the "place."

Meanwhile, Mom was still in the nursing home with Libby and by now she was just hanging onto life by a silver thread. Her arthritis throughout her body had become excruciating and she had already told us that she didn't want to live to her ninety-third birthday.

"But I won't die," she said in late summer, "until you and Maurice are married."

We set the wedding for October. I made sure I would have everything that I didn't have the first time around: a real gown, a real cake, champagne, my family and friends, real sacredness and celebration but this time my Mommy, would not be there for much as she wanted to, as she was bed-ridden in Connecticut.

The pivotal moment came for Maurice and me to make our entrance through the French doors of our Village Club House and walk down the aisle, preceded by our twelve grandbabies tossing rose petals. Outside, red and gold

leaves continued their swan song, spiraling off trees, and Dorothy, who had flown in from

Celebrating with bubbles.

Connecticut, was up front waiting to perform the ceremony. Nancy and Rob (Maurice's son-in-law) stood attentively beside us.

Arm in arm we strolled, Maurice serious and dignified and me grinning widely, floating several inches off the ground in a pair of sparkling white heels (which no one will ever again see unless I make them an artifact for the living room pedestal, as I hadn't worn anything but clogs, boots and sneakers in twenty years). My grown kids beamed at us, smiling and wet-eyed. Our twelve grandchildren encircled us and spoke special wishes one after the other while the winds of change kept blowing outside and we sealed our individual vows with a kiss.

After the ceremony, we toasted with champagne and a two-tiered chocolate cake surrounded in blue hydrangeas, as candle glow filled the room and danced in our love-struck eyes.

Then we danced. Maurice chose Ella

Maur and me dancing.

Fitzgerald's "Our Love is Here to Stay" as our song and we circled the few feet of open space, round and round.

We all came back to the house, celebrated by telling stories and stuffing our faces with leftovers. Then in the morning, Maur and I took off for the Maine Coast and visited Mom on our way up.

They told us that one minute Mom was here and present and the next she was speaking from somewhere else.

That day, Mom told me a dream she'd had. It wasn't really a dream, she said, but it changed everything. The beauty and the love that surrounded her was something she had never before experienced. It as though she was floating in a luminous bubble. It seemed to me that she had been testing the waters on the other side.

Mom had also "dreamed" of me. She had already apologized for not showing her love for me enough when I was a child and she wanted to be sure she was doing now what she had always felt through the years. She had tears of joy in her eyes as she stroked my cheek and studied me deeply. Her "dream experience" seemed to have stripped her of any guilt, resentment or bitterness that she was still clinging to, despite herself. She had become like a little dove, pale and beautiful, exuding a peace that everyone around her felt in those final days. I've heard it said that this happens. Perhaps it was the medication or a near death experience, leaving her body for higher realms and returning to let us know who she had become, how much she loved us and that she had lost all fear of dying. She was processing her transition.

Knowing that Mom pleasantly had one foot on earth and the other in another realm, I left the nursing home with an infusion of beauty, peace and joyful connection.

On the way home from our honeymoon, we stopped again for a visit. There was much kissing, exultation, foot massaging, gentle stroking, and general adoration amongst us three. Mom was ready for her exit. We said our goodbyes, knowing it would be our last time together.

"Don't forget to stop by on your way out," I begged, squeezing her delicate hand and kissing her tender cheek.

She laughingly promised that she would try but couldn't guarantee it because she wasn't sure how leaving the planet would work. Mom hadn't been able to come to the wedding, but she had vowed not to die before we were married and she hadn't. By early November she was gone.

Oh, Mom

We touched that day,
With joy I never dreamed
You knew your earthly visit was complete
Faithfully you suspected, too,
Your journey would race on
To some familiar place above the sun
And as you soared you also knew
Another chapter opened
And already had begun.

And so one fleeting kiss you gave
A wisp against my cheek
Then passed on by
Toward loving ones
Waiting at the brink

Evolution in Motion

Our Evolution:
The Microcosm and the Macrocosm

Nuclear Family/Human Family, Valentine's Day Gift,
Cape Cod Ritual

Even though Maurice didn't meet all of the requirements on my list, as we got into our lives together we were relieved and delighted to discover that we did do the right thing. After all, you never really know until you live with someone. We are fitting partners. We simply fit.

At Maurice's suggestion, one of the first things we did together was to further research my disability to see what could be done about it. I had attempted this periodically and hadn't found out much because my condition was so rare; however, Maurice was successful. He located a doctor in New York who, oddly enough, had my maiden name, Slonim, also quite uncommon. All the way into his eighties, this doc was still dedicated to solving this muscle mystery and other rare muscle diseases. He was immersed in research and seeing patients at Columbia Presbyterian Hospital and actually making some progress, so we drove to New York to meet him.

That visit changed my life. Without all of his testing and very exacting program of diet and exercise, I'd probably be in very bad shape right now. He validated that my body doesn't store glycogen, which is the fuel needed to get muscles working, so it's no wonder that I couldn't exercise or do so many normal things. He had me on the treadmill, going as slow as it would go for ten or twelve minutes, until my body finally kicked into using fatty acids as fuel, instead. Then I began to gain some endurance and learn how to use my body more efficiently. It looked like I wasn't going to end up in a wheelchair at least for a while, which is something I had feared all my life.

Now that my path had taken a wide curve into love and a welcome sense of security for my body and my mind, I was ready to delve into my wedding services, return to painting and plunge back into my studies on the Internet in search of reasons for all the turmoil and dumbing down of our culture and the human and environmental crisis looming. I was remembering some of my purpose for walking the planet at this time. The question now was, What can one person do? What could I do?

Our house sat on a steep hill, which created a lower level giving me a high ceilinged walkout basement. Maurice laid the hardwood floor himself and *voila*, I had my own space. I was able to sell my cute little Italianate house in Staunton, making a small profit just before the crash in 2008.

My life was gliding gracefully and gloriously into place. In fact, I was a bit embarrassed at thinking maybe I have a Cinderella complex as described by Collette Dowling in her book of the same name. But how could that be? Me, the feminist, the spiritual seeker, the artist who now has found my way into this loving, playful, comfortable life without the old worries? But my guilt soon faded. I knew that I had paid my dues with tedious stints at health food stores, book stores, the textile mill, the crazy gym on Forty-Second Street, the bizarre experience of serving drinks to tourists at the World's Fair and a variety of restaurants along the way, all to fill in the gaps of my ironically professional life as an employment and empowerment specialist and then lastly as an aspiring artist. I took those in-between menial jobs because I was surviving and always striving and I was, as Gloria Steinem says, "a hopeaholic." And more than that, the times they are a changing once again and once again I need to be part of it. I am not on vacation.

First Thanksgiving.

I had learned the concept of surrender on The Path and later at seminary. Surrender was a concept that meant more about trust than about giving up. The trust came from the love and the love came from trust and the more I grew and evolved, the more deeply I trusted. Surrender had been the ultimate letting go, not a decision, not a thought or emotion but a complete, whole-body, whole-mind relaxing into the knowledge that God's will would be done and with my soul's best interest at heart. It took the burden

of agonizing decisions away and increased my intuition infinitely. This took practice, a habit of paying attention and sinking down into what my body was saying as opposed to my opinionated mind. I had evolved into something new and having the support from Maurice had allowed me to do so much easier.

We all need each other so badly. We cannot do it alone. We have to step out and find the person or community that can support us in our personal evolution, which of course becomes a part of the collective evolution. Somewhere for every person there are those doing something that would be a match for their interests and their growth. Part of the surrender is that we need to let go of our expectations and be open to what spirit might bring to us when we are ready and often when we are at the very bottom of ourselves.

My surrender had opened the window for that divine intervention which had set everything in motion for my greater good. Life with Maurice never could have happened if I hadn't surrendered to the pain of leaving everything in Bloomfield and trusting in the unknown.

But as I was evolving, so was the world evolving. Ron, too, eventually remarried. On the day of our divorce, his lawyer had invited him to dinner and there at the table sat his cousin, Barbara from California, the woman who would become Ron's next wife.

Since I've been in my new life these past nine years, my business officiating weddings for all combinations of couples has brought me more love than ever before. They are in love and I am in love with them as they gaze at each other while making their vows. Tears of the soul inevitability fall.

I've returned to painting and writing, gotten to know my grandchildren a little better, and have had light and laughter accompany me along the way. But I have also shed tears. Not so wrapped up in myself anymore, I have had time to find out what else was going on in the world.

I have had the time and inclination to participate in many online seminars and workshops in these nine years. They have helped me remember my purpose, what I was born to do. It has been instrumental in helping me remember my indecision as soul when coming into this lifetime, my reticence about my parents-to-be, and my hopes to eventually become an agent of change once I had passed some very real tests.

And now the time has come. I am excited to find what lies ahead as we collectively make the effort to transform the consciousness of humanity through compassion and fearlessness. We watch the wars that have popped up like fire grass exploding across the land while the land itself shakes, burns, floods and shudders displacing hoards of humans, animals and plants. Right now refugees from Syria and other countries are trying, at great risk, to escape from indescribable horrors and women and children are being raped in the process. Our country has ceased to be a true democracy and our planet is rapidly overheating from negligence and greed. Food is being manufactured instead of grown naturally and still so many starve. Democracy in America has been bought by corporations and Wall Street right from under our noses and the belief in group supremacy of one kind over another and the fear of losing dominance has created so much hatred that there is no justice; and to top it all off, nuclear warheads wait ominously all around us, dotting the planet like a diseased body waiting for death. What will we do? What can we do?

Thousands of people are already leading the way into a radical new idea called conscious evolution by the eighty-five year old activist-visionary Barbara Marx Hubbard. She has been the author of many of these online courses that I have taken and gathered on a daily basis with hundreds of other visionaries who want to act by bringing their intrinsic gifts to the world as an integral part of what is becoming our evolutionary transformation. We call ourselves evolutionaries, people conscious of our abilities to make a leap together as individuals into the birth of a new humanity. The wisdom of indigenous people is now being heard and technology has brought us together. Timing is always perfect. Never before would we have been able to connect across the planet like this, learn from each other, envision peace and pray as one. Here are a few of my favorite thoughts from those who are on the front lines of bringing this new humanity into being:

- Carter Phipps says in his book, *Evolutionaries: Unlocking the Spiritual and Cultural Potential of Science's Greatest Idea:* "We have so much information but so little context . . . We are data rich and meaning poor."

- Abraham Joshua Heschel has said in his writings compiled by his daughter Suzannah Heschel in her book: *Essential Writings:* "Daily we should take account and ask *What have I done today to alleviate the anguish, to mitigate the evil, to prevent humiliation? . . .* What we need is the involvement of every one of us as individuals. What we need is restlessness, a constant awareness of the monstrosity of injustice."

- Charles Eisenstein says in his book, *The More Beautiful World Our Hearts Know is Possible:* "A good definition of Hell is having no choice but to tolerate the intolerable." And he also says: "Greed is the perception of scarcity and Evil is the perception of separation." These statements seem even more obvious today as we look at politics in 2016.

- Barbara Marx Hubbard says in her book, *Birth 2012:* Humanity's Great Shift to the Age of Conscious Evolution: "The birthing of a new consciousness whose time has truly come cannot be halted, in the same sense that the gestation and delivery of a baby cannot be reversed. Its birth is a *one-way journey.*" We are becoming even more aware of this as we watch the ills of society rise from under the carpet to be revealed and in that revelation we can't help but be inspired to work for change, for our evolutionary birth.

So now what lies ahead as we collectively make the effort to transform the consciousness of humanity through compassion and fearlessness, those millions of us who were born to do just that and maybe it is all of us? I have always believed that if I ever got to an old age, my life would be at its best. I've come to understand that by accepting impermanence and the belief in possibility, we are able to move forward as individuals and as a civilization. We need to develop communities of like-minded thinkers and spread out to include our connections with un-like minded thinkers so we can learn from each other and evolve together. We do not evolve in isolation.

Making the leap out of isolation, out of the multi-tasking, busy, self-focused lives we've been living, we must step into some form of action, one of faith and determination. As we step out of one reality into another, we are in mid-air, neither here nor there and it is downright uncomfortable. We have not yet landed into the new reality and we worry about tripping or falling, but it is usually these moments that allow for change, blossoming into the new, the fresh and the good.

It's hard to be solid in our optimism, I know, because of everyone else's cynicism. We can fall back into doubt. How can we not have doubts when we are called naïve by smart people all around us? And it's totally understandable, this cynicism coming as it does, from all of our past abuses and disappointments because it's not the first time we have had high hopes. We thought we had made inroads to alleviate racism and we elected a black president. There was great rejoicing but it was an event that polarized people even more. There has been an interfaith movement over these recent years but that seems to have fundamentalized people from all religions even more. Afraid of change, people cling to what they know. These polarizations have been an extreme disappointment. Perhaps it's too risky to believe things can actually change. But I wonder, can we hold truth, wisdom, inspiration and beauty in our hearts despite the whirling negativity around us? I think, perhaps if we are determined, together we can.

"In this age when history itself is on fire
In this time of the convulsion of the beast
Of the final dance of the enraged demons
May I keep faith, Lord, in Your sublime alchemy
That has ordained the mystery
That from deepest darkness births
the Highest Light."
--Andrew Harvey, *Light the Flame*

My life, like so many others, has had its share of difficulties but for most of that time I sought the Mystery and diligently tracked the Light. Thank goodness that what often seemed permanent was not. So many are discouraged right now but it's helpful to know that wonderful people and wonderful things are happening all around the world. We need to find each other because corporate media refuses to tell us about the good and true stuff. They have their own agenda. I am not a conspiracist but I do look for truth and I've never noticed how manipulated we are by the media until this year when electing a new president in America opened up the propaganda machine like never before. The only way to know the good stuff, it seems to me, is by getting involved with networks of people who have no agenda but to make things better, not worse.

Now I would like to jump from my soapbox back to the personal.

I had been pondering one day why I missed my kids on Sundays when they didn't call, or why I missed Ron on a Sunday morning over croissants and coffee when I was already so deeply and happily involved in my new life with Maurice.

I wished the phone would ring with one of my kids on the other end. Because I was enjoying everything my new life was offering, I faulted myself for having these desires. They have their own lives to live, their own children to engage with, laugh with and cry with, thank goodness, and my life was sweeter and easier than ever. So I wondered how I could be so greedy. How did my grown kids with their own families, who lived distances away, fit into this picture? I wanted them to be a bigger part of my life.

Sunday in March

It's Sunday in March
The sun is out, still cold
I want the phone to ring
Any of my children, my sister, a friend
But what would I even say, then?

So what do I want? I wonder.
I think just connection, contact, a caress on the heart
No words
I have all the words I need.

My grown babies Elizabeth, Adam and Jennifer.

So one day, I suddenly received an answer to my longing. I was ignited by a feeling in my bones, in my heart, in my mind, and in my soul that I was a fusion of everyone and, in particular, these children I have raised and the man I had raised them with. Those four people are vital to who I am. At that same moment of realization, I had integrated everyone into my being, everyone I had ever touched and everyone who had ever touched me, especially all the smiles, frowns, words and gestures from my own parents and then from my own children. But it didn't stop there. It included the woman at the market register and the conductor helping me onto the train, the

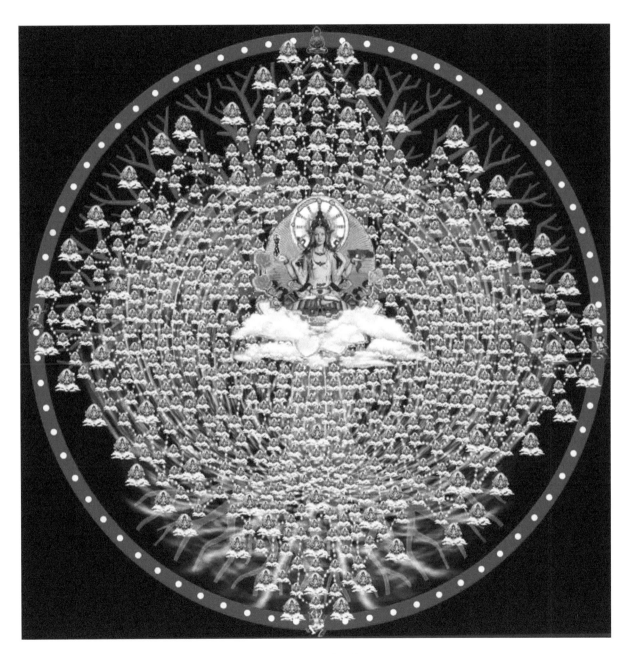

A portrait of Indra.

child in the shopping cart that smiled at me, the mean teacher I had in seventh grade, the boy who grabbed my breast when I was twelve, and all those who gifted me with fruits and flowers throughout my many lives. I am all of the many, many mothers and fathers and children of all the races. I was and am a mix of all of them. I felt this so strongly in my whole being.

"Imagine a multidimensional spider's web in the early morning covered with dew drops. And every dewdrop contains the reflection of all the other dewdrops. And, in each reflected dewdrop, the reflections of all the other dewdrops in that reflection. And so ad infinitum. That is the Buddhist conception of the universe in an image."
–Alan Watts

Epiphanies can come at any time: washing the floor, climbing a mountain and often when we're sitting as still as a stone. These are the times we are open to receive. I hate to say it but if I get a bad cold or some other physical misery that lands me in bed, I'll lie there while my mind runs wild thinking all kinds of things. Then I'll doze off and upon awakening I find myself floating around somewhere in between. That's usually when things come in for me. It was unfortunate that I'd get sick but I finally realized that I no longer need to get sick to create that open time. Sometimes I get a nudge to just stop and go sit down and inevitably the muse is waiting with a gift for me.

In that state on that day, I saw so clearly that we are each a complex, multi-faceted, many-hued human being with lifetimes following one after another and even possibly running parallel to each other. It is a mystery but I get these glimpses that I know hold reality within them. All the influences from those lifetimes, I saw, determine all of our connections, each reflecting as brilliant jewels back and forth, one to the other. In deeper reality, though, there is no "other", for we are all connected—animals, vegetables and minerals alike. It is said that the flutter of one butterfly's wing affects the whole world. There's not-so-new research proving that animals and plants respond to human thoughts, emotions and actions that are directed at them. What we think about everything changes as we grow, as we begin to see with clearer eyes, and that is good.

I was relieved to suddenly have this awareness about our circles of connection and it showed me why I care so much about my children and Ron, too. Because we are all interconnected, our personal and present families are deeply imbedded into who we are and this causes deep longing for healing whatever wounds have occurred and an ongoing connection with them. But what else is this longing about? Is it for our closest people or does it go even deeper than that? Is the longing for what our soul remembers and our mind has forgotten? Is the empty space within still partially empty even while we are giving and receiving love from our dearest loved ones? It is a complicated and delicious question to ponder.

The longing for God is partially and temporarily satisfied by these interaction with our loved ones because they carry God within them, as everyone does, and we are directly connected with them through the threads of shared experience. What underlies even that, I believe, is the longing of the reality that the soul remembers and wants to return to. I believe this longing is in each of us and we pursue it in different ways—through religion, drugs, food, meditation, prayer, sex, religion, our "toys" and even life-threatening thrills. We usually never know what it is that we are truly pursuing as we rush to relieve the yearning. The Sufis whirl round and round to sacred music, which brings them into that bliss—the Hasidic Jews and many indigenous people use sacred dance, as well, and, of course, all kinds of music bring us into the state of grace.

Nothing, though, is ever enough to permanently fill the inner void, even when we make connection with the Divine, because that filling up is ever fleeting. In my experience, the filling of the inner void can temporarily be renewed through relationships with loved ones because that is what expands the heart. And even that flees in the busyness of our days.

The family, either biological or selected, is the nucleus, our personal circle, those sitting closest to the central figure in that portrait of Indra, above, and our reciprocal influences with others spread out from there.

Beloved Us

It's beyond this world, this love,
Great Spirit that permeates our everything.

You are the pulse in my wrist,
Sweet water between my lips
You are All That Is
and All that came before.

So tell me, Oh Permeating One,
Are we each an endless stream of humanity?
With new sets of bones and skin and
dancing feet
Stepping through the generations,

Mixing it up for posterity?

Do we travel through the doorways of color,
creed,
class, gender, ability, and disability?

Could this be how we grow compassion?
Do we travel among stars that hold us close
While we decide what's next
before we come to here?

Today I know something new
and that is that I don't really know.

At last, I don't really know your Mystery
after all these years of certainty.
Now I Am open to my Self
peering in through a burning lens
to see who that might be.

Through stillness I remember
who I am not,

that bundle of opinions,
attitudes, and preferences
walking around in comfortable shoes.

That muddle of misconception about you,
Dear brothers and sisters
coming from some strange land in a far away
place
or perhaps that clapboard house next door.

Please know that I am pained by your wounds.
Your pain does not stop where you end.

Know, too, I turn to silk and fire from your joy.
This air that I breathe leaves my body
and wanders toward you to fuel you with honey.
And your exhale carries your glisten back to me.

You are a Christian.
I am a Jew.

You are a Hindu.
I am The Tao.
You are a Muslim,
a Pagan, a Jain,

And we are Buddhists, too.
What we do and how we love
makes us who we are

and Compassion is the name we will become.
For the sun that shines on you
splashes down on me.
Our laughter raises up the world.
2.
And on another note this sensual body
relishes your rice and beans,
your samosas, knishes and halvah.

It savors your curried goat and dumplings,
your satay, kim chee and perogi.

I drink in your ragas through my skin,
I embrace your chants and gospels and hymns,
Your Ave Maria, one voice davening to
fill the air,
one drum, one heart, one dream

Are we not all of That in our emergence,
Even fern, fungi, flower and moss?
And aren't we also trees?

Are we One entangled love affair,
slender tendrils intertwining
and a pebbled river fed by many streams?

Are we all of that?
Are we one furiously pulsing,
vibrant body
called YES?
Say yes.

So, we need to trust. If we consider the illusions,
deceptions and realities that are revealing

themselves at the moment and darkening the mood of the world, creating legitimate fears, then we have to ask the universe how we can help. It is indeed daunting and so much easier to keep a blind eye and busy ourselves with daily routines. But we can't afford to close our eyes anymore. If we have no solutions to today's problems, we are asked to keep peace in our own hearts, to dispel fear and hold tight with other like-minded souls the vision of a kinder world. If we can do that, I do trust that we can sweeten life on earth.

When I began this story, I mentioned that I had never been a child but was something else that I was yet to discover. That something else was a perpetual seeker, a serious child looking for meaning from the very beginning. I needed to know who I was and what the world was. Because of my abuse, I was a stranger in a strange body and a strange land. I needed to find out about the things that were not being taught at home, in school or in the synagogue. I knew that I was not fitting into expectations and that there must be something beyond this world that I felt so alien in. When my Brownie troop took a field trip to a planetarium in 1946, the guide asked, "Who would like to sign up to go to the moon? Who wants to get on the list for when we can do this?" I was the only one who signed up. Some part of me wanted out of this world.

I think those of us who have been treated badly as children get kick-started into becoming who we are meant to be because we begin looking for answers early. We want to know exactly who we are apart from the abuse. The feelings of alienation start us on that search that after all these years, has brought me to where I am now, at home in myself and happy to be living in these transitory times.

In today's faster-paced world, it's Monday and before we know, it's Friday. We are all on a fast track both inwardly and outwardly and even if some of us can't see it at the moment, we are being carried by the rising tide of the collective consciousness happening beneath the radar. It is said that we are at a tipping point at this very moment.

What may seem like bad news is good news because the radar is being penetrated, truth is emerging, things are being revealed. Humanity feels so unsettled because we are waking up. These changes are driving us into our human potential, into enlightenment on a massive scale if we can allow it. That means that anyone can start anywhere. We are all unique in our greatness and our weakness. We are in process and each of us is simply where we are in our journey to liberation but it no longer has to take a lifetime to come to that. It's the awareness that counts and the starting. The momentum can take over on its own. The journey becomes the destination and reaching the destination is only part of the journey because there is no end.

Wherever we are now is where we belong and from where we begin. It is not linear. The way I see it for each of us is that it takes place on many levels at once. What we've been talking about when we refer to our higher selves and our lower selves seems to me to end up being integrated and nuanced into one perfect self for the task at hand. When we are willing to share the insights about the control money has on our lives through the system and all its flaws, and when we are brave enough to communicate our actions and intentions wherever we are then we can become part of humanity's evolution and the universe is happy to lead us along.

Humanity has always been creeping forward, as all of life has, but throughout earth's history there have been what appeared to be sudden leaps, out of the Dark Ages, into the enlightenment and now we are there again, here again. Now there is an opening where we can bring our own unique wisdom and beauty through to the whole. We must begin to give ourselves credit, to find acceptance in who we are and to recognize our unique gifts that were given to each of us for the very purpose of bringing them to the world. Life isn't what it used to be. The children being born now and those rising to adulthood are being faced with huge responsibilities and in many ways are feeling overwhelmed by what they are inheriting on this earth. I don't need to itemize the problems they are facing because we all know what they are; however, some of them are mentioned below. We earlier generations owe the young ones the support they need in the ways they need supporting, in ways we may not even understand. We have to have faith in them, trust them and still guide them from our hearts and our integrity, but also we must listen to them because they come with the wisdom needed to make the changes that are needed. They are the future and it may scare the daylights out of them, but I believe we can, together, bring this world out of chaos and into a more compassionate and brilliant civilization.

Our willingness to move out of our old ways and embrace the new possibilities is what, to me, is evolution, and the beauty of impermanence.

"Your work is to keep cranking the flywheel that turns the gears that spin the belt in the engine of belief that keeps you and your desk in midair."
—Annie Dillard

No matter what our situation, as long as we breathe and our hearts pump blood, we still have the opportunity to, one way or another, get our innate wisdom and our gifts into the world. It has been done by those in the most dire conditions and we can do it, too, because the only horrible option to evolution is devolution.

You're song, a wished-for song.
Go through the ear to the center,
Where sky is, where wind,
Where silent knowing.

Put seeds and cover them.
Blades will sprout
Where you do your work.
—Rumi

Now, I peer into the bathroom mirror to find who lives beneath my face, who's in there today, but this time I stop in my tracks. Hmm . . . I look okay. There are wrinkles and crevices, which I expect after all these years, especially at the smile lines, but I look okay. I apply concealer, eyeliner, color to my cheeks and I must say it does the job and creates the illusion of youth, even to myself, but as soon as I put on my glasses there is the true face beneath it all.

Somehow, though, when I look in the mirror in the light of the living room window from ten feet away, it is altogether different. The planes of my face are different, the way the light falls and the shadow. I am an elder woman with more years to go but at least I have reached old. It is truly an amazing fact. These days when I catch a glance myself in the mirror, I see myself smiling. There is love there, finally love for myself after all the self-doubting, the not being "good" enough and all those internalized messages. So it seems especially urgent now with all this potential that we cherish our children dearly, protect them and support who they are. Just naturally they, in turn, will cherish others and kindness will prevail. Loving kindness is what will move us forward and moving forward is what the beauty of impermanence is all about. The messages we give them will stick for a long time to come.

So many women that I meet express despair, apathy and disappointment. They feel they've stepped over the hill and are slipping into obsolescence. What they need to know is that the ember still burns within them and can be fanned into flame at any time. They may discover, in this time of change, new passions or rekindle old ones to further their life's purpose. We grow and change and awaken and that is the energy that propels the evolution we are participating in and, at the same time, creating.

So aging is a beautiful thing when we come to the place of liberation from years of struggle and we finally accept ourselves for who we are and all that we have already given and received. Then we notice that the critic within has finally left the building.

The mythologist Jean Houston says, "The reset button of history has been set. We are moving closer into who we are and our face is the signature of that."

So as we move closer to who we are, the loose ends get tied up. Healing occurs. Forgiveness gets done and we continue moving forward on the spiral of this life.

It is sometimes hard to believe that at sixty-seven, after forty-four years of marriage to one man, I found myself beginning a new relationship with another man. Unimaginable. And now nine years later, it is as natural and sweet as cake and ice cream, which I will have on my eightieth birthday come December 2016.

On February thirteenth of this year, Maurice went out to see if any valentines had come in the mail from our kids and from each other. He bounced in the door.

"Henny's here," he announced cheerily and we were like two little kids on holiday anxious to open the package we knew contained my mother's ashes. It was not grim. I tenderly and silently opened the package, both of us glowing with curiosity. That's part of what I love about Maurice, his compassion for my deepest experiences and his playfulness, as well.

Later, I sat with the box on my lap, my palms flat against it in reverie and I felt so much love emanating from the darn thing. It struck me as odd that I was so attached to these ashes. I knew that they weren't my Mom and I had always been so callous about things like ashes and coffins and all that precious land used for burials. The soul has flown the coop, so why put so much significance on the remains? But what a lesson in humility, to think I had dismissed these rituals with so much arrogance, such a lack of sacredness, because it did matter and I cried with gratitude to have this beautiful box with the gold rim straight from the medical school where Mom had bequeathed her body in her usual compassion for others.

With all our differences in the earlier years that had kept Nance and I apart, our losses in the later years brought us close again. We wanted to get together, just us alone, to honor Mom's passing. I left for the Cape to meet for a few days and this would definitely be a special time for us, a sister's retreat. I brought the remainder of Mom's ashes for a ritual. Most of them had ended up on our respective gardens per her request, but there was a surprising amount left so we decided to do something together with the rest.

Nance and I left the B&B for the beach late afternoon to do the deed. The moon hung full, high above the rocks, orange as cadmium light. We sang our prayers and tried to light some colored candles that I had brought in my bag, but the wind won out. We told "Mom stories" and held each other tight. We were comforted by her presence and sensed her laughing with glee at our friendship, which had been so long in coming as we gifted ourselves with each other, fine dining, and the sea.

"Age does not protect you from love. But love, to some extent, protects you from age."
—Anaïs Nin

Crack in the Heart Where Love Rushes In

Beyond Forgiveness, Daddy and the Shaman, All Our Stories, Now is the Time And We are the Ones

Oh, Beloved One, no words,
No words form on my lips
Or in my throat or on this page

It is novel that I am wordless
There's just no language for this bliss
And what am I to do?

My heart cracks with expansion
And breaks in two, your kiss

Cleaving a river not wide enough
For this rushing.

So what would you have me do?

Walk into the starry sky? I will.
Kiss the spherical earth? I will.
Doze in the crook of that tree? I will.
Nuzzle my nose in the fur of that cat. I will.
Sign petitions and call senators, I will

Still I listen and tilt my inner ear to hear
Your wordless voice whispering
As I hunger for direction,
Beg you for instruction

You tell me just be still
That's all you want me to do?
Okay, I will.

Being still for awhile inevitably leads me to action, often to very simple things, maybe even what seems insignificant, a letter to the editor somewhere, or a post on Facebook that might bring a spark of something good to the reader, a call to a friend. Sometimes I cannot tell but since it was born of stillness, my little engine starts up, the muse appears and I'm off and running.

I've found in my story that writing about joy is so much harder than writing about pain. Pain is pushing to get out and so takes over the page in rapid desperation with little need to search for words. But joy, well, it can so easily sound like a Hallmark card.

Alice McDermott wrote an essay called "Too Happy for Words" in reference to motherhood. She ponders the resistance to writing about the happiness many of us derive from our pregnancies, our children's births, and from watching them grow. We read about the horrors of all that but rarely about the delights. McDermott quotes Tolstoy, who warned that "sustained joy doesn't make much of a story." Maybe not, but it makes for a rich life and mine, so far, has felt rich to me, the darkness as well as the light. Now that the joy and sense of real wellbeing have caught up with me, I consider mine a lifetime of evolution. The impermanence, the growth of states of mind and stages of consciousness is a beautiful thing that breaks through to the expansion of gratitude and love. Ron and I are good friends. His wife and I are good friends. There is beauty in the way things needed to change and because we have looked truth in the eyes, we are now an inclusive family as natural to all of us as if we are shining like stars in the same constellation. So on it goes.

I started this memoir when I was sure I had a good story to tell that would empower other women to take chances and leap into their own better life. I thought it would show how a happy ending is possible no matter what age the leap takes place. I thought that would be the end of

306

a story that ends pretty.

And then 2015 hit the fan: With the increase of suicide bombers and ISIS, our own country seething with hatred and prejudice, a country at war with itself, a world at war with itself, so many trembling with fear and rage that this ends up being an epic year. It's not a pretty ending to my story. The joy and beauty is once again shaken up and broken into pieces for us to put back together. Many of us saw this coming. It drove me to write my story, to show that no matter what age we are we can determine to heal and to participate. Writing this was a daily inquiry into the realities of my life. I'm not the only one who has come here to heal and to turn that healing into a contribution. I'm not the only one who has jumped into the joyful resonant field of conscious evolution and I'm not the only one who has transformed her negative experiences into wholeness. I have been guided to share these intimacies with anybody who can gain from them, knowing that we are all unique but that our wounds all have the same effect. In this, my eightieth year, there is much to do and I seem to be busier and more inspired then ever.

As I mentioned earlier, the Hebrew concept of tikkun says that it is our job to repair a broken world. If we each do our part from belief, from integrity, from passion and because it is something we are capable of doing, it will be an essential part that repairs the whole and from that helping sometimes comes the bonus of bliss. The state of our simple *beingness* seems to precede our *doingness* because within the state of *being* or the stillness comes the impetus of *what* to do. It is from there that what needs *doing* will come forth. That can be called our inner guidance. These twin occupations of *being and doing* ebb and flow. They allow us to experience both form and emptiness as they come into our awareness.

Empowered women are needed more than ever. Women have always been about the process rather than the product. We have known that the world within is just as important as the world without. We know compassion, we value relationship, and we long for peace. It is our nature. Collaboration is how we will get things changed. Jean Houston says, "Women are pilgrims, parents of this new world." I believe that is true but not only for us women, but also the men who are courageous enough to allow their feminine attributes to emerge in balance with their masculine—not one or the other.

Evolutionary spirituality is not a new religion or organization but a growing global movement that comes in many forms. It descends—or I should say *ascends*—from the great mystic experiences of the ancient traditions of the world in combination with new discoveries in science. Science and spirituality are now two ends joining together in a circle. We are receiving something into ourselves that is evolving us as humans who are aware of and desire to fulfill the spiritual insights of the great visionaries of all times. I really think each of us, knowingly or not, as soul, has chosen this time to be here now for the opportunity to help mid-wife the crisis of our time into the birth of this new human consciousness and the re-patterning of human nature. Now we can join the thousands of evolutionaries walking upon the earth who make up this resonant field, those we do not see making news.

The Universal Human, the person who understands our human potential and is willing to participate consciously by intention and voluntary presence in the field of like-minded folks, connected through the heart to the whole of life, is helping to co-create this new world we can all live in. Co-creation is the operative word, made mainstream by Barbara Marx Hubbard. It involves an intimate and practical process for all who wish to make the transition to the next stage of evolution. Think about it. If we went from Neanderthals to where we are now, what is to stop us from doing it again, now when we are conscious of that potential? Now is the time to awaken and to "break through what is breaking down", as she says.

Some say this ethical thrust to advance humanity has been going on since the sixties, others say since the Harmonic Convergence—one of the world's first globally synchronized meditation events which occurred in 1987. Others say it is a spontaneous shifting of human consciousness upward and yet others say it is fantasy. Whatever it is the extreme negativity of civilization is finally being revealed, the greed, the deception, the manipulation, the corruption, and all the "isms" such as sexism, racism and in this culture, ageism . . . well, you get the point. We all know what they are but they are driven not necessarily by hatred but what's underneath that which is fear, the fear of never having enough of something—money, love, power, control or an egoic sense of superiority. Terrorism and destruction are making us all think and shake our heads, since we now have immediate access to witnessing these atrocities and because they are no longer confined to foreign shores but are here right on our own turf. That reality spurs some into despair and then sometimes into action while others slip into regression, nostalgia for the past idealized world that never really was, and still others just bury their heads in the sand.

In 2011, I was listening to all the prophesies and predictions being spoken of all over the loosely called New Age movement. There would be a celebration of a new birth when the clock struck twelve in the year 2012. I wanted desperately to be ready for this transformational shift. I wanted to be clean and open enough to participate. I wanted to address whatever shadow was dominating any attitudes, opinions, emotions and actions that were a part of me. I wanted to see and clear out what was not pure, open and ready to help in this planetary transformation, which I felt, along with millions of others, was my job. I wanted to be a channel for love, because I had some vague memory of my purpose for being here and I sure didn't want to leave the planet without fulfilling that purpose.

I know that all of my healing modalities, therapy and workshops, readings and seminars were part of the journey to get me to the destination of this awakening. However, there was one identifiable piece of darkness lingering inside of me, one I was able to identify. The residue of pain I felt from my father's actions remained tucked away in a little corner of myself. I wanted to free it. I wanted to replace that residue of pain with love for him. I'm not talking about our rendezvous in space. That was only temporary, a lit match to fire up my search. So for several years I had been praying for the ability to forgive him. Saying the words would have been easy but I knew it went much deeper then that. I had to release any blame I still held in my body and that wouldn't just happen because I wanted it to.

With the help of one of Sharon Old's poems, I was reminded that my father had once been a little boy and I didn't know what had been done to him in those early years. In imagining him as a little boy as a victim, I felt a rush of compassion come over me. I knew that being a victim himself was no excuse for what he had done to me but in that moment the sensation of deep forgiveness happened. The experience felt like I had nothing to do with it. All I knew was I had prayed to have that happen and circumstances lined up to make it happen. Still, that wasn't enough. I now wanted to be able to love the man. I'm talking about open-hearted, full-bodied love and I just couldn't get there by myself.

So whom could I call for help? I knew plenty of therapists and healers but since this was more esoteric than anything I'd overcome before, the deep healing with a dead person, I needed someone special to work with me. I had the idea that seeing a shaman might be a good choice. I'd had a good experience with Raphael and the breast cancer thing, but I didn't know how to locate him. It was Maurice who found Rachel through the Four Winds Society, which offers the world's most thorough training in the philosophy and practice of shamanic energy medicine. It was founded by Alberto Villoldo, who studied for twenty-five years with the shamans of the Amazon and Andes of Peru. They combine ancient wisdom teachings with cutting-edge neuroscience.

I had two sessions with Rachel that year and had learned a lot about my journey in the hours I worked with her, so now I totally trusted her to do this extraordinary thing.

We set our intention and in her altered state, not from drugs or plants, but from wherever she goes from whatever she does with her voice and breath, she soon said, "Your father is close by. He can come now but only for a moment. Do you want to see him? Are you ready?"

I was ready.

Before the next breath he was *here*. It had nothing to do with time or space. It was all at once and he was sobbing with sorrow and remorse.

"I'm so, so sorry," he sobbed, "I don't expect you to forgive me." As he spoke my arms reached out and pulled him down onto my chest into a close and penetrating hug. Our two hearts were touching and bubbling with unexplainable grace.

"I love you," I said. I said it, over and over, holding him tight. And then it was done. He was gone as suddenly as he had come. How does that happen? How can that happen? I don't know, but it did. I just know that our reality is so much greater then our imaginations can ever dream up. Reality is beyond the senses and far flung almost into the unknowable. Some may say that it is the devil working but I believe that is just fear talking, avoidance and that's okay, too. We believe what we experience and we experience what we believe.

But a warning here: As they say, "Don't try this at home." This experience had taken an enormous amount of preparation on my part. Rachel had been in shamanic training with traditionally true shamans for years. We cannot be naïve. There are too many charlatans out there who are into power and manipulation, all too happy to take the vulnerable for a devastating ride. So I don't recommend anyone taking this lightly because without divine guidance, divine protection and inner preparation, it can bring serious trouble into one's life—as in my Harlan and Grandmaster experiences, and even worse. As Star Wars clearly shows, for every Yoda there is a Darth Vader.

I tell this part of the story because it happened and to me that means anything can happen. There's a fine line between being open to experience and using discrimination. We each have to find it for ourselves but we do have to find it. We need to discriminate who we engage with as individuals. Just because a person is a pastor, a guru, a priest, a rabbi, a lightworker or healer does not mean that person is free of their own dark agenda. We have to be alert to what is right for us and who is right for us.

Rachel was my local miracle or a moment of divine intervention, but also I delved into the Internet at just the right time. Not only did I become aware of the bad things that were happening but now I could see how it was bringing so many peace-loving people from all over the planet together in a positively great, love-filled effort to help address this new time. Simultaneously, people from every race, nation and religion are experiencing within themselves the emergence of a more universal, empathetic, spiritually awakened self. What we do get to see on the news can sadden and shock us into a kind of paralysis. What can one person do? Well, we can tumble into despair or respond by researching what interests us, pisses us off, frightens us, or delights us. We can find out how we can become part of the solution. We need to begin to look not only deep inside ourselves but at those outside our own groups for the goodness they bring to the world and we must be discreet in believing what is being force fed to us.

Through the writing of my own story, I have

311

learned that every single person has a story—a beautiful, gorgeous, tragic, humorous story, and one that may be more full of grace than we can ever know. Maya Angelou says: "There is no greater agony then bearing an untold story inside of you." And we have something to learn from every story. Our world is so polarized right now in the early part of this 21st Century that we need more than ever to hear each other's stories—not as any group, nation, race, gender or religion but as individuals. We need to recognize and try to find ways to transcend the shadow that lives in each of us, and interestingly, also lives in all of our cultures. We need to be vigilant about who within us runs our lives—our higher self or our shadow self—and we need to be vigilant in our honesty. Is it fear, rage, judgment, a sense of worthlessness or hopelessness, or is it a passion for working together for the benefit of all of humanity because we see how we are all connected?

Friendship happens through our personal stories. We become sisters and brothers. That's how we will know each other and that's how we will come together for this necessary and beautiful change that awaits our attention and our courage.

Here you are and here I am in the thick of living potential. I read somewhere that "the second coming is within us" and I agree. It is time to understand that none of us need be alone and that there's no way we can ever know the deep beauty of a stranger anymore than we can realize the deep beauty within ourselves and that knowledge can bring us into a commitment to *be* and *do* in our own way. As Marianne Williamson says, "Grownups need to be grownups, not little girls and boys."

So can we make it? Belief changes reality, as well as the other way around. Of course, I, too, have doubts that creep in, just as I'd had during the pregnancy of my first baby. I had no precedent to know what would happen. Anything could happen but I forced myself to drop the worry and quickly move into the optimism of probability that all will be perfect. It is the same now. When I fall into doubt, I immediately move into the optimism of possibility that all can be beautiful. What is the point of thinking otherwise? Where does pessimism or even worry get us? *But it doesn't excuse us from deep inquiry into our own personal motivations*. All it seems to do is bring what we do not want closer into reality by our thoughts and the energy inherent in those thoughts. So why not choose optimism and the beauty that is possible? We have nothing to lose and everything to gain.

Throughout these seven decades, I have been down on myself and fallen in love with myself over and over again. Whether it was uphill sidewalks, slanted pastures, rocky forest trails or tenement stairs, whether it was divorce, breast cancer or childhood betrayals, there was always exultation at the summit. Being willing to walk away from my life as I knew it and walk through a wider door to undreamed of possibility has made the difference. I do think believing in ourselves though we are not perfect, and believing in humanity although it seems far from perfect right now, I trust that it is only temporary. As Angela Davis said, "I am no longer accepting the things I cannot change. I am changing the things I cannot accept."

I see now how this has been my evolutionary journey, a microcosm within the macrocosm that is all of us and a reason I have also written this for my kids, so they can know who I am now beyond the woman they grew up with. We each grow in our own ways. From one evolutionary microcosm, a part of the whole macrocosm comes the capacity to flood our planet with a deeper, wider kindness and love for ourselves and for others. I knew before I came onto the planet what I needed to do here. Science and spirituality have come to meet each other in full circle. I knew when I was drifting in and out of my mother's womb what I was coming for.

Then soon after the moment of birth when God breathed that first breath into me, when I became a person, I began to forget. Or maybe I forgot when I was already one or two or three. But it has taken me close to eighty years to finally be able to recognize the purpose I began with has happened. I don't believe in accidents. I was privileged to have rolled to the curb in my eighth month with my first child. The twilight zone it placed me in at that time brought me the gift of memory. I remember the angst about coming into this life because of all that was revealed to me then. And it has happened. We must put the nuances of our differences aside and come together on the issues that are important to humanity and our beloved planet. We need to come together with

May this book inspire you to break free from whatever drags at you and help you claim your lofty potential as a vital cell in the body of humanity. These are a few of my favorite things. See what pops out for you from this list and within the books themselves. There are so many jewels in this world and one brilliant resource leads to another. Enjoy.

A FEW GOOD BOOKS:

- Arrien, Angeles: *The Second Half of Life: Opening the Eight Gates of Wisdom*

- Aurabindo Sri: *Writings of Sri Aurobindo*

- Barks, Coleman and Moyne, John (Translation): *The Essential Rumi*

- Borysenko, Joan: *A Woman's Book of Life: The Biology, Psychology and Spirituality of the Feminine Life Cycle*

- Cahill, Thomas: *The Gifts of the Jews: How a Tribe of Desert Nomads Changed the Way Everyone Thinks and Feels*

- Einstein, Albert: *The World as I See It: Out of My Later Years*

- Eisenstein, Charles: *The More Beautiful World Our Hearts Know is Possible*

- Harvey, Andrew: *The Hope: A Guide to Sacred Activism*

- Heschel, Suzannah: *Essential Writings of Abraham Joshua Heschel*

- Houston, Jean: *A Passion for the Possible: A Guide to Realizing Our True Potential*

- Barbara Marx Hubbard: *Birth 2012 and Beyond* and *Emergence: The Shift from Ego to Essence: Ten Steps to the Universal Human*

- Karpinski, Gloria: *Barefoot on Holy Ground: Twelve Lessons in Spiritual Craftsmanship*

- Newton, Michael: *Journey of Souls and Destiny of Souls*

- Nye, Naomi Shihab: *Words Under Words: Selected Poems*

- O'Donohue, John: *Beauty: The Invisible Embrace*

- Olsen, Tillie: *Silences*

- Phipps, Carter: *Evolutionaries: Unlocking the Spiritual and Cultural Potential of Science's Greatest Ideas*

- Prager, Rabbi Marcia: *The Path of Blessing*

- Salzberg, Sharon: Faith: *Trusting Your Own Deepest Experience*

- Spretnak, Charlene, Editor: *The Politics of Women's Spirituality: Essays on the Rise of Spiritual Power Within the Feminist Movement,*

- Thurman, Robert A.F. (Translator): *Tibetan Book of the Dead*

- Tolle, Eckert: *Stillness Speaks and The New Earth: Awakening to Your Life's Purpose*

- Villoldo, Alberto PhD: *Shaman, Healer, Sage: How to Heal Yourself and Others with the Energy Medicine of the Americas*

- Walker, Alice: *In Search of Our Mothers' Gardens: Womanist Prose*

- Yogananda, Paramahansa: *Autobiography of a Yogi*

MOVIES:

Chomsky, Noam *Requiem For The American Dream*

Once you see our current reality it will awaken you to your next evolutionary action, which may be inspired by the movie, *Cultural Creatives: The (R)evolution.* This can be found on the Internet.

JUST A FEW ORGANIZATIONS TO EXPLORE:

- http://www.aclu.org/join: ACLU (American Civil Liberties Union)

- http://www.eldersclimateaction.org: Elders Climate Action

- http://feminist.com: (news, activism, resources)

- http://lwv.org: League of Women Voters

- http://lwv.org: National Human Trafficking Resource Center

- http://www.theoracleinstitute.org: The Oracle Institute: An Advocate for Peace and a Vanguard for Conscious Evolution

- http://theshiftnetwork.com/vision2020: The Shift Network

- http://www.wipp.org: Women Impacting Public Policy

- https://www.zonta.org: Zonta International: Empowering Women through Service and Advocacy

Frances Curtis Barnhart is an artist, writer, teacher, mother of three, grandmother of ten, spiritual explorer and an evolutionary activist in the human potential movement.

Barnhart is a graduate of Boston University, where she majored in painting at The School of Fine and Applied Arts.

She is a published poet and author of *The New Woman Warrior's Handbook: Not for Women Only* [Illuminated Way Press, 1982]. Her work has appeared in *MS Magazine, The New York Times Magazine,* the journal *Artemis: Artists and Writers from the Blue Ridge Mountains and Beyond* and various other publications.

In 2003, she became ordained as an Interfaith Minister by The New Seminary at St. John the Divine Cathedral in New York City.

In 2006, Barnhart was remarried at the age of seventy and moved to the picturesque town of Roanoke, Virginia with her husband, Maurice Barnhart. She continues her wedding ministry and is active in evolutionary work, creating workshops for those interested in becoming more engaged in creating positive change in our transitioning world.

319

CPSIA information can be obtained
at www.ICGtesting.com
Printed in the USA
LVHW02n2316220118
563549LV00014B/145/P